ARCO

MASTER THE
POSTAL EXAMS

7th Edition

John Gosney
Dawn Rosenberg McKay

THOMSON ™

PETERSON'S

Australia • Canada • Mexico • Singapore • Spain • United Kingdom • United States

An ARCO Book

ARCO is a registered trademark of Thomson Learning, Inc., and is used herein under license by Thomson Peterson's.

About Thomson Peterson's

Thomson Peterson's (www.petersons.com) is a leading provider of education information and advice, with books and online resources focusing on education search, test preparation, and financial aid. Its Web site offers searchable databases and interactive tools for contacting educational institutions, online practice tests and instruction, and planning tools for securing financial aid. Thomson Peterson's serves 110 million education consumers annually.

Petersons.com/publishing

Check out our Web site at www.petersons.com/publishing to see if there is any new information regarding the test and any revisions or corrections to the content of this book. We've made sure the information in this book is accurate and up-to-date; however, the test format or content may have changed since the time of publication.

For more information, contact Thomson Peterson's, 2000 Lenox Drive, Lawrenceville, NJ 08648; 800-338-3282; or find us on the World Wide Web at www.petersons.com/about.

Editor: Joe Krasowski; Production Editor: Alysha Bullock; Manufacturing Manager: Ivona Skibicki; Composition Manager: Linda M. Williams; Cover Design: Christina Chattin.

ISBN-13: 978-0-7689-1987-5
ISBN-10: 0-7689-1987-8

Printed in the United States of America

10 9 8 7 6 5 4 3   08 07 06

Seventh Edition

Contents

Contents

Contents

OTHER RECOMMENDED TITLES

ARCO Master the Civil Service Exams

ARCO Civil Service Handbook

ARCO Civil Service Arithmetic & Vocabulary Review

Before You Begin

Congratulations! You have in your hands a powerful tool to ensure your best chances of getting a great score on the United States Postal Service (USPS) exams. By working through this book, taking time to practice the sample exercises, and studying the various strategies and techniques for tackling all the various question types, you will put yourself at a significant advantage for achieving a top-notch score.

This book contains information on:

- Every exam given by the USPS, including the NEW General Entrance Test Battery 473/473-C

- Job requirements

- Salary and benefits

- Working conditions

HOW TO USE THIS BOOK

This book is designed as a teach-yourself training course, complete with test-taking tips and strategies, exercises, and five full-length practice tests.

Part I provides a quick overview of important information you need to know about the USPS job market, working conditions, and job requirements.

Part II provides the exams required for specific USPS positions. It also has exercises to prepare you for every question type you will encounter on the actual exam.

Part III provides full-length practice tests, including detailed answer explanations, for Exams 473/473-C, 460, 710, 711, 911, 91, and 630. You can work through the specific practice test for the exam you are required to take.

Finally, the **Glossary** found at the back of the book provides definitions of some of the most important and frequently used terms you can expect to see during the application process.

PART I

A CAREER WITH THE U.S. POSTAL SERVICE

Benefits of the U.S. Postal Service

chapter 1

OVERVIEW

- Salary and benefits
- Training and qualifications
- Finding more information about USPS positions
- Summing it up

Remember when you were a kid and you took a field trip to your local post office? More than likely, a friendly employee gave you a tour of the mail-sorting area, demonstrated how the various computers are used (depending, of course, on your age at the time of the tour) and perhaps gave you a peek into one of the mail trucks. And, if you're like many people, you left with the impression that the only thing postal employees do is sort mail.

Most people are familiar with the duties of the city carrier and window clerk, the same friendly employees who may have given you the tour when you were young. However, very few people are aware of the many different tasks required in "sorting the mail," not to mention the enormous variety of occupations within the U.S. Postal Service (USPS). Twenty-four hours a day, mail moves through the typical large post office. It takes a lot of hard work to keep that mail moving, and all that hard work requires the involvement of many different people performing many different tasks.

The USPS employs more than 700,000 people, operates more than 37,000 post offices, and handles more than 202 billion pieces of mail per year. This group includes city carriers; data conversion operators, electronic technicians, mail handlers; mail processing clerks; rural carrier associates; and sales, services, and distribution associates. Postmasters and supervisors make up nearly 10 percent of total employment; and maintenance workers, which include automotive mechanics, building equipment mechanics, custodians, mail processing equipment mechanics, and maintenance mechanics, comprise about 4 percent. The remainder includes postal inspectors, guards, personnel workers, and secretaries.

SALARY AND BENEFITS

The USPS is an independent agency of the federal government. As such, USPS employees are federal employees who enjoy the very generous benefits offered by the government. These benefits include an automatic raise at least once a year, regular cost-of-living adjustments, liberal paid vacation and sick leave, life insurance, hospitalization, and the opportunity to join a credit union.

Salary

Salaries within the USPS are graded. Depending on the amount of time you've been employed, any promotions you might have achieved, and whether you work full- or part-time all determine your salary. The following tables illustrate salary levels for various positions with the USPS.

CITY CARRIER GRADE 1 PAY SCHEDULE
EFFECTIVE 2005

STEP	ANNUAL SALARY	HOURLY WAGE	REGULAR OVERTIME
A	$35,602	$17.12	$25.67
B	39,010	18.75	28.13
C	40,331	19.39	29.08
D	42,862	20.61	30.91
E	43,211	20.77	31.16
F	43,561	20.94	31.41
G	43,905	21.11	31.66
H	44,254	21.28	31.91
I	44,603	21.44	32.17
J	44,947	21.61	32.41
K	45,297	21.78	32.67
L	45,644	21.94	32.92
M	45,993	22.11	33.17
N	46,343	22.28	33.42
O	46,689	22.45	33.67

MAIL HANDLER GRADE 5 PAY SCHEDULE
EFFECTIVE 2004

STEP	ANNUAL SALARY	HOURLY WAGE	REGULAR OVERTIME
A	$29,461	$14.16	$21.24
B	34,832	16.75	25.13
C	37,273	17.92	26.88
D	39,637	19.06	28.59
E	39,941	19.20	28.80
F	40,250	19.35	29.03
G	40,550	19.50	29.25
H	40,857	19.64	29.46
I	41,166	19.79	29.69
J	41,468	19.94	29.91
K	41,774	20.08	30.12
L	42,075	20.23	30.35
M	42,384	20.38	30.57
N	42,689	20.52	30.78
O	42,993	20.67	31.01

FULL-TIME REGULAR APWU SALARY SCHEDULE (CLERK, MAINTENANCE, MOTOR VEHICLE, SUPPORT SERVICES) EFFECTIVE 2005

GRADE LEVEL	STEP BB	STEP AA	STEP A	STEP B	STEP C	STEP D
1	$26,079	$27,041	$28,003	$28,965	$29,927	$30,889
2	27,191	28,143	29,095	30,047	30,999	31,951
3	28,297	29,240	30,183	31,126	32,069	33,012
4			31,871	32,758	33,645	34,532
5			33,509	34,349	35,189	36,029
6			35,252	36,044	36,836	37,628
7			36,059	36,875	37,691	38,507
8						42,033
9						42,985
10						43,988
11						45,047
12						46,162

GRADE LEVEL	STEP E	STEP F	STEP G	STEP H	STEP I	STEP J
1	$31,851	$32,813	$33,775	$34,737	$35,699	$36,661
2	32,903	33,855	34,807	35,759	36,711	37,663
3	33,955	34,898	35,841	36,784	37,727	38,670
4	35,419	36,306	37,193	38,080	38,967	39,854
5	36,869	37,709	38,549	39,389	40,229	41,069
6	38,420	39,212	40,004	40,796	41,588	42,380
7	39,323	40,139	40,995	41,771	42,587	43,403
8	42,644	43,255	43,866	44,477	45,088	45,699
9	43,630	44,275	44,920	45,565	46,210	46,855
10	44,674	45,360	46,046	46,732	47,418	48,104
11	45,773	46,499	47,225	47,951	48,677	49,403
12	46,933	47,704	48,475	49,246	50,017	50,788

GRADE LEVEL	STEP K	STEP L	STEP M	STEP N	STEP O	STEP P
1	$39,613	$40,556	$41,449	$42,442	$43,385	
2	38,615	39,567	40,519	41,471	42,538	
3	38,916	39,847	40,778	41,709	42,640	
4	40,741	41,628	42,515	43,402	44,289	
5	41,909	42,749	43,589	44,429	45,269	
6	43,172	43,964	44,756	45,548	46,340	
7	44,219	45,035	45,851	46,667	47,483	
8	46,310	46,921	47,532	48,143	48,754	$49,365
9	47,500	48,145	48,790	49,435	50,080	50,725
10	48,790	49,476	50,162	50,848	51,534	52,220
11	50,129	50,855	51,581	52,307	53,033	53,759
12	51,559	52,330	53,101	53,872	54,643	55,414

NOTE

As you advance in your selected position within the USPS, you will become eligible for pay increases.

To be eligible for a periodic step increase, an employee must meet the following criteria:

* Must have received and currently be serving under a career appointment

* Must have performed in a satisfactory or outstanding manner during the waiting period

* Cannot have received an equivalent increase during the waiting period

* Must have completed the required waiting period

Health Benefits

The Federal Employees Health Benefit Plan (FEHBP), administered by the Office of Personnel Management, is among the most generous and popular of all postal benefit plans. Depending on the employee's craft and selected health-care plan, the USPS pays from 71% to about 88% of the premium.

Virtually all career USPS employees (and eligible family members) are covered by the FEHBP. Employees who are not eligible (with certain exceptions) include those serving in a temporary position lasting less than a year, such as casual and temporary employees, substitute rural carriers, and rural carrier associates. Other exclusions include non-citizens and employees paid on a contract or fee basis, including contract job cleaners and contract carriers.

Several types of plans are available, including the Service Benefit Plan (available nationwide), Employee Organization Plans (available through employee organizations such as labor unions), and Comprehensive Medical Plans (group practice plans/HMOs).

Vacation

Vacation is provided to employees for paid time off from regularly scheduled work hours. The charts below show how much vacation is accrued for full-time and part-time employees. Vacation for full-time employees is credited at the beginning of the year, while vacation for part-time employees is accrued in units of 20, 13, or 10 hours worked. Military service time (in most cases) counts towards USPS service time for determining vacation per year. (For example, if you served four years in the U.S. military prior to your employment with the

USPS, your initial vacation amount would be in the 3- to 15-year category. However, military retirees do not qualify for this time except under certain conditions.)

ANNUAL VACATION FOR FULL-TIME EMPLOYEES

YEARS OF EMPLOYMENT	VACATION
Less than 3 years	13 days
3 to 15 years	20 days
15 years or more	26 days

ANNUAL VACATION FOR PART-TIME EMPLOYEES

YEARS OF EMPLOYMENT	VACATION
Less than 3 years	13 days per 26-period leave year or 4 hours for each biweekly pay period; one hour for each unit of 20 hours in pay status
3 to 15 years	20 days per 26-period leave year or 6 hours for each full biweekly pay period, plus 4 hours in last pay period in leave year; one hour for each unit of 13 hours in pay status
15 years or more	26 days per 26-period leave year or 8 hours for each full biweekly pay period; one hour for each unit of 10 hours in pay status

Sick Leave

Sick leave is provided to employees for paid time off from regularly scheduled work hours due to illness, injury, pregnancy, and medical examinations and treatment (including dental and optical). Sick leave is accrued and credited at the end of each biweekly pay period in which it is earned. Both full- and part-time employees receive 13 sick days per year.

Court Leave

An employee is entitled to paid time off without charge to leave for service as a juror or witness. An employee is responsible for informing his or her supervisor if he or she is excused from jury or witness service for 1 day or more or for a substantial part of a day. To avoid undue hardship, an agency may adjust the schedule of an employee who works nights or weekends and is called to jury duty. (If there is no jury/witness service, there is no court leave. The employee would be charged annual leave, sick leave, or leave without pay, as appropriate.)

Family and Medical Leave

Under the Family and Medical Leave Act of 1993 (FMLA), most Federal employees are entitled to a total of up to 12 weeks of unpaid leave during any 12-month period for the following purposes:

- Birth of a son or daughter of the employee and the care of such son or daughter

- Placement of a son or daughter with the employee for adoption or foster care

- Care of spouse, son, daughter, or parent of the employee who has a serious health condition
- Serious health condition of the employee that makes the employee unable to perform the essential functions of his or her positions

Military Leave

An employee is entitled to time off at full pay for certain types of active or inactive duty in the National Guard or as a Reserve of the Armed Forces. Any full-time federal civilian employee whose appointment is not limited to one year is entitled to military leave.

Organ Donor Leave

An employee may use up to 7 days of paid leave each calendar year to serve as a bone-marrow donor. An employee also may use up to 30 days of paid leave each calendar year to serve as an organ donor. Leave for bone marrow and organ donation is a separate category of leave that is in addition to annual and sick leave.

Leave Transfer

An employee may donate annual leave directly to another federal employee who has a personal or family medical emergency and who has exhausted his or her available paid leave. Each agency must administer a voluntary leave transfer program for its employees. There is no limit on the amount of donated annual leave a leave recipient may receive from the leave donor(s). However, any unused donated leave must be returned to the leave donor(s) when the medical emergency ends.

Federal Holidays

The following 10 days are observed as holidays by the USPS:
- New Year's Day
- Martin Luther King Jr.'s Birthday
- Washington's Birthday
- Memorial Day
- Independence Day
- Labor Day
- Columbus Day
- Veterans' Day
- Thanksgiving Day
- Christmas Day

Workers' Compensation Benefits

All USPS employees are covered by the Federal Employee's Compensation Act (FECA). The program is administered by the Office of Workers' Compensation (OWCP)—United States Department of Labor. FECA entitles employees who have suffered a job-related disability to:

- Continuation of regular pay for the period of the disability, up to a maximum of 45 calendar days, for a traumatic job-related injury
- Compensation for wages lost as a result of job-related injury or illness
- Medical care for disability due to personal injuries sustained while in the performance of duty or diseases caused, aggravated, or accelerated by postal employment
- Vocational rehabilitation

TRAINING AND QUALIFICATIONS

An applicant for a postal service job must pass an examination and meet minimum age requirements. Generally, the minimum age is 18 years, but a high school graduate may begin work at 16 years if the job is not hazardous and does not require use of a motor vehicle. Many postal service jobs do not require formal education or special training. Applicants for these jobs are hired on the basis of their examination scores.

Some postal jobs do have special education or experience requirements, while some are open only to veterans.

Additional Qualifying Issues for USPS Positions

- Male applicants between the ages of 18 and 25 must be registered with the Selective Service System, unless for some reason they are exempt.
- The Immigration Reform and Control Act of 1986 applies to postal workers. All postal workers must be citizens of the United States or must be able to prove identity and right to work in the United States (permanent resident alien status—Green Card).
- Applicants should apply at the post office where they wish to work and take the entrance examination for the job they want.
- A physical examination, including drug testing, is required.
- Applicants for jobs that require strength and stamina are sometimes given a special test. For example, mail handlers must be able to lift mail sacks weighing up to 70 pounds. The names of applicants who pass the examinations are placed on a list in the order of their scores.
- Examinations for most jobs include a written test.

When a job opens, the appointing officer chooses one of the top three applicants. Others are kept on file so they can be considered for future openings.

NOTE

Any special requirements will be stated on the announcement of examination.

New employees are trained either on the job by supervisors and other experienced employees or in local training centers. Training ranges from a few days to several months, depending on the job. Advancement opportunities are available for most postal workers because a management commitment provides career development. Employees also can get preferred assignments, such as the day shift or a more desirable delivery route, as their seniority increases. When an opening occurs, employees may submit written requests, called "bids," for assignment to the vacancy. The bidder who meets the qualifications and who has the most seniority gets the job.

FINDING MORE INFORMATION ABOUT USPS POSITIONS

TIP

You also can visit www.jobsfed.com and www.usps.gov/hrisp for additional information about career opportunities with the USPS.

National job listings for the United States Postal Service can be found at the USPS Web site at www.usps.gov. Employment opportunities are broken into three categories:

- Mail Processing Jobs: maintenance, operations, transportation

- Corporate Jobs: administrative/clerical, customer service, economics, emergency preparedness, engineering, facilities, finance, human resources, information technology, law enforcement, labor relations, legal, sales, purchasing, transportation, and other corporate areas

- USPS Employees: internal positions for those who already work for the USPS

- Bargaining Unit Reassignment: This Web-based application, also known as eReassign, allows USPS employees to electronically:

  1. Submit a reassignment request via the Internet
  2. View the status of a request
  3. View offices and positions within each district

SUMMING IT UP

- USPS employees enjoy very generous benefits, including:
  - Automatic raises at least once a year
  - Regular cost-of-living adjustments
  - Liberal paid vacation, sick leave, and other forms of leave
  - Life insurance
  - Hospitalization
  - Opportunity to join a credit union
- Applicants for USPS jobs must pass an examination and meet minimum age requirements.

Postal Service Job Descriptions

OVERVIEW

- Post office clerk
- City or special carrier/special delivery messenger
- Distribution clerk—machine
- Flat sorting machine operator
- Mail handler
- Mail processor
- Mark-up clerk—automated
- Rural carrier
- Clerk-typist, clerk-stenographer, typist
- Data conversion operator
- Cleaner, custodian, laborer—custodial
- Motor-vehicle operator, tractor-trailer operator
- Garageman
- Building equipment mechanic
- Electronic technician
- Summing it up

Deciding on a job with the USPS is like deciding on any other job. Each position is unique and will appeal to different individuals for different reasons. Do you enjoy a specific type of work? If you don't really like being outdoors, then a courier route is probably not the right position for you. Perhaps you enjoy a position that is more structured compared to one that changes every minute. If that's the case, a mail sorting position might be the best fit for you.

The point is that you should try to match the job descriptions listed in this chapter with your own interests. Keep in mind, however, that all positions within the USPS are competitive, so you may need to find two or three positions that interest you, in case your position of choice doesn't happen right away.

chapter 2

POST OFFICE CLERK

Job Duties

Think back to that trip to the post office we talked about earlier. You might remember thinking that the only duties of a postal clerk are to sell stamps and to take your packages. Actually, the majority of postal clerks are distribution clerks who sort incoming and outgoing mail in workrooms. Only in a small post office will a postal clerk perform double duty of sitting behind the counter and sorting mail. Generally speaking, a post office clerk performs the following tasks:

- Sorts and distributes mail to post offices and carrier routes

- Performs a variety of services at public windows of post offices, post office branches, or stations (again, usually only in small post offices)

- Performs related duties, as assigned

Working Conditions

The postal clerk may have to perform manual work, depending on the size of the post office and the equipment in place (such as chutes and sorting machines) to help with this task. Generally speaking, work involves continuous standing, stretching, and reaching. Additionally, the postal clerk may be required to handle heavy sacks of letter mail or parcel post weighing up to 70 pounds.

As we mentioned earlier, different jobs will appeal to different people—for different reasons. However, you should be aware that some distribution clerks can become bored with the routine of sorting mail. Also, postal clerks may be required to work at night (especially in large post offices where sorting and distributing the mail is a "24/7" activity).

However, if your duties also include those of a window clerk, you will more than likely experience a wider variety of duties. You will have frequent contact with the public (which may be viewed as a benefit or drawback, depending on the type of person you are), your work will (usually) be less physically strenuous, and you won't have to work much at night. Again, each post office differs in the particular duties that are assigned to the postal clerk.

Qualifications

Qualification requirements for the position of postal clerk closely mirror the working conditions just described. Candidates must demonstrate the following:

- Ability to perform the physical duties of the position, including prolonged standing, walking, and reaching

- Ability to lift heavy sacks of mail

- 20/40 (Snellen) vision in one eye (corrective lenses permitted)

- Ability to read, without strain, printed material the size of typewritten characters (corrective lenses permitted)
- Ability to hear the conversational voice, with or without a hearing aid (for window positions)
- Emotional and mental stability
- No irremediable defect or incurable disease that prevents efficient performance of duty, or that renders them a hazard to themselves, fellow employees, or others

Testing Requirement

Applicants must pass the General Entrance Test Battery 473/473-C.

Postal clerks are represented by:

The American Postal Workers Union (APWU), AFL-CIO
1300 L St. NW
Washington, D.C. 20005
202-842-4200
www.apwu.org

ALERT!

The new Exam 473/473-C, which is replacing the old Test Battery 470, is explained in detail in Chapter 3.

CITY OR SPECIAL CARRIER/SPECIAL DELIVERY MESSENGER

Perhaps the most familiar of the positions within the postal service is that of mail carrier. Indeed, the mailperson is a fixture in our culture. Despite the rise in popularity of e-mail, it's difficult to imagine a world where there is no daily mail. You might be surprised to learn, however, that much of the postal carrier's work is done before and after they deliver the mail. Often starting as early as 6 a.m., mail carriers start their day at the post office, where they spend a few hours arranging their mail for delivery, readdressing letters to be forwarded, and taking care of other details.

Job Duties

A mail carrier typically covers a route on foot, toting a heavy load of mail in a satchel or pushing it in a cart. In outlying areas, a mail carrier may drive a car or small truck. Mail carriers and special delivery messengers perform the following tasks:

- Promptly and efficiently deliver and collect mail on foot or by vehicle under varying conditions in a prescribed area or on various routes
- Deliver parcel post from trucks and make collections of mail from various boxes or other locations
- Maintain pleasant and effective public relations with customers

Working Conditions

The mail is always delivered—regardless of the conditions. In fact, there must be an extreme weather situation for the mail to be postponed for an entire day (it may be late, of course, but that's a big difference from not going out at all).

With that thought in mind, carriers must be able to perform the following tasks:

- Drive motor vehicles in all kinds of traffic and road conditions
- Carry mail in shoulder satchels weighing as much as 35 pounds
- Load and unload sacks of mail weighing up to 70 pounds
- Serve in all kinds of weather

Despite these tough requirements, the job does have many advantages. Carriers who begin work early in the morning are finished by early afternoon. They are also free to work at their own pace as long as they cover their routes within a reasonable period of time.

Qualifications

As is the case with many positions with the USPS, carriers must be able to perform physically taxing work. Candidates must demonstrate the following:

- Ability to perform the physical duties of the position, including prolonged standing, walking, and reaching
- Ability to lift heavy sacks of mail
- 20/40 (Snellen) vision in one eye (corrective lenses permitted)
- Ability to read, without strain, printed material the size of typewritten characters (corrective lenses permitted)
- Ability to hear the conversational voice, with or without a hearing aid (for window positions)
- Emotional and mental stability
- No irremediable defect or incurable disease that prevents efficient performance of duty, or that renders them a hazard to themselves, fellow employees, or others

For positions requiring driving, applicants must have a valid state driver's license and demonstrate and maintain a safe driving record. Applicants must pass the Postal Service road test to show the ability to safely drive a vehicle of the type used on the job.

If driving a vehicle weighing less than 10,000 pounds (GVW), vision of 20/40 in one eye and the ability to read, without strain, printed material the size of typewritten characters (corrective lenses permitted). The ability to hear is not required to operate a vehicle weighing less than 10,000 pounds (GVW).

Testing Requirement

Applicants must pass the General Entrance Test Battery 473/473-C.

City or Special Carrier/Special Delivery Messengers are represented by:

National Association of Letter Carriers (NALC), AFL-CIO
100 Indiana Ave. NW
Washington, D.C. 20001-2144
202-393-4695
www.nalc.org

DISTRIBUTION CLERK—MACHINE

Job Duties

The work of the distribution clerk is more routine than that of other postal clerks, but the starting salary is higher. However, you should realize that as a distribution clerk, you may be on your feet all day. Additionally, you must be able to occasionally handle sacks of mail weighing up to 70 pounds.

Perhaps the most challenging aspect of the job (and an aspect that will either greatly appeal to you or greatly discourage you, depending on your personality type) is the way in which you must sort mail. You must memorize a complicated scheme, which will enable you to quickly and efficiently sort mail. For example, these schemes include being able to quickly read a ZIP Code and then determine how the piece of mail is to be directed.

Qualifications

The distribution clerk—machine applicant must possess sufficient levels of the following Knowledge, Skills, and Abilities (KSAs):

- Knowledge of multi-position letter sorting machine
- Ability to work without immediate supervision
- Ability to work in cooperation with follow employees to efficiently perform the duties of the position
- Ability to observe and act on visual information such as names, addresses, numbers, and shapes
- Ability to learn and recall pairings of addresses with numbers, letters, or positions
- Ability to sequence, or place mail in the proper numerical, alphabetical, or geographic order
- Ability to efficiently perform the physical duties of the position

TIP

Increased automation within the USPS has made the job of the distribution clerk quite secure. Although nothing is ever 100 percent guaranteed, this is a fact you might consider when investigating USPS positions (along with your own personal interests, of course).

- 20/40 (Snellen) vision in one eye, near acuity of 7 or higher in either eye (Titmus or Bausch and Lomb), and the ability to read, without strain, printed material the size of typewritten characters (corrective lenses permitted)

- Ability to distinguish basic colors and shades

Testing Requirement

Applicants must pass the General Entrance Test Battery 473/473-C and successfully complete dexterity training as required by management.

Distribution Clerks are represented by:

The American Postal Workers Union (APWU), AFL-CIO
1300 L St. NW
Washington, D.C. 20005
202-842-4200
www.apwu.org

FLAT SORTING MACHINE OPERATOR

Job Duties

A flat sorting machine operator's work is very similar to that of the distribution clerk. However, as a flat sorting machine operator, you will work with large, bulky packages.

You might guess that you will have to possess greater physical strength and stamina. As with the machine operator's position, increasing automation adds a good degree of security to this position.

Qualifications

The flat sorting machine operator applicant must possess sufficient levels of the following Knowledge, Skills, and Abilities (KSAs):

- Knowledge of all recall pairings of addresses with numbers, letters, or positions

- Ability to work without immediate supervision

- Ability to work in cooperation with fellow employees to efficiently perform the duties of the position

- Ability to observe and act on visual information such as names, addresses, numbers, and shapes

- Ability to sequence, or place mail in the proper numerical, alphabetical, or geographic order

- Ability to perform routine troubleshooting, such as removing jams

- Ability to efficiently perform the physical duties of the position

- 20/40 (Snellen) vision in one eye, near acuity of 7 or higher in either eye (Titmus or Bausch and Lomb), and the ability to read, without strain, printed material the size of typewritten characters (corrective lenses permitted)

- Ability to distinguish basic colors and shades

Testing Requirement

Applicants pass the General Entrance Test Battery 473/473-C, successfully complete the appropriate training program for the flat sorting machine operation, and demonstrate the ability to key 45 items per minute with 98 percent accuracy.

Flat Sorting Machine Operators are represented by:

> The American Postal Workers Union (APWU), AFL-CIO
> 1300 L St. NW
> Washington, D.C. 20005
> 202-842-4200
> www.apwu.org

MAIL HANDLER

Job Duties

As a mail handler, you will unload loads, move bulk mail, and perform other duties incidental to the movement and processing of mail.

Qualifications

The mail handler applicant must possess sufficient levels of the following Knowledge, Skills, and Abilities (KSAs):

- Minimum competency for senior-qualified positions

- Ability to perform these KSAs by describing examples of experience, education, or training, any of which may be non-postal

- Ability to perform efficiently the physical duties of the position

- Because of the extreme physical nature of this job, certain physical conditions can preclude you from taking the strength and stamina test without prior approval from your doctor (which is a requirement for this position). These conditions include hernia or rupture, back trouble, heart trouble, pregnancy, or any other condition that makes it dangerous for you to lift and carry 70-pound weights.

- 20/40 (Snellen) vision in one eye and the ability to read, without strain, printed material the size of typewritten characters (corrective lenses are permitted)

- Ability to hear the conversational voice in at least one ear (hearing aid permitted)

Testing Requirement

Applicants must pass the General Entrance Test Battery 473/473-C and pass a physical ability test.

Mail Handlers are represented by:

> National Postal Mail Handlers Union (NPMHU), AFL-CIO
> 1101 Connecticut Ave. NW, Suite 500
> Washington, D.C. 20036
> 202-833-9095
> www.npmhu.org

MAIL PROCESSOR

Job Duties

Mail processors perform a combination of tasks that are required to process the mail by utilizing a variety of mail processing equipment.

Working Conditions

You won't find the physical requirements for this position as tough as those required for mail handlers. However, you won't start at the same salary as that of a mail handler.

Qualifications

The mail processor applicant must possess sufficient levels of the following Knowledge, Skills, and Abilities (KSAs):

- Ability to perform efficiently the physical duties of the position
- 20/40 (Snellen) vision in one eye and the ability to read, without strain, printed material the size of typewritten characters (corrective lenses permitted)
- Ability to distinguish basic colors and shades

Testing Requirement

Applicants must pass the General Entrance Test Battery 473/473-C and pass a physical ability test.

Mail Processors are represented by:

> The American Postal Workers Union (APWU), AFL-CIO
> 1300 L St. NW
> Washington, D.C. 20005
> 202-842-4200
> www.apwu.org

MARK-UP CLERK—AUTOMATED

Job Duties

A mark-up clerk—automated operates an electro-mechanical operator-paced machine to process mail that is undeliverable as addressed. In doing this, the clerk operates the keyboard of a computer terminal to enter and extract data to several databases. Although you don't have to be a computer programmer to qualify for this position, you should feel comfortable working with computers, as you will need to work in several potentially different programs to enter, view, and change data.

Qualifications

The mark-up clerk—automated applicant must possess sufficient levels of the following Knowledge, Skills, and Abilities (KSAs):

- Ability to use reference materials and manuals relevant to the position
- Ability to perform effectively under the pressures of the position
- Ability to operate any office equipment appropriate to the position
- Ability to work with others
- Six months of clerical or office machine operating experience
- Ability to type will prove invaluable
- Successful completion of a four-year high school course; successful completion of business school may be substituted for the six months of clerical or office machine operating requirements
- Ability to perform efficiently the physical duties of the position
- 20/40 (Snellen) vision in one eye and the ability to read, without strain, printed material the size of typewritten characters (corrective lenses permitted)
- Ability to distinguish basic colors and shades

Testing Requirement

Given the clerically oriented requirements of this position, you'll need to demonstrate the ability to key data codes on a computer terminal at a rate of 14 correct lines per minute. This is determined by successful completion of Clerical Ability Test 710. You'll also need to pass the General Entrance Test Battery 473/473-C.

Mark-up Clerks—Automated are represented by:

The American Postal Workers Union (APWU), AFL-CIO
1300 L St. NW
Washington, D.C. 20005
202-842-4200
www.apwu.org

RURAL CARRIER

Job Duties

The work of the rural carrier combines the work of the window clerk and the letter carrier. However, the job also has special characteristics of its own.

A rural carrier begins the day with sorting and loading the mail for delivery. Then comes the drive, which may be over tough roads and through tough weather. Given the rural nature of the job, the rural carrier delivers most of the mail from the car. At the end of the day, the carrier returns to the post office with outgoing mail and money collected in various transactions.

As you might guess, you'll enjoy a great deal of independence with this position, as there is no one looking over your shoulder. However, the work can be taxing, and you will have to endure the inherent dilemmas that come with spending lots of time in the car.

Because many of the rural carrier's patrons live in remote locations (hence the word *rural* in the job title), this employee will occasionally also be required to perform all the duties of a window clerk, including accepting, collecting, and delivering all classes of mail and selling stamp supplies and money orders.

Working Conditions

In general, you should expect the following working conditions:

- You must load and deliver parcels weighing up to 70 pounds.
- You must place letters and parcels in mailboxes, requiring careful handling of the vehicle and frequent shifting from one side of the vehicle to the other.

Qualifications

NOTE

Working with the public requires maintaining pleasant and effective working relations with customers and an acceptable appearance.

The rural carrier applicant must possess sufficient levels of the following Knowledge, Skills, and Abilities (KSAs):

- Ability to read, understand, and apply written instructions
- Ability to perform basic arithmetic computations
- Ability to prepare reports and maintain records
- Ability to communicate effectively with customers
- Ability to work effectively without close supervision
- Ability to perform efficiently the arduous physical duties of the position
- 20/40 (Snellen) vision in one eye and the ability to read, without strain, printed material the size of typewritten characters (corrective lenses permitted)

Testing Requirement

Applicants must successfully complete the Rural Carrier Exam 460.

In addition to completing the Rural Carrier Exam 460, applicants must also have a valid state driver's license and a safe driving record, and must pass the Postal Service road test. Additionally, rural carriers furnish all necessary vehicle equipment for prompt handling of the mail, unless supplied by the employer.

Rural carriers are represented by:

National Rural Letter Carriers Association (NLRCA)
1630 Duke St., Fourth Floor
Alexandria, VA 22314-3465
703-684-5545
www.nrlca.org

CLERK-TYPIST, CLERK-STENOGRAPHER, TYPIST

Job Duties

A clerk-typist types records, letters, memorandums, reports, and other materials from hand-written and other drafts, or from a dictating machine. He or she sets up the material typed in accordance with prescribed format and assembles it for initialing, signing, routing, and dispatch. The clerk-typist also cuts mimeograph stencils and masters for duplication by other processes.

The miscellaneous office clerical duties of the position include: making file folders, keeping them in the prescribed order, and filing them; making and keeping routine office records; composing routine memorandums and letters relating to the business of the office, such as acknowledgments and transmittals; examining incoming and outgoing mail of the office, routing it to the appropriate persons, and controlling the time allowed for preparation of replies to incoming correspondence; receipting and delivering salary checks and filling out various personnel forms; acting as receptionist and furnishing routine information over the telephone; relieving other office personnel in their absence; and operating office machines such as the mimeograph, comptometer, and adding machine.

The clerk-stenographer performs all the functions of the clerk-typist. Also, the clerk-stenographer takes dictation, in shorthand or on a shorthand writing machine, of letters, memorandums, reports, and other materials given by the supervisor of the office and other employees. He or she then transcribes it on the typewriter or word processor, sets up the material transcribed in accordance with prescribed format, and assembles it for required initialing, signing, routing, and dispatch. In consideration of the extra training and skill required in the taking of dictation, the clerk-stenographer is rated at salary level 5 rather than at the salary level 4 of the clerk-typist.

Qualifications

The clerk-typist, clerk-stenographer, typist applicant must possess sufficient levels of the following Knowledge, Skills, and Abilities (KSAs):

- Ability to perform basic mathematical computations

- Ability to follow instructions, both written and verbal

- Ability to keep records, such as files, charts, and indexes, in an organized fashion for proper retrieval

- Ability to prepare reports and correspondence in acceptable form

- Ability to operate office machines safely and make any necessary adjustments to these machines

- Ability to perform efficiently the physical duties of the position

- 20/40 (Snellen) vision in one eye and the ability to read, without strain, printed material the size of typewritten characters (corrective lenses permitted)

- Ability to hear the conversational voice (hearing aid permitted)

Testing Requirement

To qualify for these positions, you'll need to successfully complete Clerical Abilities Exam 710, Parts A and B, which demonstrate your clerical and verbal abilities. Additionally, applicants will need to successfully complete Postal Service Test 712, which demonstrates your ability to type at a net rate of 45 words per minute in a five-minute test. Successful completion of Postal Service Test 711 is required for clerk-stenographer positions. This test demonstrates the applicant's ability to take dictation at the rate of 80 words per minute and interpret this dictation.

Clerical staff is represented by:

The American Postal Workers Union (APWU), AFL-CIO
1300 L St. NW
Washington, D.C. 20005
202-842-4200
www.apwu.org

DATA CONVERSION OPERATOR

Job Duties

Data conversion operators use a computer terminal to prepare mail for automated sorting equipment. They read typed or handwritten addresses from a letter image on the terminal screen and then select and type essential information so that an address bar code can be applied to the letter. Depending on the quality of the address information shown on the image, data conversion operators are prompted to key the five-number ZIP Code or an abbreviated version of the street and city address. Abbreviated addresses must conform to strict encoding rules so that the computer can then expand the abbreviation to a full address and find the correct ZIP + 4 code. Unlike some other types of data entry, this job is not just "key what you see."

REMOTE BAR CODING SYSTEM

Data conversion operators are the vital personnel in the Remote Bar Coding System (RBCS), a system designed to allow letter mail that cannot be read by a machine to be bar-coded and processed in the automated mail stream. RBCS technology has created a new operation called a remote encoding center (REC). RBCS has two major elements: an input subsystem (ISS) and an output subsystem (OSS).

At the processing plant, ISS takes a video picture or image of each letter and then attempts to look up the address to find a ZIP + 4 code. For letters for which the ISS computer cannot find a ZIP + 4 code, corresponding images are transmitted by telephone lines to data conversion operators at the remote encoding center for further processing. At the REC, data conversion operators working at video display terminals are presented with images one at a time. Using specific rules, operators key data for each image so that the computers can find the correct ZIP + 4 code.

At the plant, the output subsystem sprays letters with correct ZIP + 4 bar codes and performs initial sorting. Letters are then processed by bar code sorters. These elements are linked by a communication system consisting of cabling and telephone or microwave telecommunications.

Qualifications

The data conversion operator applicant must possess sufficient levels of the following Knowledge, Skills, and Abilities (KSAs):

- Ability to perform efficiently the physical duties of the position
- 20/40 (Snellen) vision in one eye and the ability to read, without strain, printed material the size of typewritten characters (corrective lenses permitted)
- Ability to distinguish basic colors and shades
- Ability to hear the conversational voice (hearing aid permitted)

Testing Requirement

Applicants must successfully complete the Clerical Abilities Exam 710 and Postal Service Exam 714 at the high standard. This demonstrates the applicant's ability to key data on a computer terminal at a rate of 35 correct lines within five minutes.

NOTE

Remote encoding centers offer a possibility for flexible scheduling. The basic work hours are between 3:00 p.m. and 1:00 a.m. Individual work schedules range between four and eight hours. RECS operate seven days a week.

Data Conversion Operators are represented by:

The American Postal Workers Union (APWU), AFL-CIO
1300 L St. NW
Washington, D.C. 20005
202-842-4200
www.apwu.org

CLEANER, CUSTODIAN, LABORER—CUSTODIAL

Job Duties

Workers who serve as cleaners, custodians, or custodial laborers are charged with the maintenance of postal buildings. These positions include routine and periodic heavy cleaning, routine maintenance (such as replacing light bulbs), and responsibility for noticing when specialized maintenance or repair work is called for and then following through to be certain that this is done at the proper time.

While the work of custodial laborers, cleaners, and custodians is not generally noticed by the public, their work is vital to the operation of post offices and to the health and safety of postal workers and patrons.

NON–U.S. VETERANS NEED NOT APPLY

The positions of cleaner, custodian, and custodial laborer are open only to veterans of the United States Armed Services. All other applications will be rejected. While these positions are at the low end of the postal pay scale, they afford the veteran an opportunity to earn a steady wage and to enjoy all the fringe benefits and security of all other postal employees.

The person who starts a career with the Postal Service as a cleaner, custodian, or custodial laborer can advance to positions of greater responsibility within the custodial service or can prepare for examinations for other positions, either more specialized jobs within building maintenance or completely different jobs such as mail handler, letter clerk, and others.

People who already work for the Postal Service in any capacity need not wait for an exam that is open to the public to be announced. After being employed at their present position for a year, they may ask to take an exam at any time. Although this request may or may not be granted, this is one special advantage of postal employees that makes the veterans-only feature of this position so valuable.

NOTE

A veteran who wants a postal career can break in at the bottom and rise rapidly.

Qualifications

The cleaner, custodian, laborer—custodial applicant must possess sufficient levels of the following Knowledge, Skills, and Abilities (KSAs):

- Ability to use hand tools, such as power cleaning equipment (waxers, polishers, mowers, and similar equipment)

- Ability to work without immediate supervision

- Ability to handle weights and loads beyond normal functions of a position (for custodian and laborer)

- Ability to perform efficiently the physical duties of the position, including standing, walking, climbing, bending, reaching, and stooping for prolonged periods of time

- 20/40 (Snellen) vision in one eye and the ability to read, without strain, printed material the size of typewritten characters (corrective lenses permitted)

Cleaners and custodial employees are represented by:

The American Postal Workers Union (APWU), AFL-CIO
1300 L St. NW
Washington, D.C. 20005
202-842-4200
www.apwu.org

MOTOR-VEHICLE OPERATOR, TRACTOR-TRAILER OPERATOR

Job Duties

What's the thing these jobs have in common? The answer is driving various Postal Service vehicles on the highway and within the lots and properties of the Postal Service.

Motor vehicle operators operate a mail truck on a regularly scheduled route to pick up and transport mail in bulk.

Tractor-trailer operators operate a heavy-duty tractor-trailer in over-the-road service, city shuttle service, or trailer spotting operations.

Qualifications

Given the specific technical training inherent to these positions (knowing how to handle a large vehicle), you'll need to have one year or more of full-time, or equivalent, employment driving 7-ton trucks or buses of at least 16 passengers. At least six months must be in driving a tractor-trailer (for the position of tractor-trailer operator). Additionally, the motor vehicle, tractor-trailer operator applicant must possess sufficient levels of the following Knowledge, Skills, and Abilities (KSAs):

- Knowledge of safety procedures for the duties common to the position

- Ability to drive under local driving conditions

- Ability to follow instructions and to prepare trip and other reports

- Ability to perform efficiently the physical duties of the position

- 30/30 (Snellen) vision in one eye and 20/50 (Snellen) vision in the other eye, with or without corrective lenses; the ability to read, without strain, printed material the size of typewritten characters (corrective lenses permitted) (for applicants required to drive vehicles 10,000 pounds [CVW] or more)

- Ability to hear the conversational voice in one ear (hearing aids permitted)
- Emotional and mental stability

Testing Requirement

These positions are filled by rated application. Applicants must successfully complete Postal Service Exam 91, which demonstrates an applicant's ability to understand instructions and fill out forms, and the Postal Service road test to demonstrate an ability to safely drive a vehicle of the type used on the job.

In addition, applicants:

- Must have a valid state driver's license
- Must demonstrate and maintain a safe driving record

Motor vehicle employees are represented by:

The American Postal Workers Union (APWU), AFL-CIO
1300 L St. NW
Washington, D.C. 20005
202-842-4200
www.apwu.org

GARAGEMAN

Job Duties

The position of garageman requires routine services to properly maintain motor vehicles. Obviously, this position requires an applicant to be comfortable with—and most importantly, enjoy—working on motor vehicles.

Qualifications

The garageman applicant must possess sufficient levels of the following Knowledge, Skills, and Abilities (KSAs):

- Ability to assemble and disassemble mechanical equipment
- Ability to work without immediate supervision
- Ability to work with others
- 20/40 (Snellen) vision in one eye and the ability to read, without strain, printed material the size of typewritten characters (corrective lenses are permitted)
- Ability to distinguish basic colors and shades
- Ability to hear the conversational voice (hearing aids permitted)

Testing Requirement

This position is filled by rated application. Applicants must successfully complete Postal Service Exam 91, which demonstrates an applicant's ability to understand instructions and fill out forms, and the Postal Service road test to demonstrate an ability to safely drive a vehicle of the type used on the job.

In addition, applicants:

- Must have a valid state driver's license
- Must have and maintain a safe driving record

Garagemen are represented by:

The American Postal Workers Union (APWU), AFL-CIO
1300 L St. NW
Washington, D.C. 20005
202-842-4200
www.apwu.org

BUILDING EQUIPMENT MECHANIC

Job Duties

Building equipment mechanics perform a variety of tasks (some highly specialized), including:

- Troubleshooting and performing complex maintenance work on building and building equipment systems
- Performing preventive maintenance inspections of building, building equipment, and building systems
- Maintaining and operating a large automated air conditioning system and a large heating system

Qualifications

Given the nature of the job, applicants are required to have at least a basic understanding of several maintenance-related topics, including:

- Basic mechanics
- Basic electricity
- Basic electronics
- Safety procedures and equipment
- Lubrication materials and procedures
- Cleaning materials and procedures
- National Electrical Code (NEC)

- Refrigeration

- Heating, ventilation, and air conditioning (HVAC)

- Plumbing

In addition, the building equipment mechanic applicant must possess sufficient levels of the following Knowledge, Skills, and Abilities (KSAs):

- Knowledge of basic and complex mathematics

- Ability to apply theoretical knowledge to practical applications

- Ability to detect patterns

- Ability to use written reference materials

- Ability to communicate in writing and orally

- Ability to follow instructions

- Ability to work under pressure

- Ability to work with others

- Ability to work without immediate supervision

- Ability to work from heights

- Ability to use hand tools

- Ability to use portable power tools

- Ability to use shop power equipment

- Ability to use technical drawings

- Ability to use test equipment

- Ability to solder

- 20/40 (Snellen) vision in one eye and the ability to read, without strain, printed material the size of typewritten characters (corrective lenses permitted)

- Ability to distinguish basic colors and shades

- Ability to hear the conversational voice in a noisy environment and to identify environmental sounds, such as equipment running or unusual noises (hearing aids permitted)

Testing Requirement

Applicants must successfully complete General Maintenance Exam 931.

In addition, applicants must:

- Complete a prescribed training course (for some positions)

- Be able to operate powered industrial equipment

- Have a valid state driver's license, and demonstrate and maintain a safe driving record (for driving positions)

- Pass the Postal Service road test to show the ability to safely drive a vehicle of the type used on the job (for driving positions)
- Consent to driving motor vehicles in all kinds of traffic and road conditions

Maintenance employees are represented by:

The American Postal Workers Union (APWU), AFL-CIO
1300 L St. NW
Washington, D.C. 20005
202-842-4200
www.apwu.org

ELECTRONIC TECHNICIAN

Job Duties

An electrical technician must independently perform the full range of diagnostic preventive maintenance, alignment, and calibrations, as well as overhaul tasks on both hardware and software on a variety of equipment and systems. These technicians also apply advanced technical knowledge to solve complex problems.

Qualifications

In addition, the electronic technician applicant must possess sufficient levels of the following Knowledge, Skills, and Abilities (KSAs):

- Knowledge of basic mechanics
- Knowledge of basic electricity
- Knowledge of basic electronics and digital electronics
- Knowledge of safety procedures and equipment
- Knowledge of basic computer concepts
- Knowledge of basic and complex mathematics
- Ability to apply theoretical knowledge to practical applications
- Ability to detect patterns
- Ability to use written reference materials
- Ability to communicate in writing and orally
- Ability to follow instructions
- Ability to work under pressure
- Ability to work with others
- Ability to work without immediate supervision
- Ability to work from heights

NOTE

Similar to the maintenance position mentioned previously, the electrical technician may be called upon to possess a specific knowledge base.

- Ability to use hand tools
- Ability to use portable power tools
- Ability to use technical drawings
- Ability to use test equipment
- Ability to solder
- 20/40 (Snellen) vision in one eye and the ability to read, without strain, printed material the size of typewritten characters (corrective lenses permitted)
- Ability to distinguish basic colors and shades
- Ability to hear the conversational voice in a noisy environment and to identify environmental sounds, such as equipment running or unusual noises (hearing aids permitted)

Testing Requirement

Applicants must complete the Electronic Technician Exam 932.

In addition, applicants:

- May be required to complete a prescribed training course
- Must be able to operate powered industrial equipment

For positions requiring driving, applicants:

- Must produce a valid state driver's license and have and maintain a safe driving record
- Must pass the Postal Service road test to show an ability to safely drive a vehicle of the type used on the job
- Must be able to drive motor vehicles in all kinds of traffic and road conditions

Electronic Technicians are represented by:

The American Postal Workers Union (APWU), AFL-CIO
1300 L St. NW
Washington, D.C. 20005
202-842-4200
www.apwu.org

SUMMING IT UP

- USPS jobs come with working conditions, qualifications, and testing requirements unique to each specific job.

- Try to match a job with your own interests.

- All USPS positions are competitive, so you may need to find two or three positions that interest you, in case your position of choice doesn't happen right away.

PART II

FAMILIARIZE YOURSELF WITH THE TESTS

Get to Know the Tests

chapter 3

OVERVIEW

- What's it all about?
- Parts of the tests
- Test-taking instructions
- Filling in answer sheets
- Score determination and reporting
- General test-taking strategies
- Summing it up

WHAT'S IT ALL ABOUT?

Anxiety prior to taking a test is normal. You've spent many hours studying and preparing for the exam, and you want to get the best score possible. In addition, you probably think (and rightly so) that this test may be just a bit more important than some of those spelling tests you took back in elementary school. This is your career, and you want to prove to yourself and others that you're capable of achieving the highest performance.

Although the postal exams are a bit unusual (as compared to other tests), there really is no reason for you to be overly nervous. If you've put in the time studying for the exam, if you use common sense, and if you don't panic, you'll be well on your way to achieving a good score.

This chapter is designed to help alleviate even more of your pre-test anxiety by introducing you to the format of the tests. Then, as you study the rest of this book, you'll have plenty of opportunity to practice the various question types. By test day, you still might be a bit nervous, but you shouldn't encounter any surprises.

This chapter provides you with an introduction to Postal Exams 460 and 473/473-C. But you may be asking yourself, "Hey, wait a minute! The previous chapters of this book mention several different tests. What about them?" Although you may encounter different question types if you take an exam other than the 460 or 473/473-C, the vast majority of questions will be very similar to the ones you encounter—and practice—in this book. So although we may be describing only 460 or 473/473-C questions, you can be assured that if you master these tests, you will be very well prepared, no matter what additional test you may be required to take. These two exams are used to fill more than 90 percent of all full-time USPS positions.

Exam 460 is used to fill Rural Carrier and Rural Carrier Associate positions.

Now the big news!

The new Exam 473/473-C was launched in December 2004 to replace old Exam 470. The exam is called Exam 473 when it is given to fill all entry-level Processing, Distribution, Delivery, and Retail positions. However, the City Carrier position is in highest demand. Therefore, that test is occasionally given to fill that one job classification. When the test is given just to fill City Carrier positions, it is called Exam 473-C. Regardless of which exam you take, however, the content is identical. The only thing different about the two is the name it is given. As a result, we will refer to Exam 473/473-C simply as Exam 473.

PARTS OF THE TESTS

NOTE

Exam 473 is used by the Postal Service to evaluate job-related skills. However, it is not a true aptitude test of your abilities.

The new Exam 473 contains traditional topics such as address checking and coding and memory but also contains other job-related behaviors such as:

- Forms completion
- Customer service and interpersonal skills

The following table describes the Exam parts/subject matter covered, time allotted for each part, and number of questions in each part.

EXAM PART	TIME ALLOTTED	NUMBER OF QUESTIONS
Part A: Address Checking	11 Minutes	60
Part B: Forms Completion	15 Minutes	30
Part C: Section 1—Coding	6 Minutes	36
Part C: Section 2—Memory	7 Minutes	36
Part D: Personal Characteristics and Experience Inventory	90 Minutes	236

Don't fall into the trap of thinking that you must possess certain innate talents to get a high score. On the contrary, preparing for this test will definitely increase your chances of doing well on it. The question types are extremely coachable and get easier with practice. Use your desire for getting hired as a key motivator throughout the test preparation process.

The remaining chapters of this book, as well as the full-length sample exams, will help you practice the various question types.

TEST-TAKING INSTRUCTIONS

You must not underestimate the importance of following all the rules and procedures required at the test center. This includes following all of the examiner's test-taking instructions and filling in the answer sheets correctly.

Instructions read by the examiner are intended to ensure that neither you nor any other applicant has an unfair advantage when taking the exam. Any infraction of the rules is considered cheating.

- Listen to what the examiner says at all times. Be prepared to immediately act on any exam changes to content, question type, directions, or time limits.

- Follow all instructions the examiner gives you. If you do not understand any of the examiner's instructions, ask questions.

- Don't begin working on any part of the test until told to do so.

- Stop working as soon as the examiner tells you to do so. Remember that your ability to follow instructions is considered in the hiring process.

- If you finish a test part before time is called, review your work for that test part. Although you cannot go on or back to any other part of the test, you have the chance to review answers that you are unsure of or to guess, if guessing is a good strategy for that test part. Use whatever extra time you have wisely.

- Don't work on any other part of the test than the one you are told to work on. Be certain to check that you're working on the right test part immediately. While working in the wrong section could be an inadvertent error on your part, it would not leave a favorable impression and probably could put you out of the running.

ALERT!

If you cheat, your test paper will not be scored and you will not be eligible for appointment.

FILLING IN ANSWER SHEETS

You will be required to fill in required personal information on the sample answer sheet sent to you by the Postal Service to be admitted to the test center. You cannot take the test without doing this. At the center of the answer sheet, you will be instructed to transfer the personal information you filled in on the sample answer sheet to the actual answer sheet.

How to Enter Your Answer

Exam 473 is machine-scored, so you must be careful to fill in your answer sheets clearly and accurately. You will be given instructions in the test kit sent to you by the Postal Service. You also will be given ample opportunity to perfect your skills in the practice material in this book.

SCORE DETERMINATION AND REPORTING

When the exam is over, the examiner will collect your test booklet and answer sheet. Your answer sheet will be sent to the National Test Administration Center in Merrifield, Virginia, where a machine will scan your answers and mark them as either right or wrong.

Reporting Scaled Scores

Your raw score is not your final score:

1. The Postal Service determines your raw scores for each test part.

2. Your part scores are combined according to a certain formula.

3. Your raw score is converted to a scaled score, on a scale of 1 to 100.

The entire process of conversion from raw to scaled score is confidential.

A total scaled score of 70 is a passing score. The names of all persons with 70 or more are placed on an eligibility list (called the register) that remains valid for two years. The register is ordered according to score rankings—the highest scores are at the top of the list. Hiring then takes place from the top of the list as vacancies occur. Many candidates prepare rigorously for this test and strive for perfect scores. In fact, most applicants who are hired score between 90 percent and 100 percent.

How Did You Do?

The scoring process may take 6–10 weeks, or even longer. Be patient. The process could take many months, but you remain eligible for employment for two years after taking the test. If you pass the exam, you will receive notice of your scaled score. As the hiring process nears your number, you will be notified to appear for the remaining steps of the hiring process:

1. Drug testing

2. Psychological interview

3. Physical performance tests, according to the requirements of the position

4. Alphanumeric typing test

If you fail the exam, you will not be informed of your score. You will simply be notified that you have failed and will not be considered for postal employment. Of course, this number will vary per exam administration. Use this number as a reality check for setting a serious study schedule. And while this is a high failure rate, don't let it shake your confidence. Your preparation will give you better odds of getting a higher score than many of the candidates.

GENERAL TEST-TAKING STRATEGIES

Learn the Directions for Each Question Type

Don't waste time during the test reading directions. You will be given the instructions by the Postal Service in your exam kit; know them inside and out. This book also gives you the most recent directions used on Exam 473. Remember, though, to listen to the examiner for an announcement that something has changed.

Skip Questions When Stumped

When you cannot answer a question for Parts A–C, skip the question and come back to it after finishing the other questions in that part of the test. Circle the number of the question in your test booklet to indicate the question skipped, and remember to skip the appropriate space on your answer sheet. A later section discusses whether you should guess.

Avoid Perfectionism

You are not expected to answer every question in Parts A and B. Don't be a perfectionist and waste time on questions you cannot answer. This kind of attitude can restrict the number of questions you attempt to answer, which will lower your score. Come back to the difficult questions if you have extra time to spare.

Use a stopwatch or a kitchen timer for accurate measurement; this will give you a sense of your optimal pace to apply on the actual test. Not doing this will handicap your chances for a higher score.

Know How Much Time You Have

To do well on Exam 473, you must work quickly within the time limits allowed. The examiner will probably inform you at periodic intervals of how much time you have left. Check your wristwatch as a backup, but don't become obsessed by watching the clock. Your time is better spent answering the questions. This means practicing for the test as much as possible, knowing what to expect, and following the strategies provided in this book.

Build a Test-Smart Attitude

By practicing as much as possible for Exam 473, you will gain confidence in yourself, which in turn will help you succeed on the actual test. Having a test-smart attitude also will help build your competitive spirit, an essential factor in doing well on this highly competitive examination.

TIP

Use the practice tests in this book to get used to the quick pace of the test and the stringent time limitations for each test part. Adhere to these time limitations without exception.

NOTE

Keeping track of time does not imply that you should rush through a section and answer questions carelessly. You must be in control of the situation to do your best.

Use the Test Booklet as Scratch Paper

You may find it beneficial to make notes or draw lines or arrows in the test booklet to help solve certain test questions. This may focus your thoughts and channel your energy to help solve the question. However, you don't want to spend too much time doing this. If it doesn't help you, just go on to the next question.

Eliminate Obviously Incorrect Answers

This common test-taking strategy can be used to different degrees on each test part except Part A, which has only two answer choices. To use this strategy, you must usually read all the answer choices listed to eliminate incorrect answers before choosing the correct answer. This prevents you from picking a red herring (a deliberately misleading answer choice) as the answer.

SUMMING IT UP

- Exam 473/473-C was launched in December 2004 and replaces Exam 470.

- Exam 473 contains traditional topics such as address checking and coding and memory but also contains other job-related behaviors such as:
  - Forms completion
  - Customer service and interpersonal skills

- The best way to prepare for the exam is to understand the test prior to taking it and by mastering some proven test-taking strategies.

Score Higher on Address-Checking Questions

chapter 4

OVERVIEW

- Strategies to score higher
- Address-checking techniques
- Summing it up

STRATEGIES TO SCORE HIGHER

Although everyone will respond to the tests differently, you can use the following tips and guidelines to assist you in answering these questions.

- **Read for differences only.** Once you spot a difference between the two given addresses, mark your answer sheet with a "D" and go immediately to the next question.

- **Vocalize your reading.** This doesn't mean simply reading out loud, but rather reading exactly what is listed. For example, if you see "St." don't read it as "Street," but as "ess–t." This will help you to focus on the exact details.

- **Know your state and territory abbreviations.** You should be familiar with conventional abbreviations as well as the two-letter capitalized abbreviations used with ZIP Codes.

Don't worry about memorizing this list. The point of having it included here is to demonstrate how easy it is to mistake one abbreviation for another. If you vocalize what you see, you should (hopefully) hear the differences. And remember: Your task is not to read for meaning, but to spot differences.

State	Conventional Abbreviation	Zip Code Abbreviation
Alabama	Ala.	AL
Alaska	n/a	AK
American Samoa	Amer. Samoa	AS
Arizona	Ariz.	AZ
Arkansas	Ark.	AR
California	Calif.	CA
Colorado	Colo.	CO
Connecticut	Conn.	CT
Delaware	Del.	DE
District of Columbia	D.C.	DC
Florida	Fla.	FL
Georgia	Ga.	GA
Guam	n/a	GU
Hawaii	n/a	HI
Idaho	n/a	ID
Illinois	Ill.	IL
Indiana	Ind.	IN
Iowa	n/a	IA
Kansas	Kans.	KS
Kentucky	Ky.	KY
Louisiana	La.	LA
Maine	n/a	ME
Maryland	Md.	MD
Massachusetts	Mass.	MA
Michigan	Mich.	MI
Minnesota	Minn.	MN
Mississippi	Miss.	MS
Missouri	Mo.	MO
Montana	Mont.	MT
Nebraska	Nebr.	NE
Nevada	Nev.	NV
New Hampshire	N.H.	NH
New Jersey	N.J.	NJ
New Mexico	N.Mex.	NM
New York	N.Y.	NY
North Carolina	N.C.	NC
North Dakota	N.Dak.	ND
Ohio	n/a	OH
Oklahoma	Okla.	OK
Oregon	Oreg.	OR
Pennsylvania	Pa.	PA
Puerto Rico	P.R.	PR
Rhode Island	R.I.	RI
South Carolina	S.C.	SC
South Dakota	S.Dak.	SD
Tennessee	Tenn.	TN
Texas	Tex.	TX

State	Conventional Abbreviation	Zip Code Abbreviation
Utah	n/a	UT
Vermont	Vt.	VT
Virginia	Va.	VA
Virgin Islands	V.I.	VI
Washington	Wash.	WA
West Virginia	W.Va.	WV
Wisconsin	Wis.	WI
Wyoming	Wyo.	WY

- **Use your hands.** Don't be afraid to use your index finger under or alongside the addresses being compared. This will help you to keep your place and to focus on just one line at a time.

- **Take the question apart.** Try to break the addresses into parts: For example, first compare the street name, then the ZIP Code and so on for each of the two items to be compared. This will help to make the comparison more manageable.

- **Read from right to left.** This can be very difficult for some people (remember, English-speakers read left to right, so this may take some practice if English—and many other languages—is your natural tongue). However, you might be surprised at how this forces your brain to focus on the details instead of on, for all practical purposes, extraneous information.

- **Play the numbers game.** You can expect to find many differences in numbers, so keep a close eye on this when you are making your comparison. Questions with two items that are not alike will often have differences in the number of digits as well as differences in the order of digits.

- **Watch for differences in abbreviations.** Similar to differences in numbers, you'll find many different types of standard abbreviations. You'll also find that it's very easy to misread these, especially when comparing two items.

TIP

Remember you aren't expected to answer all the questions in the time given. Just try to work as quickly and as accurately as possible, and avoid guessing if you start to run out of time.

ADDRESS-CHECKING TECHNIQUES

Vocalizing

Sound out the following abbreviations and numbers:

NY

CA

OR

VA

AL

HA

MT

MA

IL

TX

68919

10001

3694

Ct

Pkwy

Cir

Sample Questions

> **Directions:** Use your index finger or pointer and compare the following addresses. Are they alike or different? For each question, compare the address in the left column with the address in the right column. If the two addresses are **ALIKE** in every way, write "A" next to the question number. If the two addresses are **DIFFERENT** in any way, write "D" next to the question number.

1. 5115 Colchester Rd   5115 Calchester Rd

2. 4611 N Randall Pl   4611 N Randall Pl

3. 17045 Pascack Cir   17045 Pascack Cir

4. 3349 Palma del Mar Blvd   3346 Palma del Mar Blvd

5. 13211 E 182nd Ave   13211 E 182nd Ave

6. Francisco WY 82636   Francisco WI 82636

7. 6198 N Albritton Rd   6198 N Albretton Rd

8. 11230 Twinflower Cir   11230 Twintower Cir

9. 6191 MacDonald Station Rd   6191 MacDonald Station Rd

10. 1587 Vanderbilt Dr N   1587 Vanderbilt Dr S

Answer Key

1. D	3. A	5. A	7. D	9. A
2. A	4. D	6. D	8. D	10. D

Sample Questions

Directions: Break the following addresses into parts. Are they alike or different? For each question, compare the address in the left column with the address in the right column. If the two addresses are **ALIKE** in every way, write "A" next to the question number. If the two addresses are **DIFFERENT** in any way, write "D" next to the question number.

1. 3993 S Freemont Ter   3993 S Freemount Ter
2. 3654 S Urbane Dr   3564 S Urbane Cir
3. 1408 Oklahoma Ave NE   1408 Oklahoma Ave NE
4. 6201 Meadowland Ln   6201 Meadowlawn Ln
5. 5799 S Rockaway Ln   15799 S Rockaway Ln
6. 3782 SE Verrazanno Bay   37872 SE Verrazanno Bay
7. 2766 N Thunderbird Ct   2766 N Thunderbird Ct
8. 2166 N Elmmorado Ct   2166 N Eldorado Ct
9. 10538 Innsbruck Ln   10538 Innsbruck Ln
10. 888 Powerville Rd   883 Powerville Rd

Answer Key

1. D	3. A	5. D	7. A	9. A
2. D	4. D	6. D	8. D	10. D

Sample Questions

Directions: Reading from right to left, compare the following addresses. Are they alike or different? For each question, compare the address in the left column with the address in the right column. If the two addresses are **ALIKE** in every way, write "A" next to the question number. If the two addresses are **DIFFERENT** in any way, write "D" next to the question number.

1. 4202 N Bainbridge Rd   4202 N Bainbridge Rd

2. 300 E Roberta Ave   3000 E Roberta Ave

3. Quenemo KS 66528   Quenemo KS 66528

4. 13845 Donahoo St   13345 Donahoo St

5. 10466 Gertrude NE   10466 Gertrude NE

6. 2733 N 105th Ave   2773 N 105th Ave

7. 3100 N Wyandotte Cir   3100 N Wyandottte Ave

8. 11796 Summerville Dr   11769 Summerville Dr

9. Wilburnum Miss 65566   Vilburnum Miss 65566

10. 9334 Kindleberger Rd   9334 Kindleberger Rd

Answer Key

1. A	3. A	5. A	7. D	9. D
2. D	4. D	6. D	8. D	10. A

Sample Questions

> **Directions:** Answer "A" if the two numbers are exactly alike and "D" if the two numbers are different in any way.

1. 2003	2003	
2. 75864	75864	
3. 7300	730	
4. 50105	5016	
5. 2184	2184	
6. 8789	8789	
7. 36001	3601	
8. 1112	1112	
9. 89900	8990	
10. 07035	07035	

Answer Key

1. A	3. D	5. A	7. D	9. D
2. A	4. D	6. A	8. A	10. A

EXERCISE

Directions: For each question, compare the address in the left column with the address in the right column. If the two addresses are **ALIKE** in every way, write "A" next to the question number. If the two addresses are **DIFFERENT** in any way, write "D" next to the question number.

1. 8690 W 134th St   8960 W 134th St

2. 1912 Berkshire Rd   1912 Berkshire Wy

3. 5331 W Professor St   5331 W Proffesor St

4. Philadelphia PA 19124   Philadelphia PN 19124

5. 7450 Gaguenay St   7450 Saguenay St

6. 8650 Christy St   8650 Christey St

7. Lumberville PA 18933   Lumberville PA 1998333

8. 114 Alabama Ave NW   114 Alabama Av NW

9. 1756 Waterford St   1756 Waterville St

10. 2214 Wister Wy   2214 Wister Wy

11. 2974 Repplier Rd   2974 Repplier Dr

12. Essex CT 06426   Essex CT 06426

13. 7676 N Bourbon St   7616 N Bourbon St

14. 2762 Rosengarten Wy   2762 Rosengarden Wy

15. 239 Windell Ave   239 Windell Ave

16. 4667 Edgeworth Rd   4677 Edgeworth Rd

17. 2661 Kennel St Se   2661 Kennel St Sw

18. Alamo TX 78516   Alamo TX 78516

19. 3709 Columbine St   3709 Columbine St

20. 9699 W 14th St   9699 W 14th Rd

21. 2207 Markland Ave   2207 Markham Ave

22. Los Angeles CA 90013   Los Angeles CA 90018

23. 4608 N Warnock St   4806 N Warnock St

24. 7718 S Summer St   7718 S Sumner St

25. New York NY 10016   New York NY 10016

26. 4514 Ft Hamilton Pk   4514 Ft Hamilton Pk

27. 5701 Kosciusko St   5701 Koscusko St

28. 5422 Evergreen St   4522 Evergreen St

29. Gainsville FL 43611   Gainsville FL 32611

30. 5018 Church St   5018 Church Ave

31. 1079 N Blake St   1097 N Blake St

32. 8072 W 20th Rd   80702 W 20th Dr

33. Onoro ME 04473   Orono ME 04473

34. 2175 Kimbell Rd   2175 Kimball Rd

35. 1243 Mermaid St   1243 Mermaid St

36. 4904 SW 134th St   4904 SW 134th St

37. 1094 Hancock St   1049 Hancock St

38. Des Moines IA 50311   Des Moines IA 50311

39. 4832 S Rinaldi Rd   48323 S rinaldo Rd

40. 2015 Dorchester Rd   2015 Dorchester Rd

41. 5216 Woodbine St   5216 Woodburn St

42. Boulder CO 80302   Boulder CA 80302

43. 4739 N Marion St   479 N Marion St

44. 3720 Nautilus Wy   3270 Nautilus Way

45. 3636 Gramercy Pk   3636 Gramercy Pk

46. 757 Johnson Ave   757 Johnston Ave

47. 3045 Brighton 12th St	3045 Brighton 12th St
48. 237 Ovington Ave	237 Ovington Ave
49. Kalamazoo MI	49007 Kalamazoo MI 49007
50. Lissoula MT 59812	Missoula MS59812
51. Stillwater OK 74704	Stillwater OK 47404
52. 47446 Empire Blvd	4746 Empire Bldg
53. 6321 St Johns Pl	6321 St Johns Pl
54. 2242 Vanderbilt Ave	2242 Vanderbilt Ave
55. 542 Ditmas Blvd	542 Ditmars Blvd
56. 4603 W Argyle Rd	4603 W Argyle Rd
57. 653 Knickerbocker Ave NE	653 Knickerbocker Ave NE
58. 3651 Midwood Terr	3651 Midwood Terr
59. Chapel Hill NC 27514	Chaple Hill NC 27514
60. 3217 Vernon Pl NW	3217 Vernon Dr NW
61. 1094 Rednor Pkwy	1049 Rednor Pkwy
62. 986 S Doughty Blvd	986 S Douty Blvd
63. Lincoln NE 68508	Lincoln NE 65808
64. 1517 LaSalle Ave	1517 LaSalle Ave
65. 3857 S Morris St	3857 S Morriss St
66. 6104 Saunders Expy	614 Saunders Expy
67. 2541 Appleton St	2541 Appleton Rd
68. Washington DC 20052	Washington DC 20052
69. 6439 Kessler Blvd S	6439 Kessler Blvd S
70. 4786 Catalina Dr	4786 Catalana Dr
71. 132 E Hampton Pkwy	1322 E Hampton Pkwy

exercises

72. 1066 Goethe Sq S		1066 Geothe Sq S
73. 1118 Jerriman Wy		1218 Jerriman Wy
74. 5798 Grand Central Pkwy		57998 Grand Central Pkwy
75. Delaware OH 43015		Delaware OK 43015
76. Corvallis OR 973313		Corvallis OR 97331
77. 4231 Keating Ave N		4231 Keating Av N
78. 5689 Central Pk Pl		5869 Central Pk Pl
79. 1108 Lyndhurst Dr		1108 Lyndhurst Dr
80. 842 Chambers Ct		842 Chamber Ct
81. Athens OH 45701		Athens GA 45701
82. Tulsa OK 74171		Tulsa OK 71471
83. 6892 Beech Grove Ave		6892 Beech Grove Ave
84. 2939 E Division St		2929 W Division St
85. 1554 Pitkin Ave		1554 Pitkin Ave
86. 905 St Edwards Plz		950 St Edwards Plz
87. 1906 W 152nd St		1906 W 152nd St
88. 3466 Glenmore Ave		3466 Glenville Ave
89. Middlebury VT 05753		Middleberry VT 05753
90. Evanston IL 60201		Evanston IN 60201
91. 9401 W McDonald Ave		9401 W MacDonald Ave
92. 55527 Albermarle Rd		5527 Albermarle Rd
93. 9055 Carter Dr		9055 Carter Dr
94. Greenvale NY 11548		Greenvale NY 11458
95. 1149 Cherry Gr S		1149 Cherry Gr S

ANSWER KEY

1. D	20. D	39. D	58. A	77. D
2. D	21. D	40. A	59. D	78. D
3. D	22. D	41. D	60. D	79. A
4. D	23. D	42. D	61. D	80. D
5. D	24. D	43. D	62. D	81. D
6. D	25. A	44. D	63. D	82. D
7. D	26. A	45. A	64. A	83. A
8. D	27. D	46. D	65. D	84. D
9. D	28. D	47. A	66. D	85. A
10. A	29. D	48. A	67. D	86. D
11. D	30. D	49. A	68. A	87. A
12. A	31. D	50. D	69. A	88. D
13. D	32. D	51. D	70. D	89. D
14. D	33. D	52. D	71. D	90. D
15. A	34. D	53. A	72. D	91. D
16. D	35. A	54. A	73. D	92. D
17. D	36. A	55. D	74. D	93. A
18. A	37. D	56. A	75. D	94. D
19. A	38. A	57. A	76. D	95. A

answers

SUMMING IT UP

- Address-checking questions carry the highest penalties for guessing.

- Score higher by learning the test-taking strategies for address-checking questions.

- Reading for differences and vocalization are the two best techniques for answering address-checking questions.

Score Higher on Forms Completion Questions

OVERVIEW

- Strategies to score higher
- Forms completion techniques
- Summing it up

STRATEGIES TO SCORE HIGHER

Your score on the forms completion section is based on the number of items you answer correctly. There is no penalty for guessing on this part of the test. It is to your advantage to respond to each item, even if you have to guess.

FORMS COMPLETION TECHNIQUES

Here are some proven tips to help you do your best on forms completion questions:

- **Study each form carefully.** Each form is different and calls for different information in the various sections. You should take time to study the forms carefully before responding to the items to be sure you know what information is requested.

- **Answer the questions you know the answers to first.** Once you answer the questions you are confident about, you can return to those questions you passed the first time around. Be careful, however. If you return to an item, make sure you mark the correct answer on your answer sheet. It is easy to lose your place and darken the wrong circle.

- **As time permits, go back and try to answer the more difficult questions.** If you are able to narrow down a question to one or two possible answers, it would benefit you to make an educated guess.

EXERCISE

Directions: Answer each question based on the information provided in the sample forms provided.

Authorization to Hold Mail

➤ We can hold your mail for a minimum of **3**, but not for more than **30 days.**

NOTE: *Complete and give to your letter carrier or mail to the post office that delivers your mail.*

Postmaster: Please hold mail for:

Name(s)

☐ **A.** Please deliver all accumulated mail and resume normal delivery on the ending date shown below.

Address *(Number, street, apt./suite no., city, state, ZIP + 4)*

☐ **B.** I will pick up all accumulated mail when I return and understand that mail delivery will not resume until I do.

Beginning Date	Ending Date *(May only be changed by the customer in writing)*	Customer Signature

For Post Office Use Only

Date Received **1.**		
Clerk **2.**		Bin Number **3.**
Carrier **4.**		Route Number **5.**

(Complete this section only if customer selected option B)

6. ☐ Accumulated mail has been picked up.	Resume Delivery of Mail *(Date)* **7.**	By **8.**

---

1. Which of these would be a correct entry for Box 2?
   - **(A)** Rural Route 3
   - **(B)** $2.90
   - **(C)** 9/12/06
   - **(D)** Josh Kidd

2. Where would you enter 7/27/06?
   - **(A)** Box 1
   - **(B)** Box 2
   - **(C)** Box 3
   - **(D)** Box 4

3. Which of these would be a correct entry for Box 6?
   - **(A)** A check mark
   - **(B)** 10/07/06
   - **(C)** 1/13/06 to 2/27/06
   - **(D)** Amy McDonnell

4. Which of these would be a correct entry for Box 7?
   - **(A)** A check mark
   - **(B)** 12/20/06
   - **(C)** 6351 Hardin Road
   - **(D)** 19134

exercises

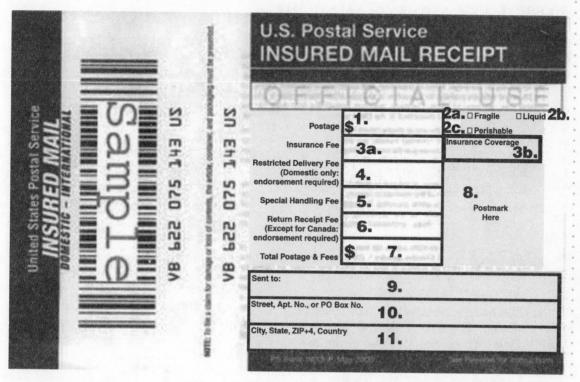

5. Where would you check that the item is liquid?

 (A) Box 2a
✓(B) Box 2b
 (C) Box 2c
 (D) Box 3b

6. Where would you enter the special handling fee?

 (A) Box 1
 (B) Box 3a
✓(C) Box 5
 (D) Box 7

7. What would be the correct entry for Box 1?

 (A) A check mark
 (B) A postmark
✓(C) $2.50
 (D) 12456

8. You could enter fees in all of the following boxes EXCEPT

 (A) Box 1
 (B) Box 4
 (C) Box 7
✓(D) Box 11

ANSWER KEY AND EXPLANATIONS

Exercise

1. D	3. A	5. B	7. C
2. A	4. B	6. C	8. D

1. **The correct answer is (D).** Box 2 is labeled Clerk. Therefore, Josh Kidd is the correct answer.

2. **The correct answer is (A).** Box 1 is labeled Date Received. Therefore, 7/27/06 would be entered in Box 1.

3. **The correct answer is (A).** Box 6 contains a check box. Therefore, a check mark is the correct answer.

4. **The correct answer is (B).** Box 7 is labeled Resume Delivery of Mail *(Date)*. Therefore, 12/20/06 is the correct answer.

5. **The correct answer is (B).** Box 2b is a check box labeled Liquid. Therefore, Box 2b is where you would place a check mark indicating an item is liquid.

6. **The correct answer is (C).** Box 5 is labeled Special Handling Fee. Therefore, Box 5 is the correct answer.

7. **The correct answer is (C).** Box 1 is labeled Postage. Therefore, $2.50 is the correct answer.

8. **The correct answer is (D).** Boxes 1, 4, and 7 are all fee boxes. Box 11 is labeled City, State, ZIP+4, Country. Therefore, Box 11 is the correct answer.

SUMMING IT UP

- Your score on the forms completion section is based on the number of items you answer correctly. There is no penalty for guessing on this part of the test.

- Learn the proven tips to help you do your best on forms completion questions.

Score Higher on Coding and Memory Questions

OVERVIEW

- Strategies to score higher
- Coding and memory techniques
- Explanation of coding guide
- Summing it up

STRATEGIES TO SCORE HIGHER

Exam 473 consists of a section on Coding and Memory. This is a test of your ability to use codes quickly and accurately, both with a coding guide visible and from memory without using a guide. You will be shown a coding guide, along with several items that must be assigned a code. To the best of your ability, you must look up the correct code for each item and record your responses. During the first section, you will be allowed to look at the coding guide while you assign codes. During the second section, you must assign codes based on your memory of the same coding guide. While the coding guide is visible, try to memorize as many of the codes as you can. These are the same codes that will be used in the memory section.

During the actual test you are not permitted to look at the codes when answering the items in the Memory section, nor are you permitted to write down addresses during the memorization period.

Scoring

Your score is based on the number of items you answer correctly minus one-third of the number of items you answer incorrectly. In both sections, your score depends on how many items you can accurately assign a code to in the time allowed. You may not be able to assign a code to all of the items before time runs out, but you should do your best to assign codes to as many items as you can with a high degree of accuracy.

chapter 6

CODING AND MEMORY TECHNIQUES

During the actual test, you will have several opportunities to work with the coding guide and practice memorizing the codes for each range of addresses before answering them based on memory. Here are some techniques for scoring high on coding and memory questions:

- **Answer questions you know first.** You have an allotted amount of time to answer all the questions. Do not waste time on a question you can't immediately answer.

- **Narrow down a question to a couple of possible answers.** If you can do this, it might be advantageous to make an educated guess.

- **Work as quickly and accurately as possible.** You are not expected to answer all the items in the time allowed.

- **Take advantage of the practice time and memorization periods made available to you.**

NOTE

The same coding guide will be used throughout the test.

EXPLANATION OF CODING GUIDE

The first column of the coding guide shows each **Address Range.** The second column of the coding guide shows a one-letter code for the **Delivery Route** that serves the address ranges listed in that row. You may assume that addresses run in order between the lowest and highest addresses listed.

EXERCISE 1

Directions: Circle the correct delivery route for each address based on the following coding guide. Work as quickly and accurately as possible. Time yourself on this exercise. You should stop after 2 minutes to give yourself an idea of what this portion of the test is like under timed conditions.

CODING GUIDE

ADDRESS RANGE	DELIVERY ROUTE
1–99 Washington Avenue 10–200 Cedar Street 5–15 Tyson Avenue	A
100–200 Washington Avenue 16–30 Tyson Avenue	B
10000–12000 Agate Street 1–10 Lancaster Avenue 201–1500 Hardin Road	C
All mail that doesn't fall into one of the address ranges listed above	D

Address		Delivery Route		
1. 12 Washington Avenue	A	B	C	D
2. 11500 Agate Street	A	B	C	D
3. 1256 Hardin Road	A	B	C	D
4. 11 Lancaster Avenue	A	B	C	D
5. 24 Cedar Street	A	B	C	D
6. 9 Tyson Avenue	A	B	C	D
7. 3035 Aramingo Avenue	A	B	C	D
8. 1187 Lancaster Avenue	A	B	C	D
9. 456 Hardin Road	A	B	C	D
10. 176 Washington Avenue	A	B	C	D
11. 2880 Tulip Street	A	B	C	D
12. 157 Cedar Street	A	B	C	D
13. 84 Washington Avenue	A	B	C	D
14. 15400 Agate Street	A	B	C	D
15. 27 Glenn Drive	A	B	C	D

ANSWER KEY

1. A	4. D	7. D	10. B	13. A
2. C	5. A	8. D	11. D	14. D
3. C	6. A	9. C	12. A	15. D

EXERCISE 2

Directions: Take 3 minutes to memorize the coding guide on page 67. You may not take any notes when memorizing the coding guide, but you can write in the test booklet while you are answering the questions. Circle the correct delivery route for each address based on the following coding guide. DO NOT refer to the coding guide when working through the exercise. Work as quickly and accurately as possible. Time yourself on this exercise. You should stop after 3 minutes to give yourself an idea of what this portion of the test is like under timed conditions.

Address	Delivery Route			
1. 10320 Agate Street	A	B	C	D
2. 203 Hardin Road	A	B	C	D
3. 215 Cedar Street	A	B	C	D
4. 7 Lancaster Avenue	A	B	C	D
5. 27 Tyson Avenue	A	B	C	D
6. 14 Lancaster Avenue	A	B	C	D
7. 56 Pacific Street	A	B	C	D
8. 1217 Edge Hill Road	A	B	C	D
9. 942 Hardin Road	A	B	C	D
10. 98 Washington Avenue	A	B	C	D
11. 3012 Mercer Street	A	B	C	D
12. 914 Agate Street	A	B	C	D
13. 172 Washington Avenue	A	B	C	D
14. 11000 Agate Street	A	B	C	D
15. 300 Hardin Road	A	B	C	D

ANSWER KEY

1. C	4. C	7. D	10. A	13. B
2. C	5. B	8. D	11. D	14. C
3. D	6. D	9. C	12. D	15. C

SUMMING IT UP

- Your score on the memory and coding sections of the test is based on the number of items you answer correctly minus one-third of the number of items you answer incorrectly.

- There is a guessing penalty on this section of the test.

- The same coding guide is used in both the coding and memory sections of the test.

Score Higher on Number Series Questions

chapter 7

OVERVIEW

- Strategies to score higher
- Number series techniques
- Summing it up

STRATEGIES TO SCORE HIGHER

Don't worry too much about these types of questions, especially if you don't have very advanced math skills. You're not going to be asked to do algebra, but rather simple addition, subtraction, multiplication, and division. Best of all, you can solve most of these questions quickly, and there is no penalty for guessing.

Here's a good tip on guessing: If you must guess, make all your guesses the same letter. By the law of averages, this may give you a better chance of hitting the right answer.

NUMBER SERIES TECHNIQUES

So you're a bit anxious about working with numbers. Well, put your fears aside. Remember, the test isn't going to ask you to break out the calculus (or a simple calculator, for that matter). As usual, you'll need to work with as much speed and efficiency as you can muster. However, if you try to remember the following tips, you may find that this type of question isn't as frightening as you thought.

- In number series with one pattern, look for the following number arrangements:

  1. Simple ascending (increasing) or descending (decreasing) numbers, where the same number is added to or subtracted from each number in a series

  2. Alternating ascending or descending numbers, where two different numbers are alternately added to or subtracted from each number in a series

3. Simple or alternating multiplication or division

4. Simple repetition, where one or more number in the series is repeated immediately before or after addition or subtraction or other arithmetic operation

5. Repetition of a number pattern by itself

6. Unusual pattern

- In number series with two or more patterns, look for the following kinds of patterns:

  1. Random number (not one of the numbers in the series)

  2. Introduced and repeated number in a one-pattern series

  3. Two or more alternating series of two or more distinct patterns

  4. Two or more alternating series of patterns, plus repetitive or random numbers

  5. Two or more alternating patterns that include simple multiplication and division

  6. Unusual alternating or combination arrangements

- Solve at a glance. Look for simple number series that jump out at you, such as 1 2 3 1 2 3. Also be on the lookout for patterns that are either adding or subtracting to get the next number, such as 20 21 22 23 or 35 34 33 32.

- Vocalize for meaning. With all those numbers flying around, it might be easy for your eye (and, thus, your brain) to get confused, mistakenly reading a number for something else. That's why it sometimes helps to vocalize (or, say quietly to yourself) what you are reading. You might be able to hear a pattern more quickly—and more accurately—than if you had just looked at it.

- When you spot a difference, mark it down. By "difference," we mean that you should immediately mark any change in the number series that you find. For example, if you're reading and you notice that the series is increasing by 2 (for example, 2 4 6 8) write down that difference in the numbers of the series (again, in this case, 2). If you can't figure it out with addition and subtraction, try multiplication and division. Number series that use multiplication and division are fairly rare. However, you shouldn't discount this possibility entirely—just remember to try addition and subtraction first.

NOTE

Remember, most series are either ascending, descending, or a combination of the two.

- Know how to spot repeating and random numbers. Repeating and random numbers may not be so obvious. Be sure to mark up the question in your test booklet—this will help you spot these types of numbers more easily than if you simply try to see them in your brain.

EXERCISE 1

Directions: To the left of the answer choices is a series of numbers that follows some definite order. Look at the numbers in the series at the left and find out what order they follow. Then decide what the next two numbers in the series would be if the same order were continued. Circle the letter of the correct answer.

1. 8 9 10 8 9 10 8   **(A)** 8 9   **(B)** 9 10   **(C)** 9 8   **(D)** 10 8   **(E)** 8 10

2. 16 16 15 15 14 14 13   **(A)** 12 13   **(B)** 14 13   **(C)** 12 11   **(D)** 12 10   **(E)** 13 12

3. 2 6 10 2 14 18 2   **(A)** 2 22   **(B)** 2 26   **(C)** 22 26   **(D)** 22 2   **(E)** 26 2

4. 30 28 27 25 24 22 21   **(A)** 21 20   **(B)** 19 18   **(C)** 20 19   **(D)** 20 18   **(E)** 21 21

5. 25 25 22 22 19 19 16   **(A)** 18 18   **(B)** 16 16   **(C)** 16 13   **(D)** 15 15   **(E)** 15 13

6. 9 17 24 30 35 39 42   **(A)** 43 44   **(B)** 44 46   **(C)** 44 45   **(D)** 45 49   **(E)** 46 50

7. 28 31 34 37 40 43 46   **(A)** 49 52   **(B)** 47 49   **(C)** 50 54   **(D)** 49 53   **(E)** 51 55

8. 17 17 24 24 31 31 38   **(A)** 38 39   **(B)** 38 17   **(C)** 38 45   **(D)** 38 44   **(E)** 39 50

9. 87 83 79 75 71 67 63   **(A)** 62 61   **(B)** 63 59   **(C)** 60 56   **(D)** 59 55   **(E)** 59 54

10. 8 9 11 14 18 23 29   **(A)** 35 45   **(B)** 32 33   **(C)** 38 48   **(D)** 34 40   **(E)** 36 44

11. 4 8 12 16 20 24   **(A)** 26 28   **(B)** 28 30   **(C)** 30 28   **(D)** 28 32   **(E)** 28 29

12. 3 4 1 3 4 1 3   **(A)** 4 1   **(B)** 4 5   **(C)** 4 3   **(D)** 1 2   **(E)** 4 4

exercises

ANSWER KEY AND EXPLANATIONS

1. B	4. B	7. A	10. E
2. E	5. C	8. C	11. D
3. C	6. C	9. D	12. A

1. **The correct answer is (B).** The series is simply a repetition of the sequence 8 9 10.

2. **The correct answer is (E).** This series is a simple descending series combined with repetition. Each number is first repeated and then decreased by 1.

3. **The correct answer is (C).** This pattern is +4, then repeat the number 2.

4. **The correct answer is (B).** This pattern is not as easy to spot as the ones in the previous questions. If you write in the direction and degree of change between each number, you can see that this is an alternating descending series with the pattern −2, −1, −2, −1, etc.

5. **The correct answer is (C).** The rule here is: repeat, −3, repeat, −3, repeat, −3.

6. **The correct answer is (C).** The rule here is: +8, +7, +6, +5, +4, +3, +2.

7. **The correct answer is (A).** This is a simple +3 rule.

8. **The correct answer is (C).** Each number repeats itself, then increases by +7.

9. **The correct answer is (D).** Here the rule is: −4.

10. **The correct answer is (E).** The rule here is: +1, +2, +3, +4, +5, +6, +7, +8.

11. **The correct answer is (D).** This is a simple ascending series, where each number increases by 4.

12. **The correct answer is (A).** This series is simply a repetition of the sequence 3 4 1.

EXERCISE 2

Directions: To the left of the answer choices is a series of numbers that follows some definite order. Look at the numbers in the series at the left and find out what order they follow. Then decide what the next two numbers in the series would be if the same order were continued. Circle the letter of the correct answer.

1. 12 26 15 26 18 26 21   **(A)** 21 24   **(B)** 24 26   **(C)** 21 26   **(D)** 26 24   **(E)** 26 25

2. 72 67 69 64 66 61 63   **(A)** 58 60   **(B)** 65 62   **(C)** 60 58   **(D)** 65 60   **(E)** 60 65

3. 81 10 29 81 10 29 81   **(A)** 29 10   **(B)** 81 29   **(C)** 10 29   **(D)** 81 10   **(E)** 29 81

4. 91 91 90 88 85 81 76   **(A)** 71 66   **(B)** 70 64   **(C)** 75 74   **(D)** 70 65   **(E)** 70 63

5. 22 44 29 37 36 30 43   **(A)** 50 23   **(B)** 23 50   **(C)** 53 40   **(D)** 40 53   **(E)** 50 57

6. 0 1 1 0 2 2 0   **(A)** 0 0   **(B)** 0 3   **(C)** 3 3   **(D)** 3 4   **(E)** 2 3

7. 32 34 36 34 36 38 36   **(A)** 34 32   **(B)** 36 34   **(C)** 36 38   **(D)** 38 40   **(E)** 38 36

8. 26 36 36 46 46 56 56   **(A)** 66 66   **(B)** 56 66   **(C)** 57 57   **(D)** 46 56   **(E)** 26 66

9. 64 63 61 58 57 55 52   **(A)** 51 50   **(B)** 52 49   **(C)** 50 58   **(D)** 50 47   **(E)** 51 49

10. 4 6 8 7 6 8 10 9 8   **(A)** 7 9   **(B)** 11 12   **(C)** 12 14   **(D)** 7 10   **(E)** 10 12

11. 57 57 52 47 47 42 37   **(A)** 32 32   **(B)** 37 32   **(C)** 37 37   **(D)** 32 27   **(E)** 27 27

12. 13 26 14 25 16 23 19   **(A)** 20 21   **(B)** 20 22   **(C)** 20 23   **(D)** 20 24   **(E)** 22 25

13. 15 27 39 51 63 75 87   **(A)** 97 112   **(B)** 99 111   **(C)** 88 99   **(D)** 89 99   **(E)** 90 99

14. 2 0 2 2 2 4 2 6 2 8   **(A)** 2 2   **(B)** 2 8   **(C)** 2 10   **(D)** 2 12   **(E)** 2 16

15. 19 18 18 17 17 17 16   **(A)** 16 16   **(B)** 16 15   **(C)** 15 15   **(D)** 15 14   **(E)** 16 17

16. 55 53 44 51 49 44 47   **(A)** 45 43   **(B)** 46 45   **(C)** 46 44   **(D)** 44 44   **(E)** 45 44

17. 100 81 64 49 36 25 16   **(A)** 8 4   **(B)** 8 2   **(C)** 9 5   **(D)** 9 4   **(E)** 9 3

18. 2 2 4 6 8 18 16   **(A)** 32 64   **(B)** 32 28   **(C)** 54 32   **(D)** 32 54   **(E)** 54 30

19. 47 43 52 48 57 53 62   **(A)** 58 54   **(B)** 67 58   **(C)** 71 67   **(D)** 58 67   **(E)** 49 58

20. 38 38 53 48 48 63 58   **(A)** 58 58   **(B)** 58 73   **(C)** 73 73   **(D)** 58 68   **(E)** 73 83

21. 12 14 16 13 15 17 14   **(A)** 17 15   **(B)** 15 18   **(C)** 17 19   **(D)** 15 16   **(E)** 16 18

22. 30 30 30 37 37 37 30   **(A)** 30 30   **(B)** 30 37   **(C)** 37 37   **(D)** 37 30   **(E)** 31 31

23. 75 52 69 56 63 59 57   **(A)** 58 62   **(B)** 55 65   **(C)** 51 61   **(D)** 61 51   **(E)** 63 55

24. 176 88 88 44 44 22 22   **(A)** 22 11   **(B)** 11 11   **(C)** 11 10   **(D)** 11 5   **(E)** 22 10

ANSWER KEY AND EXPLANATIONS

1. D	6. C	11. B	16. E	21. E
2. A	7. D	12. C	17. D	22. A
3. C	8. A	13. B	18. C	23. D
4. E	9. E	14. C	19. D	24. B
5. B	10. E	15. A	20. B	

1. **The correct answer is (D).** This is a +3 series, with the number 26 between terms.
   $12\ ^{+3}\ 26\ 15\ ^{+3}\ 26\ 18\ ^{+3}\ 26\ 21\ ^{+3}\ 26\ 24$

2. **The correct answer is (A).** You may read this as a −5, +2 series:
   $72\ ^{-5}\ 67\ ^{+2}\ 69\ ^{-5}\ 64\ ^{+2}\ 66\ ^{-5}\ 61\ ^{+2}\ 63\ ^{-5}\ 58\ ^{+2}\ 60$

   or as two alternating −3 series.

   $$\overset{-3\qquad -3\qquad -3\qquad -3}{72\ \ 67\ \ 69\ \ 64\ \ 66\ \ 61\ \ 63\ \ 58\ \ 60}$$
   $$\underset{-3\qquad -3\qquad -3}{}$$

3. **The correct answer is (C).** By inspection or grouping, the sequence 81 10 29 repeats itself.

4. **The correct answer is (E).** Write in the numbers for this one.
   $91\ ^{-0}\ 91\ ^{-1}\ 90\ ^{-2}\ 88\ ^{-3}\ 85\ ^{-4}\ 81\ ^{-5}\ 76\ ^{-6}\ 70\ ^{-7}\ 63$

5. **The correct answer is (B).** Here we have two distinct alternating series.

   $$\overset{+7\qquad +7\qquad +7\qquad +7}{22\ \ 44\ \ 29\ \ 37\ \ 36\ \ 30\ \ 43\ \ 23\ \ 50}$$
   $$\underset{-7\qquad -7\qquad -7}{}$$

6. **The correct answer is (C).** The digit 0 intervenes after each repeating number of a simple +1 and repeat series.
   $0\ 1\ ^r\ 1\ ^{+1}\ 0\ 2\ ^r\ 2\ ^{+1}\ 0\ 3\ ^r\ 3$

7. **The correct answer is (D).** Group the numbers into threes. Each succeeding group of three begins with a number two higher than the first number of the preceding group of three. Within each group, the pattern is +2, +2.

8. **The correct answer is (A).** The pattern is +10, repeat the number, +10, repeat the number.
   $26\ ^{+10}\ 36\ ^r\ 36\ ^{+10}\ 46\ ^r\ 46\ ^{+10}\ 56\ ^r\ 56\ ^{+10}\ 66\ ^r\ 66$

9. **The correct answer is (E).** The pattern is −1, −2, −3; −1, −2, −3, and so on. If you can't see it, write it in for yourself.

10. **The correct answer is (E).** Here the pattern is +2, +2, −1, −1; +2, +2, −1, −1.
    $4\ +2\ 6\ +2\ 8\ −1\ 7\ −1\ 6\ +2\ 8\ +2\ 10\ −1\ 9\ −1\ 8\ +2\ 10\ +2\ 12$ The series that is given to you is a little bit longer than most to better assist you in establishing this extra long pattern.

11. **The correct answer is (B).** This is a −5 pattern with every other term repeated.
    $57\ ^r\ 57\ ^{-5}\ 52\ ^{-5}\ 47\ ^r\ 47\ ^{-5}\ 42\ ^{-5}\ 37\ ^r\ 37\ ^{-5}\ 32$

    $$\overset{+1\qquad +2\qquad +3\qquad +4}{13\ \ 26\ \ 14\ \ 25\ \ 16\ \ 23\ \ 19\ \ 20\ \ 23}$$
    $$\underset{-1\qquad -2\qquad -3}{}$$

12. **The correct answer is (C).** This series consists of two alternating series.

13. **The correct answer is (B).** This is a simple +12 series.

14. **The correct answer is (C).** This digit 02 intervenes before each number of a simple +2 series.
    $2\ 0\ ^{+2}\ 2\ 2\ ^{+2}\ 2\ 4\ ^{+2}\ 2\ 6\ ^{+2}\ 2\ 8\ ^{+2}\ 2\ 10$

15. **The correct answer is (A).** Each number is repeated one time more than the number before it: 19 appears only once, 18 twice, 17 three times and, if the series were extended beyond the question, 16 would appear four times.

16. **The correct answer is (E).** This is a −2 series, with the number 44 appearing after every two numbers of the series. You probably can see this now without writing it out.

17. **The correct answer is (D).** The series consists of the squares of the numbers from 2 to 10, in descending order.

$$\overbrace{2 \quad 2 \quad 4 \quad 6 \quad 8 \quad 18 \quad 16 \quad 54 \quad 32}^{\times 2 \quad \times 2 \quad \times 2 \quad \times 2}$$
$$\underbrace{}_{\times 3 \quad \times 3 \quad \times 3}$$

18. **The correct answer is (C).** This is a tricky alternating series question.

19. **The correct answer is (D).** The progress of this series is −4, +9; −4, +9.

20. **The correct answer is (B).** This series is not really difficult, but you may have to write it out to see it.
38 ^{r} 38 $^{+15}$ 53 $^{-5}$ 48 ^{r} 48 $^{+15}$ 63 $^{-5}$ 58 ^{r} 58 $^{+15}$ 73
You may also see this as two alternating +10 series, with the numbers ending in 8 repeated.

21. **The correct answer is (E).** Group into groups of three numbers. Each +2 group begins one step up from the previous group.

22. **The correct answer is (A).** By inspection, you can see that this series is nothing more than the number 30 repeated three times and the number 37 repeated three times. You have no further clues, so you must assume that the series continues with the number 30 repeated three times.

23. **The correct answer is (D).** Here are two alternating series:

$$\overbrace{75 \quad 52 \quad 69 \quad 56 \quad 63 \quad 59 \quad 57 \quad 61 \quad 51}^{-6 \qquad -6 \qquad -6 \qquad -6}$$
$$\underbrace{}_{+4 \qquad +3 \qquad +2}$$

24. **The correct answer is (B).** The pattern is divide by 2 and repeat the number, divide by 2 and repeat the number.
176 $^{÷2}$ 88 ^{r} 88 $^{÷2}$ 44 ^{r} 44 $^{÷2}$ 22 ^{r} 22 $^{÷2}$ 11 ^{r} 11

SUMMING IT UP

- Number series questions do not require advanced math skills.

- There is no penalty for guessing on this section of the test.

- There are proven techniques you should master to score high on number series questions.

Score Higher on Oral Instruction Questions

OVERVIEW

- Strategies to score higher
- Oral instruction techniques
- Summing it up

STRATEGIES TO SCORE HIGHER

It always pays to be a good listener, and you'll find that oral instruction questions are no exception. Unlike other types of questions you'll encounter, oral instruction questions require you to focus your attention on another individual (or more precisely, the sound of his or her voice) rather than simply the test booklet. However, like all questions on the exam, you'll score your highest if you concentrate, relax, and are well prepared. The information in this chapter will help you to do just that.

ORAL INSTRUCTION TECHNIQUES

- **Pay attention to the instructions.** We've stressed in previous chapters that concentration is important. Well, with oral instruction questions, attention is paramount! Unlike other questions, if you "space out" during this portion of the exam, you can't simply "re-read" the question in your booklet. Try to stay focused!

- **Mark your answer sheet as instructed.** Unlike other questions, you will not answer the oral instruction questions in sequential order on your answer sheet. In fact, you will skip around the page, filling in answers in the order specified. (Actually, you will not use all the answer spaces provided to you!)

- **Work from left to right.** If the instructions say to mark the "fourth letter," it will be the fourth letter from the left, no exceptions. Of course, if the instructions tell you differently (for example, if they say, "Please put a circle around the fifth letter from the right"), then you'll obviously need to make an exception from reading left to right. Again, listen closely!

- **Don't waste time changing answers.** If you are about to enter a choice on your answer sheet, and suddenly realize you've already filled in that choice (i.e., you've made that choice from another question), don't make a change. Wait for the next set of instructions, and move on.

If you find that you've blackened two answer spaces for the same question, erase one of them only if you have time, and if you won't get distracted and fall behind in the instructions.

EXERCISE 1 ANSWER SHEET

1. Ⓐ Ⓑ Ⓒ Ⓓ Ⓔ	23. Ⓐ Ⓑ Ⓒ Ⓓ Ⓔ	45. Ⓐ Ⓑ Ⓒ Ⓓ Ⓔ	67. Ⓐ Ⓑ Ⓒ Ⓓ Ⓔ
2. Ⓐ Ⓑ Ⓒ Ⓓ Ⓔ	24. Ⓐ Ⓑ Ⓒ Ⓓ Ⓔ	46. Ⓐ Ⓑ Ⓒ Ⓓ Ⓔ	68. Ⓐ Ⓑ Ⓒ Ⓓ Ⓔ
3. Ⓐ Ⓑ Ⓒ Ⓓ Ⓔ	25. Ⓐ Ⓑ Ⓒ Ⓓ Ⓔ	47. Ⓐ Ⓑ Ⓒ Ⓓ Ⓔ	69. Ⓐ Ⓑ Ⓒ Ⓓ Ⓔ
4. Ⓐ Ⓑ Ⓒ Ⓓ Ⓔ	26. Ⓐ Ⓑ Ⓒ Ⓓ Ⓔ	48. Ⓐ Ⓑ Ⓒ Ⓓ Ⓔ	70. Ⓐ Ⓑ Ⓒ Ⓓ Ⓔ
5. Ⓐ Ⓑ Ⓒ Ⓓ Ⓔ	27. Ⓐ Ⓑ Ⓒ Ⓓ Ⓔ	49. Ⓐ Ⓑ Ⓒ Ⓓ Ⓔ	71. Ⓐ Ⓑ Ⓒ Ⓓ Ⓔ
6. Ⓐ Ⓑ Ⓒ Ⓓ Ⓔ	28. Ⓐ Ⓑ Ⓒ Ⓓ Ⓔ	50. Ⓐ Ⓑ Ⓒ Ⓓ Ⓔ	72. Ⓐ Ⓑ Ⓒ Ⓓ Ⓔ
7. Ⓐ Ⓑ Ⓒ Ⓓ Ⓔ	29. Ⓐ Ⓑ Ⓒ Ⓓ Ⓔ	51. Ⓐ Ⓑ Ⓒ Ⓓ Ⓔ	73. Ⓐ Ⓑ Ⓒ Ⓓ Ⓔ
8. Ⓐ Ⓑ Ⓒ Ⓓ Ⓔ	30. Ⓐ Ⓑ Ⓒ Ⓓ Ⓔ	52. Ⓐ Ⓑ Ⓒ Ⓓ Ⓔ	74. Ⓐ Ⓑ Ⓒ Ⓓ Ⓔ
9. Ⓐ Ⓑ Ⓒ Ⓓ Ⓔ	31. Ⓐ Ⓑ Ⓒ Ⓓ Ⓔ	53. Ⓐ Ⓑ Ⓒ Ⓓ Ⓔ	75. Ⓐ Ⓑ Ⓒ Ⓓ Ⓔ
10. Ⓐ Ⓑ Ⓒ Ⓓ Ⓔ	32. Ⓐ Ⓑ Ⓒ Ⓓ Ⓔ	54. Ⓐ Ⓑ Ⓒ Ⓓ Ⓔ	76. Ⓐ Ⓑ Ⓒ Ⓓ Ⓔ
11. Ⓐ Ⓑ Ⓒ Ⓓ Ⓔ	33. Ⓐ Ⓑ Ⓒ Ⓓ Ⓔ	55. Ⓐ Ⓑ Ⓒ Ⓓ Ⓔ	77. Ⓐ Ⓑ Ⓒ Ⓓ Ⓔ
12. Ⓐ Ⓑ Ⓒ Ⓓ Ⓔ	34. Ⓐ Ⓑ Ⓒ Ⓓ Ⓔ	56. Ⓐ Ⓑ Ⓒ Ⓓ Ⓔ	78. Ⓐ Ⓑ Ⓒ Ⓓ Ⓔ
13. Ⓐ Ⓑ Ⓒ Ⓓ Ⓔ	35. Ⓐ Ⓑ Ⓒ Ⓓ Ⓔ	57. Ⓐ Ⓑ Ⓒ Ⓓ Ⓔ	79. Ⓐ Ⓑ Ⓒ Ⓓ Ⓔ
14. Ⓐ Ⓑ Ⓒ Ⓓ Ⓔ	36. Ⓐ Ⓑ Ⓒ Ⓓ Ⓔ	58. Ⓐ Ⓑ Ⓒ Ⓓ Ⓔ	80. Ⓐ Ⓑ Ⓒ Ⓓ Ⓔ
15. Ⓐ Ⓑ Ⓒ Ⓓ Ⓔ	37. Ⓐ Ⓑ Ⓒ Ⓓ Ⓔ	59. Ⓐ Ⓑ Ⓒ Ⓓ Ⓔ	81. Ⓐ Ⓑ Ⓒ Ⓓ Ⓔ
16. Ⓐ Ⓑ Ⓒ Ⓓ Ⓔ	38. Ⓐ Ⓑ Ⓒ Ⓓ Ⓔ	60. Ⓐ Ⓑ Ⓒ Ⓓ Ⓔ	82. Ⓐ Ⓑ Ⓒ Ⓓ Ⓔ
17. Ⓐ Ⓑ Ⓒ Ⓓ Ⓔ	39. Ⓐ Ⓑ Ⓒ Ⓓ Ⓔ	61. Ⓐ Ⓑ Ⓒ Ⓓ Ⓔ	83. Ⓐ Ⓑ Ⓒ Ⓓ Ⓔ
18. Ⓐ Ⓑ Ⓒ Ⓓ Ⓔ	40. Ⓐ Ⓑ Ⓒ Ⓓ Ⓔ	62. Ⓐ Ⓑ Ⓒ Ⓓ Ⓔ	84. Ⓐ Ⓑ Ⓒ Ⓓ Ⓔ
19. Ⓐ Ⓑ Ⓒ Ⓓ Ⓔ	41. Ⓐ Ⓑ Ⓒ Ⓓ Ⓔ	63. Ⓐ Ⓑ Ⓒ Ⓓ Ⓔ	85. Ⓐ Ⓑ Ⓒ Ⓓ Ⓔ
20. Ⓐ Ⓑ Ⓒ Ⓓ Ⓔ	42. Ⓐ Ⓑ Ⓒ Ⓓ Ⓔ	64. Ⓐ Ⓑ Ⓒ Ⓓ Ⓔ	86. Ⓐ Ⓑ Ⓒ Ⓓ Ⓔ
21. Ⓐ Ⓑ Ⓒ Ⓓ Ⓔ	43. Ⓐ Ⓑ Ⓒ Ⓓ Ⓔ	65. Ⓐ Ⓑ Ⓒ Ⓓ Ⓔ	87. Ⓐ Ⓑ Ⓒ Ⓓ Ⓔ
22. Ⓐ Ⓑ Ⓒ Ⓓ Ⓔ	44. Ⓐ Ⓑ Ⓒ Ⓓ Ⓔ	66. Ⓐ Ⓑ Ⓒ Ⓓ Ⓔ	88. Ⓐ Ⓑ Ⓒ Ⓓ Ⓔ

WORKSHEET

> **Directions:** Listen carefully to the instructions read to you from page 85 and mark each item on this worksheet as directed. Then complete each question by marking the answer sheet on the previous page as directed. For each direction, you will darken the answer sheet for an appropriate number-letter combination.

1.   13   23   2   19   6

2.   E   B   D   E   C   A   B

3. | 30 __ | 18 __ | 5 __ | 14 __ | 7 __ |

4.   (26 __)   (16 __)   (23 __)   (23 __)   (27 __)

5. | 63 __ | 16 __ | 78 __ | 48 __ |

6.   12 ____   5 ____   22 ____

7.   (14 __)   (1 __)   (36 __)   (7 __)   (19 __)

8.   26 ____   86 ____

9. 57   63   11   78   90   32   45   70   69

10. 16   30   13   25   10   14   23   26   19

11.
9:12 __A   9:28 __B   9:24 __C   9:11 __D   9:32 __E

12.
47 __   10 __   26 __   8 __   25 __

13.
__A   __B   __C   __D   __E

14.
3 __   32 __   45 __   10 __

15.
72 __   81 __   49 __   ABLE   EASY   DESK

16. X X O X O O O X O X X O X X

17.
22 __   3 __   21 __   28 __

18.
21 __   38 __   29 __   31 __

19. __ A   __ C   __ E

EXERCISE 1

> **Directions:** Give the following instructions to a friend and have him or her read them aloud to you at the rate of 80 words per minute. (Do NOT read aloud the words in parentheses.) Do NOT read them to yourself. Your friend will need a watch with a second hand. Listen carefully and do exactly what your friend tells you to do with the worksheet and answer sheet. Your friend will tell you some things to do with each item on the worksheet. After each set of instructions, your friend will give you time to mark your answer by darkening a circle on the sample answer sheet. Since B and D sound very much alike, your friend will say "B as in baker" when he or she means B and "D as in dog" when he or she means D.

Look at line 1 on the worksheet. (Pause slightly.) Draw a line under the fourth number in the line. (Pause 2 seconds.) Now, on your answer sheet, find the number under which you just drew the line and darken space A for that number. (Pause 5 seconds.)

Look at the letters in line 2 on the worksheet. (Pause slightly.) Draw a line under the fifth letter in the line. Now, on your answer sheet, find number 59 (pause 2 seconds) and darken the space for the letter under which you drew a line. (Pause 5 seconds.)

Look at the letters in line 2 on the worksheet again. (Pause slightly.) Now draw two lines under the third letter in the line. (Pause 2 seconds.) Now, on your answer sheet, find number 65 (pause 2 seconds) and darken the space for the letter under which you drew two lines. (Pause 5 seconds.)

Look at line 3 on the worksheet. (Pause slightly.) Write an E in the last box. (Pause 2 seconds.) Now, on your answer sheet, find the number in that box and darken space E for that number. (Pause 5 seconds.)

Now look at line 3 again. (Pause slightly.) Write an A in the first box. (Pause 2 seconds.) Now, on your answer sheet, find the number in that box and darken space A for that number. (Pause 5 seconds.)

Look at line 4. The number in each circle is the number of packages in a mail sack. In the circle for the sack holding the largest number of packages, write a B as in baker. (Pause 2 seconds.) Now, on your answer sheet, darken the space for the number-letter combination that is in the circle you just wrote in. (Pause 5 seconds.)

Look at line 4 again. In the circle for the sack holding the smallest number of packages, write an E. (Pause 2 seconds.) Now, on your answer sheet, darken the space for the number-letter combination that is in the circle you just wrote in. (Pause 5 seconds.)

Look at the drawings on line 5 on the worksheet. The four boxes are trucks for carrying mail. (Pause slightly.) The truck with the highest number is to be loaded first. Write B as in baker on the line beside the highest number. (Pause 2 seconds.) Now, on your answer sheet, darken the space for the number-letter combination that is in the box you just wrote in. (Pause 5 seconds.)

Look at line 6 on the worksheet. (Pause slightly.) Next to the middle number write the letter D as in dog. (Pause 2 seconds.) Now, on your answer sheet, find the space for the number beside which you wrote and darken space D as in dog. (Pause 5 seconds.)

Look at the five circles in line 7 on the worksheet. Write B as in baker on the blank in the second circle. (Pause 2 seconds.) Now, on your answer sheet, darken the space for the number-letter combination that is in the circle you just wrote in. (Pause 5 seconds.)

Now take the worksheet again and write C on the blank in the third circle on line 7. (Pause 2 seconds.) Now, on your answer sheet, darken the space for the number-letter combination that is in the circle you just wrote in. (Pause 5 seconds.)

Now look at line 8 on the worksheet. (Pause slightly.) Write an A on the line next to the right-hand number. (Pause 2 seconds.) Now, on your answer sheet, find the space for the number beside which you wrote and darken box A. (Pause 5 seconds.)

Look at line 9 on the worksheet. (Pause slightly.) Draw a line under every number that is more than 60 but less than 70. (Pause 12 seconds.) Now, on your answer sheet, for each number that you drew a line under, darken space C. (Pause 25 seconds.)

Look at line 10 on the worksheet. (Pause slightly.) Draw a line under every number that is more than 5 and less than 15. (Pause 10 seconds.) Now, on your answer sheet, for each number that you drew a line under, darken space D as in dog. (Pause 25 seconds.)

Look at line 11 on the worksheet. (Pause slightly.) In each circle there is a time when the mail must leave. In the circle for the latest time, write on the line the last two figures of the time. (Pause 5 seconds.) Now, on your answer sheet, darken the space for the number-letter combination that is in the circle you just wrote in. (Pause 5 seconds.)

Look at the five boxes in line 12 on your worksheet. (Pause slightly.) If 6 is less than 3, put an E in the fourth box. (Pause slightly.) If 6 is not less than 3, put a B as in baker in the first box. (Pause 10 seconds.) Now, on your answer sheet, darken the space for the number-letter combination that is in the box you just wrote in. (Pause 5 seconds.)

Now look at line 13 on the worksheet. (Pause slightly.) There are five circles. Each circle has a letter. (Pause slightly.) In the second circle, write the answer to this question: Which of the following numbers is smallest: 72, 51, 88, 71, 58? (Pause 10 seconds.) Now, on your answer sheet, darken the space for the number-letter combination that is in the circle you just wrote in. (Pause 5 seconds.) In the third circle on the same line, write 28. (Pause 2 seconds.) Now, on your answer sheet, darken the space for the number-letter combination that is in the circle you just wrote in. (Pause 5 seconds.) In the fourth circle do nothing. In the fifth circle write the answer to this question: How many months are there in a year? (Pause 5 seconds.) Now, on your answer sheet, darken the space for the number-letter combination that is in the circle you just wrote in. (Pause 5 seconds.)

Look at line 14 on your worksheet. (Pause slightly.) There are two circles and two boxes of different sizes with numbers in them. (Pause slightly.) If 2 is smaller than 4 and if 7 is less than 3, write A in the larger circle. (Pause slightly.) Otherwise write B as in baker in the smaller box. (Pause 10 seconds.) Now, on your answer sheet, darken the space for the number-letter combination in the box or circle in which you just wrote. (Pause 5 seconds.)

Look at the boxes and words in line 15 on the worksheet. (Pause slightly.) Write the second letter of the first word in the third box. (Pause 5 seconds.) Write the first letter of the second word in the first box. (Pause 5 seconds.) Write the first letter of the third word in the second box. (Pause 5 seconds.) Now, on your answer sheet, darken the spaces for the number-letter combinations that are in the three boxes you just wrote in. (Pause 15 seconds.)

Look at line 16 on the worksheet. (Pause slightly.) Draw a line under every "0" in the line. (Pause 5 seconds.) Count the number of lines that you have drawn, subtract 2, and write that number at the end of the line. (Pause 5 seconds.) Now, on your answer sheet, find that number and darken space D as in dog for that number. (Pause 5 seconds.)

Look at line 17 on the worksheet. (Pause slightly.) If the number in the left-hand circle is smaller than the number in the right-hand circle, add 2 to the number in the left-hand circle, and change the number in that circle to this number. (Pause 8 seconds.) Then write B as in baker next to the new number. (Pause slightly.) Next, write E beside the number in the smaller box. (Pause 3 seconds.) Then, on your answer sheet, darken the spaces for the number-letter combinations that are in the box and circle you just wrote in. (Pause 5 seconds.)

Look at line 18 on the worksheet. (Pause slightly.) If in a year October comes before September, write A in the box with the smallest number. (Pause slightly.) If it does not, write C in the box with the largest number. (Pause 10 seconds.) Now, on your answer sheet, darken the space for the number-letter combination that is in the box you just wrote in. (Pause 5 seconds.)

Look at line 19 on the worksheet. (Pause slightly.) On the line beside the second letter, write the highest of these numbers: 12, 56, 42, 39, 8. (Pause 2 seconds.) Now, on your answer sheet, darken the space of the number-letter combination you just wrote. (Pause 5 seconds.)

ANSWER KEY

Correctly Filled Answer Sheet

1. (A) ● (C) (D) (E)	23. (A) (B) (C) (D) (E)	45. (A) ● (C) (D) (E)	67. (A) (B) (C) (D) (E)
2. (A) (B) (C) (D) (E)	24. (A) ● (C) (D) (E)	46. (A) (B) (C) (D) (E)	68. (A) (B) (C) (D) (E)
3. (A) (B) (C) (D) ●	25. (A) (B) (C) (D) (E)	47. (A) ● (C) (D) (E)	69. (A) (B) ● (D) (E)
4. (A) (B) (C) ● (E)	26. (A) (B) (C) (D) (E)	48. (A) (B) (C) (D) (E)	70. (A) (B) (C) (D) (E)
5. (A) (B) (C) ● (E)	27. (A) ● (C) (D) (E)	49. (A) ● (C) (D) (E)	71. (A) (B) (C) (D) (E)
6. (A) (B) (C) (D) (E)	28. (A) (B) ● (D) (E)	50. (A) (B) (C) (D) (E)	72. (A) (B) (C) (D) ●
7. (A) (B) (C) (D) ●	29. (A) (B) (C) (D) (E)	51. (A) ● (C) (D) (E)	73. (A) (B) (C) (D) (E)
8. (A) (B) (C) (D) (E)	30. ● (B) (C) (D) (E)	52. (A) (B) (C) (D) (E)	74. (A) (B) (C) (D) (E)
9. (A) (B) (C) (D) (E)	31. (A) (B) (C) (D) (E)	53. (A) (B) (C) (D) (E)	75. (A) (B) (C) (D) (E)
10. (A) (B) (C) ● (E)	32. (A) (B) (C) (D) ●	54. (A) (B) (C) (D) (E)	76. (A) (B) (C) (D) (E)
11. (A) (B) (C) (D) (E)	33. (A) (B) (C) (D) (E)	55. (A) (B) (C) (D) (E)	77. (A) (B) (C) (D) (E)
12. (A) (B) (C) (D) ●	34. (A) (B) (C) (D) (E)	56. (A) (B) ● (D) (E)	78. (A) ● (C) (D) (E)
13. (A) (B) (C) ● (E)	35. (A) (B) (C) (D) (E)	57. (A) (B) (C) (D) (E)	79. (A) (B) (C) (D) (E)
14. (A) (B) (C) ● (E)	36. (A) (B) ● (D) (E)	58. (A) (B) (C) (D) (E)	80. (A) (B) (C) (D) (E)
15. (A) (B) (C) (D) (E)	37. (A) (B) (C) (D) (E)	59. (A) (B) ● (D) (E)	81. (A) (B) (C) ● (E)
16. (A) (B) (C) (D) ●	38. (A) (B) ● (D) (E)	60. (A) (B) (C) (D) (E)	82. (A) (B) (C) (D) (E)
17. (A) (B) (C) (D) (E)	39. (A) (B) (C) (D) (E)	61. (A) (B) (C) (D) (E)	83. (A) (B) (C) (D) (E)
18. (A) (B) (C) (D) (E)	40. (A) (B) (C) (D) (E)	62. (A) (B) (C) (D) (E)	84. (A) (B) (C) (D) (E)
19. ● (B) (C) (D) (E)	41. (A) (B) (C) (D) (E)	63. (A) (B) ● (D) (E)	85. (A) (B) (C) (D) (E)
20. (A) (B) (C) (D) (E)	42. (A) (B) (C) (D) (E)	64. (A) (B) (C) (D) (E)	86. ● (B) (C) (D) (E)
21. (A) (B) (C) (D) (E)	43. (A) (B) (C) (D) (E)	65. (A) (B) (C) ● (E)	87. (A) (B) (C) (D) (E)
22. (A) (B) (C) (D) (E)	44. (A) (B) (C) (D) (E)	66. (A) (B) (C) (D) (E)	88. (A) (B) (C) (D) (E)

Correctly Filled Worksheet

1.   13   23   2   <u>19</u>   6

2.   E   B   <u>D</u>   E   <u>C</u>   A   B

3. | 30 <u>A</u> | 18 __ | 5 __ | 14 __ | 7 <u>E</u> |

4.   (26 __) (16 <u>E</u>) (23 __) (23 __) (27 <u>B</u>)

5. | 63 __ | 16 __ | 78 <u>B</u> | 48 __ |

6.   12 ____   5 <u>d</u>   22 ____

7.   (14 __) (1 <u>B</u>) (36 <u>C</u>) (7 __) (19 __)

8.   26 ____   86 <u>A</u>

9.   57   <u>63</u>   11   78   90   32   45   70   <u>69</u>

10.   16   30   <u>13</u>   25   <u>10</u>   <u>14</u>   23   26   19

11.   (9:12 __ A) (9:28 __ B) (9:24 __ C) (9:11 __ D) (9:32 <u>32</u> E)

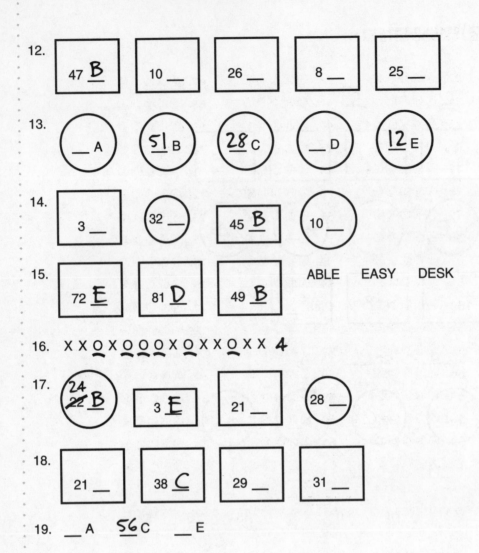

12. [47 _B_] [10 __] [26 __] [8 __] [25 __]

13. (__ A) (_51_ B) (_28_ C) (__ D) (_12_ E)

14. [3 __] (32 __) [45 _B_] (10 __)

15. [72 _E_] [81 _D_] [49 _B_]   ABLE   EASY   DESK

16. X X O X O O O X O X X O X X **4**

17. (24 22 _B_) [3 _E_] [21 __] (28 __)

18. [21 __] [38 _C_] [29 __] [31 __]

19. __ A   _56_ C   __ E

EXERCISE 2 ANSWER SHEET

1. Ⓐ Ⓑ Ⓒ Ⓓ Ⓔ	23. Ⓐ Ⓑ Ⓒ Ⓓ Ⓔ	45. Ⓐ Ⓑ Ⓒ Ⓓ Ⓔ	67. Ⓐ Ⓑ Ⓒ Ⓓ Ⓔ
2. Ⓐ Ⓑ Ⓒ Ⓓ Ⓔ	24. Ⓐ Ⓑ Ⓒ Ⓓ Ⓔ	46. Ⓐ Ⓑ Ⓒ Ⓓ Ⓔ	68. Ⓐ Ⓑ Ⓒ Ⓓ Ⓔ
3. Ⓐ Ⓑ Ⓒ Ⓓ Ⓔ	25. Ⓐ Ⓑ Ⓒ Ⓓ Ⓔ	47. Ⓐ Ⓑ Ⓒ Ⓓ Ⓔ	69. Ⓐ Ⓑ Ⓒ Ⓓ Ⓔ
4. Ⓐ Ⓑ Ⓒ Ⓓ Ⓔ	26. Ⓐ Ⓑ Ⓒ Ⓓ Ⓔ	48. Ⓐ Ⓑ Ⓒ Ⓓ Ⓔ	70. Ⓐ Ⓑ Ⓒ Ⓓ Ⓔ
5. Ⓐ Ⓑ Ⓒ Ⓓ Ⓔ	27. Ⓐ Ⓑ Ⓒ Ⓓ Ⓔ	49. Ⓐ Ⓑ Ⓒ Ⓓ Ⓔ	71. Ⓐ Ⓑ Ⓒ Ⓓ Ⓔ
6. Ⓐ Ⓑ Ⓒ Ⓓ Ⓔ	28. Ⓐ Ⓑ Ⓒ Ⓓ Ⓔ	50. Ⓐ Ⓑ Ⓒ Ⓓ Ⓔ	72. Ⓐ Ⓑ Ⓒ Ⓓ Ⓔ
7. Ⓐ Ⓑ Ⓒ Ⓓ Ⓔ	29. Ⓐ Ⓑ Ⓒ Ⓓ Ⓔ	51. Ⓐ Ⓑ Ⓒ Ⓓ Ⓔ	73. Ⓐ Ⓑ Ⓒ Ⓓ Ⓔ
8. Ⓐ Ⓑ Ⓒ Ⓓ Ⓔ	30. Ⓐ Ⓑ Ⓒ Ⓓ Ⓔ	52. Ⓐ Ⓑ Ⓒ Ⓓ Ⓔ	74. Ⓐ Ⓑ Ⓒ Ⓓ Ⓔ
9. Ⓐ Ⓑ Ⓒ Ⓓ Ⓔ	31. Ⓐ Ⓑ Ⓒ Ⓓ Ⓔ	53. Ⓐ Ⓑ Ⓒ Ⓓ Ⓔ	75. Ⓐ Ⓑ Ⓒ Ⓓ Ⓔ
10. Ⓐ Ⓑ Ⓒ Ⓓ Ⓔ	32. Ⓐ Ⓑ Ⓒ Ⓓ Ⓔ	54. Ⓐ Ⓑ Ⓒ Ⓓ Ⓔ	76. Ⓐ Ⓑ Ⓒ Ⓓ Ⓔ
11. Ⓐ Ⓑ Ⓒ Ⓓ Ⓔ	33. Ⓐ Ⓑ Ⓒ Ⓓ Ⓔ	55. Ⓐ Ⓑ Ⓒ Ⓓ Ⓔ	77. Ⓐ Ⓑ Ⓒ Ⓓ Ⓔ
12. Ⓐ Ⓑ Ⓒ Ⓓ Ⓔ	34. Ⓐ Ⓑ Ⓒ Ⓓ Ⓔ	56. Ⓐ Ⓑ Ⓒ Ⓓ Ⓔ	78. Ⓐ Ⓑ Ⓒ Ⓓ Ⓔ
13. Ⓐ Ⓑ Ⓒ Ⓓ Ⓔ	35. Ⓐ Ⓑ Ⓒ Ⓓ Ⓔ	57. Ⓐ Ⓑ Ⓒ Ⓓ Ⓔ	79. Ⓐ Ⓑ Ⓒ Ⓓ Ⓔ
14. Ⓐ Ⓑ Ⓒ Ⓓ Ⓔ	36. Ⓐ Ⓑ Ⓒ Ⓓ Ⓔ	58. Ⓐ Ⓑ Ⓒ Ⓓ Ⓔ	80. Ⓐ Ⓑ Ⓒ Ⓓ Ⓔ
15. Ⓐ Ⓑ Ⓒ Ⓓ Ⓔ	37. Ⓐ Ⓑ Ⓒ Ⓓ Ⓔ	59. Ⓐ Ⓑ Ⓒ Ⓓ Ⓔ	81. Ⓐ Ⓑ Ⓒ Ⓓ Ⓔ
16. Ⓐ Ⓑ Ⓒ Ⓓ Ⓔ	38. Ⓐ Ⓑ Ⓒ Ⓓ Ⓔ	60. Ⓐ Ⓑ Ⓒ Ⓓ Ⓔ	82. Ⓐ Ⓑ Ⓒ Ⓓ Ⓔ
17. Ⓐ Ⓑ Ⓒ Ⓓ Ⓔ	39. Ⓐ Ⓑ Ⓒ Ⓓ Ⓔ	61. Ⓐ Ⓑ Ⓒ Ⓓ Ⓔ	83. Ⓐ Ⓑ Ⓒ Ⓓ Ⓔ
18. Ⓐ Ⓑ Ⓒ Ⓓ Ⓔ	40. Ⓐ Ⓑ Ⓒ Ⓓ Ⓔ	62. Ⓐ Ⓑ Ⓒ Ⓓ Ⓔ	84. Ⓐ Ⓑ Ⓒ Ⓓ Ⓔ
19. Ⓐ Ⓑ Ⓒ Ⓓ Ⓔ	41. Ⓐ Ⓑ Ⓒ Ⓓ Ⓔ	63. Ⓐ Ⓑ Ⓒ Ⓓ Ⓔ	85. Ⓐ Ⓑ Ⓒ Ⓓ Ⓔ
20. Ⓐ Ⓑ Ⓒ Ⓓ Ⓔ	42. Ⓐ Ⓑ Ⓒ Ⓓ Ⓔ	64. Ⓐ Ⓑ Ⓒ Ⓓ Ⓔ	86. Ⓐ Ⓑ Ⓒ Ⓓ Ⓔ
21. Ⓐ Ⓑ Ⓒ Ⓓ Ⓔ	43. Ⓐ Ⓑ Ⓒ Ⓓ Ⓔ	65. Ⓐ Ⓑ Ⓒ Ⓓ Ⓔ	87. Ⓐ Ⓑ Ⓒ Ⓓ Ⓔ
22. Ⓐ Ⓑ Ⓒ Ⓓ Ⓔ	44. Ⓐ Ⓑ Ⓒ Ⓓ Ⓔ	66. Ⓐ Ⓑ Ⓒ Ⓓ Ⓔ	88. Ⓐ Ⓑ Ⓒ Ⓓ Ⓔ

WORKSHEET

> **Directions:** Listen carefully to the instructions read to you from page 95 and mark each item on the worksheet as directed. Then complete each question by marking the answer sheet on the previous page as directed. For each direction, you will darken the answer sheet for an appropriate number-letter combination.

1.   A   B   B   D   C   D   E   D

2.   24   12   17   11   14   20

3.   [41 __]   [62 __]   [18 __]   (27 __)   (73 __)   (10 __)

4.   ___B   ___D   ___C   ___E   ___A

5.   76   14   67   46   11   74

6.   (___A)   (___E)   (△ ___B)   (___C)   (___D)

7.   [9 __]   [46 __]   [34 __]   LETTER   PARCEL

8.   G   G   G   G   G   G   G   G

9.   (79 __)   (46 __)   (32 __)

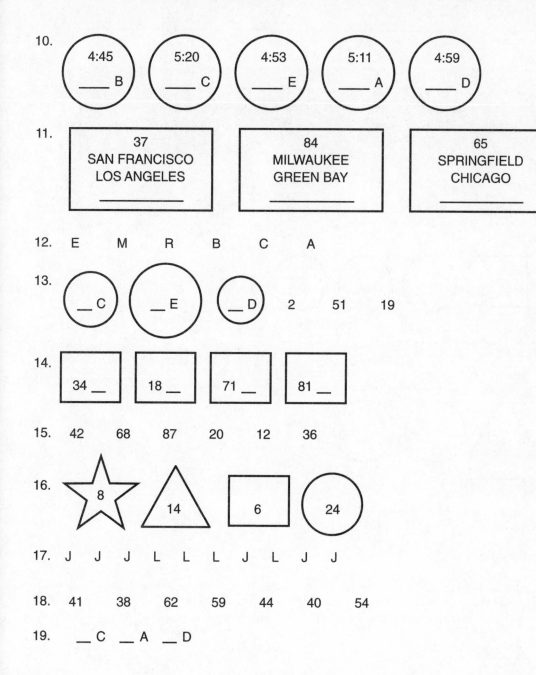

10.
4:45 ___ B   5:20 ___ C   4:53 ___ E   5:11 ___ A   4:59 ___ D

11.
| 37 SAN FRANCISCO LOS ANGELES _____ | 84 MILWAUKEE GREEN BAY _____ | 65 SPRINGFIELD CHICAGO _____ |

12.   E   M   R   B   C   A

13.   ___ C   ___ E   ___ D   2   51   19

14. | 34 __ | 18 __ | 71 __ | 81 __ |

15.   42   68   87   20   12   36

16.   8   14   6   24

17.   J   J   J   L   L   L   J   L   J   J

18.   41   38   62   59   44   40   54

19.   __ C   __ A   __ D

EXERCISE 2

> **Directions:** Give the following instructions to a friend and have him or her read them aloud to you at the rate of 80 words per minute. (Do NOT read aloud the words in parentheses.) Do NOT read them to yourself. Your friend will need a watch with a second hand. Listen carefully and do exactly what your friend tells you to do with the worksheet and answer sheet. Your friend will tell you some things to do with each item on the worksheet. After each set of instructions, your friend will give you time to mark your answer by darkening a circle on the sample answer sheet. Since B and D sound very much alike, your friend will say "B as in baker" when he or she means B and "D as in dog" when he or she means D.

Look at line 1 on your worksheet. (Pause slightly.) Circle the seventh letter on line 1. (Pause 5 seconds.) Now, on your answer sheet, find number 83 and for number 83 darken the space for the letter you just circled. (Pause 5 seconds.)

Look at line 2 on your worksheet. (Pause slightly.) Draw a line under all the odd numbers between 12 and 20. (Pause 5 seconds.) Now, on your answer sheet, darken space B as in baker for all the numbers under which you drew a line. (Pause 5 seconds.)

Look at line 2 again. (Pause slightly.) Find the number that is two times another number on line 2 and circle it. (Pause 5 seconds.) Now, on your answer sheet, darken space A for the number you just circled. (Pause 5 seconds.)

Look at line 3 on your worksheet. (Pause slightly.) Write the letter C in the middle box. (Pause 2 seconds.) Now, on your answer sheet, darken the space for the number-letter combination in the figure you just wrote in. (Pause 5 seconds.)

Look at line 3 again. (Pause slightly.) Write the letter D as in dog in the left-hand circle. (Pause 2 seconds.) Now, on your answer sheet, darken the space for the number-letter combination in the figure you just wrote in. (Pause 5 seconds.)

Look at line 4 on your worksheet. (Pause slightly.) If first-class mail costs more than bulk-rate mail, write the number 22 on the third line; if not, write the number 19 on the fourth line. (Pause 5 seconds.) Now, on your answer sheet, darken the space for the number-letter combination on the line you just wrote on. (Pause 5 seconds.)

Look at line 4 again. (Pause slightly.) Write the number 31 on the second line from the left. (Pause 2 seconds.) Now, on your answer sheet, darken the space for the number-letter combination on the line on which you just wrote. (Pause 5 seconds.)

Look at line 5 on your worksheet. (Pause slightly.) Find the highest number on line 5 and draw a line under the number. (Pause 2 seconds.) Now, on your answer sheet, find the number under which you just drew a line and darken space E for that number. (Pause 5 seconds.)

Look at line 5 again. (Pause slightly.) Find the lowest number on line 5 and draw two lines under the number. (Pause 2 seconds.) Now, on your answer sheet, find the number under which you just drew two lines and darken space A for that number. (Pause 5 seconds.)

Look at line 6 on your worksheet. (Pause slightly.) Write the number 57 in the figure that differs from the others on line 6. (Pause 2 seconds.) Now, on your answer sheet, darken the number-letter combination that is in the figure in which you just wrote. (Pause 5 seconds.)

Look at line 7 on your worksheet. (Pause slightly.) Write the second letter of the second word in the first box. (Pause 5 seconds.) Write the fifth letter of the first word in the third box. (Pause 5 seconds.) Write the fourth letter of the second word in the second box. (Pause 5 seconds.) Now, on your answer sheet, darken the number-letter combinations in all three boxes. (Pause 15 seconds.)

Look at line 8 on your worksheet. (Pause slightly.) Count the number of G's on line 8 and divide the number of G's by 2. Write that number at the end of the line. (Pause 5 seconds.) Now, on your answer sheet, darken space D as in dog for the number you wrote at the end of line 8. (Pause 5 seconds.)

Look at line 9 on your worksheet. (Pause slightly.) Write the letter B as in baker in the middle-sized circle. (Pause 2 seconds.) Now, on your answer sheet, darken the space for the number-letter combination in the circle in which you just wrote. (Pause 5 seconds.)

Look at line 10 on your worksheet. (Pause slightly.) The time in each circle represents the last scheduled pickup of the day from a street letterbox. Find the circle with the earliest pickup time and write the last two figures of that time on the line in the circle. (Pause 10 seconds.) Now, on your answer sheet, darken the space for the number-letter combination in the circle you just wrote in. (Pause 5 seconds.)

Look at line 10 again. (Pause slightly.) Find the circle with the latest pickup time and write the last two figures of that time on the line in the circle. (Pause 10 seconds.) Now, on your answer sheet, darken the space for the number-letter combination in the circle in which you just wrote. (Pause 5 seconds.)

Look at line 11 on your worksheet. (Pause slightly.) Mail directed for San Francisco and Los Angeles is to be placed in box 37; mail for Milwaukee and Green Bay, in box 84; mail for Springfield and Chicago, in box 65. Find the box for mail being sent to Green Bay and write the letter A in the box. (Pause 2 seconds.) Now, on your answer sheet, darken the number-letter combination for the box you just wrote in. (Pause 5 seconds.)

Look at line 11 again. (Pause slightly.) Mr. Green lives in Springfield. Find the box in which to put Mr. Green's mail and write E on the line. (Pause 2 seconds.) Now, on your answer sheet, darken the space for the number-letter combination in the box in which you just wrote. (Pause 5 seconds.)

Look at line 12 on your worksheet. (Pause slightly.) Find the letter on line 12 that is not in the word CREAM and draw a line under the letter. (Pause 2 seconds.) Now, on your answer sheet, find number 38 and darken the space for the letter under which you just drew a line. (Pause 5 seconds.)

Look at line 13 on your worksheet. (Pause slightly.) Write the smallest number in the largest circle. (Pause 2 seconds.) Write the largest number in the left-hand circle. (Pause 2 seconds.) Now, on your answer sheet, darken the number-letter combinations that are in the circles in which you just wrote. (Pause 10 seconds.)

Look at line 14 on your worksheet. (Pause slightly.) If there are 36 inches in a foot, write B as in baker in the first box; if not, write D as in dog in the third box. (Pause 5 seconds.) Now, on your answer sheet, darken the number-letter combination that is in the box in which you just wrote. (Pause 5 seconds.)

Look at line 14 again. (Pause slightly.) Find the box that contains a number in the teens and write B as in baker in that box. (Pause 2 seconds.) Now, on your answer sheet, darken the number-letter combination that is in the box in which you just wrote. (Pause 5 seconds.)

Look at line 15 on your worksheet. (Pause slightly.) Circle the only number on line 15 that is not divisible by 2. (Pause 2 seconds.) Now, on your answer sheet, darken space A for the number you circled. (Pause 5 seconds.)

Look at line 16 on your worksheet. (Pause slightly.) If the number in the circle is greater than the number in the box, write the letter E in the box; if not, write the letter E in the circle. (Pause 5 seconds.) Now, on your answer sheet, darken the number-letter combination that is in the figure in which you just wrote. (Pause 5 seconds.)

Look at line 16 again. (Pause slightly.) If the number in the triangle is smaller than the number in the figure directly to its left, write the letter A in the triangle; if not, write the letter C in the triangle. (Pause 5 seconds.) Now, on your answer sheet, darken the number-letter combination that is in the figure you just wrote in. (Pause 5 seconds.)

Look at line 17 on your worksheet. (Pause slightly.) Count the number of J's on line 17, multiply the number of J's by 5, and write that number at the end of the line. (Pause 5 seconds.) Now, on your answer sheet, find the number you just wrote at the end of the line and darken space C for that number. (Pause 5 seconds.)

Look at line 18 on your worksheet. (Pause slightly.) Draw one line under the number that is at the middle of line 18. (Pause 5 seconds.) Now, on your answer sheet, darken space B as in baker for the number under which you just drew a line. (Pause 5 seconds.)

Look at line 18 again. (Pause slightly.) Draw two lines under each odd number that falls between 35 and 45. (Pause 10 seconds.) Now, on your answer sheet, darken space D as in dog for each number under which you drew two lines. (Pause 5 seconds.)

Look at line 19 on your worksheet. (Pause slightly.) Next to the last letter on line 19, write the first number you hear: 53, 18, 6, 75. (Pause 2 seconds.) Now, on your answer sheet, darken the space for the number-letter combination you just wrote. (Pause 5 seconds.)

ANSWER KEY

Correctly Filled Answer Sheet

1. Ⓐ Ⓑ Ⓒ Ⓓ Ⓔ	23. Ⓐ Ⓑ Ⓒ Ⓓ Ⓔ	45. Ⓐ ● Ⓒ Ⓓ Ⓔ	67. Ⓐ Ⓑ Ⓒ Ⓓ Ⓔ
2. Ⓐ Ⓑ Ⓒ Ⓓ ●	24. ● Ⓑ Ⓒ Ⓓ Ⓔ	46. Ⓐ Ⓑ ● Ⓓ Ⓔ	68. Ⓐ Ⓑ Ⓒ Ⓓ Ⓔ
3. Ⓐ Ⓑ Ⓒ Ⓓ Ⓔ	25. Ⓐ Ⓑ Ⓒ Ⓓ Ⓔ	47. Ⓐ Ⓑ Ⓒ Ⓓ Ⓔ	69. Ⓐ Ⓑ Ⓒ Ⓓ Ⓔ
4. Ⓐ Ⓑ Ⓒ ● Ⓔ	26. Ⓐ Ⓑ Ⓒ Ⓓ Ⓔ	48. Ⓐ Ⓑ Ⓒ Ⓓ Ⓔ	70. Ⓐ Ⓑ Ⓒ Ⓓ Ⓔ
5. Ⓐ Ⓑ Ⓒ Ⓓ Ⓔ	27. Ⓐ Ⓑ Ⓒ ● Ⓔ	49. Ⓐ Ⓑ Ⓒ Ⓓ Ⓔ	71. Ⓐ Ⓑ Ⓒ ● Ⓔ
6. Ⓐ Ⓑ Ⓒ Ⓓ ●	28. Ⓐ Ⓑ Ⓒ Ⓓ Ⓔ	50. Ⓐ Ⓑ Ⓒ Ⓓ Ⓔ	72. Ⓐ Ⓑ Ⓒ Ⓓ Ⓔ
7. Ⓐ Ⓑ Ⓒ Ⓓ Ⓔ	29. Ⓐ Ⓑ Ⓒ Ⓓ Ⓔ	51. Ⓐ Ⓑ ● Ⓓ Ⓔ	73. Ⓐ Ⓑ Ⓒ Ⓓ Ⓔ
8. Ⓐ Ⓑ Ⓒ Ⓓ Ⓔ	30. Ⓐ Ⓑ ● Ⓓ Ⓔ	52. Ⓐ Ⓑ Ⓒ Ⓓ Ⓔ	74. Ⓐ Ⓑ Ⓒ Ⓓ Ⓔ
9. ● Ⓑ Ⓒ Ⓓ Ⓔ	31. Ⓐ Ⓑ Ⓒ ● Ⓔ	53. Ⓐ Ⓑ Ⓒ ● Ⓔ	75. Ⓐ Ⓑ Ⓒ Ⓓ Ⓔ
10. Ⓐ Ⓑ Ⓒ Ⓓ Ⓔ	32. Ⓐ Ⓑ Ⓒ Ⓓ Ⓔ	54. Ⓐ Ⓑ Ⓒ Ⓓ Ⓔ	76. Ⓐ Ⓑ Ⓒ Ⓓ ●
11. ● Ⓑ Ⓒ Ⓓ Ⓔ	33. Ⓐ Ⓑ Ⓒ Ⓓ Ⓔ	55. Ⓐ Ⓑ Ⓒ Ⓓ Ⓔ	77. Ⓐ Ⓑ Ⓒ Ⓓ Ⓔ
12. Ⓐ Ⓑ Ⓒ Ⓓ Ⓔ	34. Ⓐ Ⓑ Ⓒ Ⓓ ●	56. Ⓐ Ⓑ Ⓒ Ⓓ Ⓔ	78. Ⓐ Ⓑ Ⓒ Ⓓ Ⓔ
13. Ⓐ Ⓑ Ⓒ Ⓓ Ⓔ	35. Ⓐ Ⓑ Ⓒ Ⓓ Ⓔ	57. Ⓐ ● Ⓒ Ⓓ Ⓔ	79. Ⓐ ● Ⓒ Ⓓ Ⓔ
14. Ⓐ Ⓑ ● Ⓓ Ⓔ	36. Ⓐ Ⓑ Ⓒ Ⓓ Ⓔ	58. Ⓐ Ⓑ Ⓒ Ⓓ Ⓔ	80. Ⓐ Ⓑ Ⓒ Ⓓ Ⓔ
15. Ⓐ Ⓑ Ⓒ Ⓓ Ⓔ	37. Ⓐ Ⓑ Ⓒ Ⓓ Ⓔ	59. Ⓐ ● Ⓒ Ⓓ Ⓔ	81. Ⓐ Ⓑ Ⓒ Ⓓ Ⓔ
16. Ⓐ Ⓑ Ⓒ Ⓓ Ⓔ	38. Ⓐ ● Ⓒ Ⓓ Ⓔ	60. Ⓐ Ⓑ Ⓒ Ⓓ Ⓔ	82. Ⓐ Ⓑ Ⓒ Ⓓ Ⓔ
17. Ⓐ ● Ⓒ Ⓓ Ⓔ	39. Ⓐ Ⓑ Ⓒ Ⓓ Ⓔ	61. Ⓐ Ⓑ Ⓒ Ⓓ Ⓔ	83. Ⓐ Ⓑ Ⓒ Ⓓ ●
18. Ⓐ ● Ⓒ Ⓓ Ⓔ	40. Ⓐ Ⓑ Ⓒ Ⓓ Ⓔ	62. Ⓐ Ⓑ ● Ⓓ Ⓔ	84. ● Ⓑ Ⓒ Ⓓ Ⓔ
19. Ⓐ Ⓑ Ⓒ Ⓓ Ⓔ	41. Ⓐ Ⓑ Ⓒ ● Ⓔ	63. Ⓐ Ⓑ Ⓒ Ⓓ Ⓔ	85. Ⓐ Ⓑ Ⓒ Ⓓ Ⓔ
20. Ⓐ Ⓑ ● Ⓓ Ⓔ	42. Ⓐ Ⓑ Ⓒ Ⓓ Ⓔ	64. Ⓐ Ⓑ Ⓒ Ⓓ Ⓔ	86. Ⓐ Ⓑ Ⓒ Ⓓ Ⓔ
21. Ⓐ Ⓑ Ⓒ Ⓓ Ⓔ	43. Ⓐ Ⓑ Ⓒ Ⓓ Ⓔ	65. Ⓐ Ⓑ Ⓒ Ⓓ ●	87. ● Ⓑ Ⓒ Ⓓ Ⓔ
22. Ⓐ Ⓑ ● Ⓓ Ⓔ	44. Ⓐ Ⓑ Ⓒ Ⓓ Ⓔ	66. Ⓐ Ⓑ Ⓒ Ⓓ Ⓔ	88. Ⓐ Ⓑ Ⓒ Ⓓ Ⓔ

Correctly Filled Worksheet

1. A   B   B   D   C   D   (E)   D

2. (24)   12   <u>17</u>   11   14   20

3.

| 41 _ | 62 C | 18 _ | 27 D | 73 _ | 10 _ |

4. __ B   <u>31</u> D   <u>22</u> C   ___ E   ___ A

5. <u>76</u>   14   67   46   <u>11</u>   74

6.

___ A   ___ E   57 B   ___ C   ___ D

7.

| 9 A | 46 C | 34 E | LETTER   PARCEL |

8. G   G   G   G   G   G   G   G   4

9.

79 B   46 __   32 __

10.

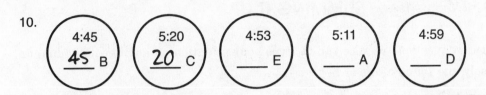

4:45 <u>45</u> B   5:20 <u>20</u> C   4:53 ___ E   5:11 ___ A   4:59 ___ D

11.

37 SAN FRANCISCO LOS ANGELES _____	84 MILWAUKEE GREEN BAY <u>A</u>	65 SPRINGFIELD CHICAGO <u>E</u>

12. E   M   R   <u>B</u>   C   A

13.

<u>51</u> C   <u>2</u> E   ___ D   2   51   19

14.

34 __	18 <u>B</u>	71 <u>D</u>	81 __

15. 42   68   (87)   20   12   36

16.

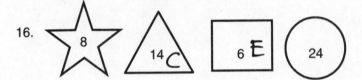

8   14 C   6 E   24

17. J   J   J   L   L   L   J   L   J   J 30

18. <u>41</u>   38   62   <u>59</u>   44   40   54

19. __ C   __ A   <u>53</u> D

answers

SUMMING IT UP

- Oral instruction questions require you to focus your attention on another individual or, more precisely, the sound of his or her voice.

- It is important to learn the four techniques for scoring high on the oral instruction section of the test.

Personal Characteristics and Experience Inventory

OVERVIEW

- **Strategies to score higher**
- **Personal characteristics and experience inventory techniques**
- **Summing it up**

One of the most interesting aspects of Exam 473 is a section called the Personal Characteristics and Experience Inventory. Understanding its role as a service provider, the USPS has developed this section in an effort to identify potential employees who have the customer service and interpersonal skills necessary to succeed in certain positions with the USPS.

The test-taker is asked to answer 236 questions in 90 minutes. The items in this section assess several personal characteristics, tendencies, or experiences related to performing effectively as an USPS employee.

STRATEGIES TO SCORE HIGHER

- **Read each item carefully and decide which of the responses is most true about you.** For some items, more than one response may fit. However, be sure to mark only one response for each item.

- **Whenever possible, respond to the questions or statements in terms of what you have done, felt, or believed in a work setting.** If you cannot relate the questions or statements to your work experiences, base your responses on other similar experiences, such as school or volunteer opportunities. Simply stated, draw on whatever experiences you have had to respond to the item.

This part of the test is divided into three sections. One section includes items with four choices, ranging from "Strongly agree" to "Strongly disagree." Another section includes items with four responses, ranging from "Very often" to "Rarely or never." The final section includes items with anywhere from four to nine response choices.

chapter 9

PERSONAL CHARACTERISTICS AND EXPERIENCE INVENTORY TECHNIQUES

Although you cannot prepare for this section of the exam, there are steps you can take to help you reduce potential errors.

- **Read each statement carefully before choosing a response.**
- **Do not try to out-think the question or statement.** Respond to each item based on your personal experiences and not on what you "think" is the correct answer.

The types of questions you can expect to see on this section of the test include:

> **Q**   I work best with minimal supervison.
> - **(A)**   Strongly agree
> - **(B)**   Agree
> - **(C)**   Disagree
> - **(D)**   Strongly disagree

> **Q**   You plan things carefully and in advance.
> - **(A)**   Very often
> - **(B)**   Often
> - **(C)**   Sometimes
> - **(D)**   Rarely

> **Q**   What type of work do you like best?
> - **(A)**   Tasks that require sitting or standing for long periods of time
> - **(B)**   Tasks that require working at a very fast pace
> - **(C)**   Tasks that require decision making
> - **(D)**   Tasks that involve repetitive activity
> - **(E)**   I like all types of work
> - **(F)**   Not sure

SUMMING IT UP

- The Personal Characteristics and Experience Inventory section was developed to identify potential employees who have the requisite personality traits to work for the USPS.

- The questions asked in this section are based on one's personal experiences. Although you cannot prepare for this section of the exam, there are steps you can take to help you reduce potential errors.

PART III

FIVE PRACTICE TESTS

PRACTICE TEST 1: EXAMS 473/473-C AND 460 ANSWER SHEET

Part A: Address Checking

1. Ⓐ Ⓑ Ⓒ Ⓓ	13. Ⓐ Ⓑ Ⓒ Ⓓ	25. Ⓐ Ⓑ Ⓒ Ⓓ	37. Ⓐ Ⓑ Ⓒ Ⓓ	49. Ⓐ Ⓑ Ⓒ Ⓓ
2. Ⓐ Ⓑ Ⓒ Ⓓ	14. Ⓐ Ⓑ Ⓒ Ⓓ	26. Ⓐ Ⓑ Ⓒ Ⓓ	38. Ⓐ Ⓑ Ⓒ Ⓓ	50. Ⓐ Ⓑ Ⓒ Ⓓ
3. Ⓐ Ⓑ Ⓒ Ⓓ	15. Ⓐ Ⓑ Ⓒ Ⓓ	27. Ⓐ Ⓑ Ⓒ Ⓓ	39. Ⓐ Ⓑ Ⓒ Ⓓ	51. Ⓐ Ⓑ Ⓒ Ⓓ
4. Ⓐ Ⓑ Ⓒ Ⓓ	16. Ⓐ Ⓑ Ⓒ Ⓓ	28. Ⓐ Ⓑ Ⓒ Ⓓ	40. Ⓐ Ⓑ Ⓒ Ⓓ	52. Ⓐ Ⓑ Ⓒ Ⓓ
5. Ⓐ Ⓑ Ⓒ Ⓓ	17. Ⓐ Ⓑ Ⓒ Ⓓ	29. Ⓐ Ⓑ Ⓒ Ⓓ	41. Ⓐ Ⓑ Ⓒ Ⓓ	53. Ⓐ Ⓑ Ⓒ Ⓓ
6. Ⓐ Ⓑ Ⓒ Ⓓ	18. Ⓐ Ⓑ Ⓒ Ⓓ	30. Ⓐ Ⓑ Ⓒ Ⓓ	42. Ⓐ Ⓑ Ⓒ Ⓓ	54. Ⓐ Ⓑ Ⓒ Ⓓ
7. Ⓐ Ⓑ Ⓒ Ⓓ	19. Ⓐ Ⓑ Ⓒ Ⓓ	31. Ⓐ Ⓑ Ⓒ Ⓓ	43. Ⓐ Ⓑ Ⓒ Ⓓ	55. Ⓐ Ⓑ Ⓒ Ⓓ
8. Ⓐ Ⓑ Ⓒ Ⓓ	20. Ⓐ Ⓑ Ⓒ Ⓓ	32. Ⓐ Ⓑ Ⓒ Ⓓ	44. Ⓐ Ⓑ Ⓒ Ⓓ	56. Ⓐ Ⓑ Ⓒ Ⓓ
9. Ⓐ Ⓑ Ⓒ Ⓓ	21. Ⓐ Ⓑ Ⓒ Ⓓ	33. Ⓐ Ⓑ Ⓒ Ⓓ	45. Ⓐ Ⓑ Ⓒ Ⓓ	57. Ⓐ Ⓑ Ⓒ Ⓓ
10. Ⓐ Ⓑ Ⓒ Ⓓ	22. Ⓐ Ⓑ Ⓒ Ⓓ	34. Ⓐ Ⓑ Ⓒ Ⓓ	46. Ⓐ Ⓑ Ⓒ Ⓓ	58. Ⓐ Ⓑ Ⓒ Ⓓ
11. Ⓐ Ⓑ Ⓒ Ⓓ	23. Ⓐ Ⓑ Ⓒ Ⓓ	35. Ⓐ Ⓑ Ⓒ Ⓓ	47. Ⓐ Ⓑ Ⓒ Ⓓ	59. Ⓐ Ⓑ Ⓒ Ⓓ
12. Ⓐ Ⓑ Ⓒ Ⓓ	24. Ⓐ Ⓑ Ⓒ Ⓓ	36. Ⓐ Ⓑ Ⓒ Ⓓ	48. Ⓐ Ⓑ Ⓒ Ⓓ	60. Ⓐ Ⓑ Ⓒ Ⓓ

Part B: Forms Completion

1. Ⓐ Ⓑ Ⓒ Ⓓ	7. Ⓐ Ⓑ Ⓒ Ⓓ	13. Ⓐ Ⓑ Ⓒ Ⓓ	19. Ⓐ Ⓑ Ⓒ Ⓓ	25. Ⓐ Ⓑ Ⓒ Ⓓ
2. Ⓐ Ⓑ Ⓒ Ⓓ	8. Ⓐ Ⓑ Ⓒ Ⓓ	14. Ⓐ Ⓑ Ⓒ Ⓓ	20. Ⓐ Ⓑ Ⓒ Ⓓ	26. Ⓐ Ⓑ Ⓒ Ⓓ
3. Ⓐ Ⓑ Ⓒ Ⓓ	9. Ⓐ Ⓑ Ⓒ Ⓓ	15. Ⓐ Ⓑ Ⓒ Ⓓ	21. Ⓐ Ⓑ Ⓒ Ⓓ	27. Ⓐ Ⓑ Ⓒ Ⓓ
4. Ⓐ Ⓑ Ⓒ Ⓓ	10. Ⓐ Ⓑ Ⓒ Ⓓ	16. Ⓐ Ⓑ Ⓒ Ⓓ	22. Ⓐ Ⓑ Ⓒ Ⓓ	28. Ⓐ Ⓑ Ⓒ Ⓓ
5. Ⓐ Ⓑ Ⓒ Ⓓ	11. Ⓐ Ⓑ Ⓒ Ⓓ	17. Ⓐ Ⓑ Ⓒ Ⓓ	23. Ⓐ Ⓑ Ⓒ Ⓓ	29. Ⓐ Ⓑ Ⓒ Ⓓ
6. Ⓐ Ⓑ Ⓒ Ⓓ	12. Ⓐ Ⓑ Ⓒ Ⓓ	18. Ⓐ Ⓑ Ⓒ Ⓓ	24. Ⓐ Ⓑ Ⓒ Ⓓ	30. Ⓐ Ⓑ Ⓒ Ⓓ

Part C: Coding and Memory

SECTION 1: CODING

1. Ⓐ Ⓑ Ⓒ Ⓓ	9. Ⓐ Ⓑ Ⓒ Ⓓ	16. Ⓐ Ⓑ Ⓒ Ⓓ	23. Ⓐ Ⓑ Ⓒ Ⓓ	30. Ⓐ Ⓑ Ⓒ Ⓓ
2. Ⓐ Ⓑ Ⓒ Ⓓ	10. Ⓐ Ⓑ Ⓒ Ⓓ	17. Ⓐ Ⓑ Ⓒ Ⓓ	24. Ⓐ Ⓑ Ⓒ Ⓓ	31. Ⓐ Ⓑ Ⓒ Ⓓ
3. Ⓐ Ⓑ Ⓒ Ⓓ	11. Ⓐ Ⓑ Ⓒ Ⓓ	18. Ⓐ Ⓑ Ⓒ Ⓓ	25. Ⓐ Ⓑ Ⓒ Ⓓ	32. Ⓐ Ⓑ Ⓒ Ⓓ
4. Ⓐ Ⓑ Ⓒ Ⓓ	12. Ⓐ Ⓑ Ⓒ Ⓓ	19. Ⓐ Ⓑ Ⓒ Ⓓ	26. Ⓐ Ⓑ Ⓒ Ⓓ	33. Ⓐ Ⓑ Ⓒ Ⓓ
5. Ⓐ Ⓑ Ⓒ Ⓓ	13. Ⓐ Ⓑ Ⓒ Ⓓ	20. Ⓐ Ⓑ Ⓒ Ⓓ	27. Ⓐ Ⓑ Ⓒ Ⓓ	34. Ⓐ Ⓑ Ⓒ Ⓓ
6. Ⓐ Ⓑ Ⓒ Ⓓ	14. Ⓐ Ⓑ Ⓒ Ⓓ	21. Ⓐ Ⓑ Ⓒ Ⓓ	28. Ⓐ Ⓑ Ⓒ Ⓓ	35. Ⓐ Ⓑ Ⓒ Ⓓ
7. Ⓐ Ⓑ Ⓒ Ⓓ	15. Ⓐ Ⓑ Ⓒ Ⓓ	22. Ⓐ Ⓑ Ⓒ Ⓓ	29. Ⓐ Ⓑ Ⓒ Ⓓ	36. Ⓐ Ⓑ Ⓒ Ⓓ
8. Ⓐ Ⓑ Ⓒ Ⓓ				

SECTION 2: MEMORY

1. Ⓐ Ⓑ Ⓒ Ⓓ	9. Ⓐ Ⓑ Ⓒ Ⓓ	16. Ⓐ Ⓑ Ⓒ Ⓓ	23. Ⓐ Ⓑ Ⓒ Ⓓ	30. Ⓐ Ⓑ Ⓒ Ⓓ
2. Ⓐ Ⓑ Ⓒ Ⓓ	10. Ⓐ Ⓑ Ⓒ Ⓓ	17. Ⓐ Ⓑ Ⓒ Ⓓ	24. Ⓐ Ⓑ Ⓒ Ⓓ	31. Ⓐ Ⓑ Ⓒ Ⓓ
3. Ⓐ Ⓑ Ⓒ Ⓓ	11. Ⓐ Ⓑ Ⓒ Ⓓ	18. Ⓐ Ⓑ Ⓒ Ⓓ	25. Ⓐ Ⓑ Ⓒ Ⓓ	32. Ⓐ Ⓑ Ⓒ Ⓓ
4. Ⓐ Ⓑ Ⓒ Ⓓ	12. Ⓐ Ⓑ Ⓒ Ⓓ	19. Ⓐ Ⓑ Ⓒ Ⓓ	26. Ⓐ Ⓑ Ⓒ Ⓓ	33. Ⓐ Ⓑ Ⓒ Ⓓ
5. Ⓐ Ⓑ Ⓒ Ⓓ	13. Ⓐ Ⓑ Ⓒ Ⓓ	20. Ⓐ Ⓑ Ⓒ Ⓓ	27. Ⓐ Ⓑ Ⓒ Ⓓ	34. Ⓐ Ⓑ Ⓒ Ⓓ
6. Ⓐ Ⓑ Ⓒ Ⓓ	14. Ⓐ Ⓑ Ⓒ Ⓓ	21. Ⓐ Ⓑ Ⓒ Ⓓ	28. Ⓐ Ⓑ Ⓒ Ⓓ	35. Ⓐ Ⓑ Ⓒ Ⓓ
7. Ⓐ Ⓑ Ⓒ Ⓓ	15. Ⓐ Ⓑ Ⓒ Ⓓ	22. Ⓐ Ⓑ Ⓒ Ⓓ	29. Ⓐ Ⓑ Ⓒ Ⓓ	36. Ⓐ Ⓑ Ⓒ Ⓓ
8. Ⓐ Ⓑ Ⓒ Ⓓ				

Part D: Personal Characteristics and Experience Inventory

1. Ⓐ Ⓑ Ⓒ Ⓓ Ⓔ Ⓕ Ⓖ Ⓗ Ⓘ
2. Ⓐ Ⓑ Ⓒ Ⓓ Ⓔ Ⓕ Ⓖ Ⓗ Ⓘ
3. Ⓐ Ⓑ Ⓒ Ⓓ Ⓔ Ⓕ Ⓖ Ⓗ Ⓘ
4. Ⓐ Ⓑ Ⓒ Ⓓ Ⓔ Ⓕ Ⓖ Ⓗ Ⓘ
5. Ⓐ Ⓑ Ⓒ Ⓓ Ⓔ Ⓕ Ⓖ Ⓗ Ⓘ
6. Ⓐ Ⓑ Ⓒ Ⓓ Ⓔ Ⓕ Ⓖ Ⓗ Ⓘ
7. Ⓐ Ⓑ Ⓒ Ⓓ Ⓔ Ⓕ Ⓖ Ⓗ Ⓘ
8. Ⓐ Ⓑ Ⓒ Ⓓ Ⓔ Ⓕ Ⓖ Ⓗ Ⓘ
9. Ⓐ Ⓑ Ⓒ Ⓓ Ⓔ Ⓕ Ⓖ Ⓗ Ⓘ
10. Ⓐ Ⓑ Ⓒ Ⓓ Ⓔ Ⓕ Ⓖ Ⓗ Ⓘ
11. Ⓐ Ⓑ Ⓒ Ⓓ Ⓔ Ⓕ Ⓖ Ⓗ Ⓘ
12. Ⓐ Ⓑ Ⓒ Ⓓ Ⓔ Ⓕ Ⓖ Ⓗ Ⓘ
13. Ⓐ Ⓑ Ⓒ Ⓓ Ⓔ Ⓕ Ⓖ Ⓗ Ⓘ
14. Ⓐ Ⓑ Ⓒ Ⓓ Ⓔ Ⓕ Ⓖ Ⓗ Ⓘ
15. Ⓐ Ⓑ Ⓒ Ⓓ Ⓔ Ⓕ Ⓖ Ⓗ Ⓘ
16. Ⓐ Ⓑ Ⓒ Ⓓ Ⓔ Ⓕ Ⓖ Ⓗ Ⓘ
17. Ⓐ Ⓑ Ⓒ Ⓓ Ⓔ Ⓕ Ⓖ Ⓗ Ⓘ
18. Ⓐ Ⓑ Ⓒ Ⓓ Ⓔ Ⓕ Ⓖ Ⓗ Ⓘ
19. Ⓐ Ⓑ Ⓒ Ⓓ Ⓔ Ⓕ Ⓖ Ⓗ Ⓘ
20. Ⓐ Ⓑ Ⓒ Ⓓ Ⓔ Ⓕ Ⓖ Ⓗ Ⓘ
21. Ⓐ Ⓑ Ⓒ Ⓓ Ⓔ Ⓕ Ⓖ Ⓗ Ⓘ
22. Ⓐ Ⓑ Ⓒ Ⓓ Ⓔ Ⓕ Ⓖ Ⓗ Ⓘ
23. Ⓐ Ⓑ Ⓒ Ⓓ Ⓔ Ⓕ Ⓖ Ⓗ Ⓘ
24. Ⓐ Ⓑ Ⓒ Ⓓ Ⓔ Ⓕ Ⓖ Ⓗ Ⓘ
25. Ⓐ Ⓑ Ⓒ Ⓓ Ⓔ Ⓕ Ⓖ Ⓗ Ⓘ
26. Ⓐ Ⓑ Ⓒ Ⓓ Ⓔ Ⓕ Ⓖ Ⓗ Ⓘ
27. Ⓐ Ⓑ Ⓒ Ⓓ Ⓔ Ⓕ Ⓖ Ⓗ Ⓘ
28. Ⓐ Ⓑ Ⓒ Ⓓ Ⓔ Ⓕ Ⓖ Ⓗ Ⓘ
29. Ⓐ Ⓑ Ⓒ Ⓓ Ⓔ Ⓕ Ⓖ Ⓗ Ⓘ
30. Ⓐ Ⓑ Ⓒ Ⓓ Ⓔ Ⓕ Ⓖ Ⓗ Ⓘ
31. Ⓐ Ⓑ Ⓒ Ⓓ Ⓔ Ⓕ Ⓖ Ⓗ Ⓘ
32. Ⓐ Ⓑ Ⓒ Ⓓ Ⓔ Ⓕ Ⓖ Ⓗ Ⓘ
33. Ⓐ Ⓑ Ⓒ Ⓓ Ⓔ Ⓕ Ⓖ Ⓗ Ⓘ
34. Ⓐ Ⓑ Ⓒ Ⓓ Ⓔ Ⓕ Ⓖ Ⓗ Ⓘ
35. Ⓐ Ⓑ Ⓒ Ⓓ Ⓔ Ⓕ Ⓖ Ⓗ Ⓘ

36. Ⓐ Ⓑ Ⓒ Ⓓ Ⓔ Ⓕ Ⓖ Ⓗ Ⓘ
37. Ⓐ Ⓑ Ⓒ Ⓓ Ⓔ Ⓕ Ⓖ Ⓗ Ⓘ
38. Ⓐ Ⓑ Ⓒ Ⓓ Ⓔ Ⓕ Ⓖ Ⓗ Ⓘ
39. Ⓐ Ⓑ Ⓒ Ⓓ Ⓔ Ⓕ Ⓖ Ⓗ Ⓘ
40. Ⓐ Ⓑ Ⓒ Ⓓ Ⓔ Ⓕ Ⓖ Ⓗ Ⓘ
41. Ⓐ Ⓑ Ⓒ Ⓓ Ⓔ Ⓕ Ⓖ Ⓗ Ⓘ
42. Ⓐ Ⓑ Ⓒ Ⓓ Ⓔ Ⓕ Ⓖ Ⓗ Ⓘ
43. Ⓐ Ⓑ Ⓒ Ⓓ Ⓔ Ⓕ Ⓖ Ⓗ Ⓘ
44. Ⓐ Ⓑ Ⓒ Ⓓ Ⓔ Ⓕ Ⓖ Ⓗ Ⓘ
45. Ⓐ Ⓑ Ⓒ Ⓓ Ⓔ Ⓕ Ⓖ Ⓗ Ⓘ
46. Ⓐ Ⓑ Ⓒ Ⓓ Ⓔ Ⓕ Ⓖ Ⓗ Ⓘ
47. Ⓐ Ⓑ Ⓒ Ⓓ Ⓔ Ⓕ Ⓖ Ⓗ Ⓘ
48. Ⓐ Ⓑ Ⓒ Ⓓ Ⓔ Ⓕ Ⓖ Ⓗ Ⓘ
49. Ⓐ Ⓑ Ⓒ Ⓓ Ⓔ Ⓕ Ⓖ Ⓗ Ⓘ
50. Ⓐ Ⓑ Ⓒ Ⓓ Ⓔ Ⓕ Ⓖ Ⓗ Ⓘ
51. Ⓐ Ⓑ Ⓒ Ⓓ Ⓔ Ⓕ Ⓖ Ⓗ Ⓘ
52. Ⓐ Ⓑ Ⓒ Ⓓ Ⓔ Ⓕ Ⓖ Ⓗ Ⓘ
53. Ⓐ Ⓑ Ⓒ Ⓓ Ⓔ Ⓕ Ⓖ Ⓗ Ⓘ
54. Ⓐ Ⓑ Ⓒ Ⓓ Ⓔ Ⓕ Ⓖ Ⓗ Ⓘ
55. Ⓐ Ⓑ Ⓒ Ⓓ Ⓔ Ⓕ Ⓖ Ⓗ Ⓘ
56. Ⓐ Ⓑ Ⓒ Ⓓ Ⓔ Ⓕ Ⓖ Ⓗ Ⓘ
57. Ⓐ Ⓑ Ⓒ Ⓓ Ⓔ Ⓕ Ⓖ Ⓗ Ⓘ
58. Ⓐ Ⓑ Ⓒ Ⓓ Ⓔ Ⓕ Ⓖ Ⓗ Ⓘ
59. Ⓐ Ⓑ Ⓒ Ⓓ Ⓔ Ⓕ Ⓖ Ⓗ Ⓘ
60. Ⓐ Ⓑ Ⓒ Ⓓ Ⓔ Ⓕ Ⓖ Ⓗ Ⓘ
61. Ⓐ Ⓑ Ⓒ Ⓓ Ⓔ Ⓕ Ⓖ Ⓗ Ⓘ
62. Ⓐ Ⓑ Ⓒ Ⓓ Ⓔ Ⓕ Ⓖ Ⓗ Ⓘ
63. Ⓐ Ⓑ Ⓒ Ⓓ Ⓔ Ⓕ Ⓖ Ⓗ Ⓘ
64. Ⓐ Ⓑ Ⓒ Ⓓ Ⓔ Ⓕ Ⓖ Ⓗ Ⓘ
65. Ⓐ Ⓑ Ⓒ Ⓓ Ⓔ Ⓕ Ⓖ Ⓗ Ⓘ
66. Ⓐ Ⓑ Ⓒ Ⓓ Ⓔ Ⓕ Ⓖ Ⓗ Ⓘ
67. Ⓐ Ⓑ Ⓒ Ⓓ Ⓔ Ⓕ Ⓖ Ⓗ Ⓘ
68. Ⓐ Ⓑ Ⓒ Ⓓ Ⓔ Ⓕ Ⓖ Ⓗ Ⓘ
69. Ⓐ Ⓑ Ⓒ Ⓓ Ⓔ Ⓕ Ⓖ Ⓗ Ⓘ
70. Ⓐ Ⓑ Ⓒ Ⓓ Ⓔ Ⓕ Ⓖ Ⓗ Ⓘ

71. Ⓐ Ⓑ Ⓒ Ⓓ Ⓔ Ⓕ Ⓖ Ⓗ Ⓘ
72. Ⓐ Ⓑ Ⓒ Ⓓ Ⓔ Ⓕ Ⓖ Ⓗ Ⓘ
73. Ⓐ Ⓑ Ⓒ Ⓓ Ⓔ Ⓕ Ⓖ Ⓗ Ⓘ
74. Ⓐ Ⓑ Ⓒ Ⓓ Ⓔ Ⓕ Ⓖ Ⓗ Ⓘ
75. Ⓐ Ⓑ Ⓒ Ⓓ Ⓔ Ⓕ Ⓖ Ⓗ Ⓘ
76. Ⓐ Ⓑ Ⓒ Ⓓ Ⓔ Ⓕ Ⓖ Ⓗ Ⓘ
77. Ⓐ Ⓑ Ⓒ Ⓓ Ⓔ Ⓕ Ⓖ Ⓗ Ⓘ
78. Ⓐ Ⓑ Ⓒ Ⓓ Ⓔ Ⓕ Ⓖ Ⓗ Ⓘ
79. Ⓐ Ⓑ Ⓒ Ⓓ Ⓔ Ⓕ Ⓖ Ⓗ Ⓘ
80. Ⓐ Ⓑ Ⓒ Ⓓ Ⓔ Ⓕ Ⓖ Ⓗ Ⓘ
81. Ⓐ Ⓑ Ⓒ Ⓓ Ⓔ Ⓕ Ⓖ Ⓗ Ⓘ
82. Ⓐ Ⓑ Ⓒ Ⓓ Ⓔ Ⓕ Ⓖ Ⓗ Ⓘ
83. Ⓐ Ⓑ Ⓒ Ⓓ Ⓔ Ⓕ Ⓖ Ⓗ Ⓘ
84. Ⓐ Ⓑ Ⓒ Ⓓ Ⓔ Ⓕ Ⓖ Ⓗ Ⓘ
85. Ⓐ Ⓑ Ⓒ Ⓓ Ⓔ Ⓕ Ⓖ Ⓗ Ⓘ
86. Ⓐ Ⓑ Ⓒ Ⓓ Ⓔ Ⓕ Ⓖ Ⓗ Ⓘ
87. Ⓐ Ⓑ Ⓒ Ⓓ Ⓔ Ⓕ Ⓖ Ⓗ Ⓘ
88. Ⓐ Ⓑ Ⓒ Ⓓ Ⓔ Ⓕ Ⓖ Ⓗ Ⓘ
89. Ⓐ Ⓑ Ⓒ Ⓓ Ⓔ Ⓕ Ⓖ Ⓗ Ⓘ
90. Ⓐ Ⓑ Ⓒ Ⓓ Ⓔ Ⓕ Ⓖ Ⓗ Ⓘ
91. Ⓐ Ⓑ Ⓒ Ⓓ Ⓔ Ⓕ Ⓖ Ⓗ Ⓘ
92. Ⓐ Ⓑ Ⓒ Ⓓ Ⓔ Ⓕ Ⓖ Ⓗ Ⓘ
93. Ⓐ Ⓑ Ⓒ Ⓓ Ⓔ Ⓕ Ⓖ Ⓗ Ⓘ
94. Ⓐ Ⓑ Ⓒ Ⓓ Ⓔ Ⓕ Ⓖ Ⓗ Ⓘ
95. Ⓐ Ⓑ Ⓒ Ⓓ Ⓔ Ⓕ Ⓖ Ⓗ Ⓘ
96. Ⓐ Ⓑ Ⓒ Ⓓ Ⓔ Ⓕ Ⓖ Ⓗ Ⓘ
97. Ⓐ Ⓑ Ⓒ Ⓓ Ⓔ Ⓕ Ⓖ Ⓗ Ⓘ
98. Ⓐ Ⓑ Ⓒ Ⓓ Ⓔ Ⓕ Ⓖ Ⓗ Ⓘ
99. Ⓐ Ⓑ Ⓒ Ⓓ Ⓔ Ⓕ Ⓖ Ⓗ Ⓘ
100. Ⓐ Ⓑ Ⓒ Ⓓ Ⓔ Ⓕ Ⓖ Ⓗ Ⓘ
101. Ⓐ Ⓑ Ⓒ Ⓓ Ⓔ Ⓕ Ⓖ Ⓗ Ⓘ
102. Ⓐ Ⓑ Ⓒ Ⓓ Ⓔ Ⓕ Ⓖ Ⓗ Ⓘ
103. Ⓐ Ⓑ Ⓒ Ⓓ Ⓔ Ⓕ Ⓖ Ⓗ Ⓘ
104. Ⓐ Ⓑ Ⓒ Ⓓ Ⓔ Ⓕ Ⓖ Ⓗ Ⓘ
105. Ⓐ Ⓑ Ⓒ Ⓓ Ⓔ Ⓕ Ⓖ Ⓗ Ⓘ

106. Ⓐ Ⓑ Ⓒ Ⓓ Ⓔ Ⓕ Ⓖ Ⓗ Ⓘ
107. Ⓐ Ⓑ Ⓒ Ⓓ Ⓔ Ⓕ Ⓖ Ⓗ Ⓘ
108. Ⓐ Ⓑ Ⓒ Ⓓ Ⓔ Ⓕ Ⓖ Ⓗ Ⓘ
109. Ⓐ Ⓑ Ⓒ Ⓓ Ⓔ Ⓕ Ⓖ Ⓗ Ⓘ
110. Ⓐ Ⓑ Ⓒ Ⓓ Ⓔ Ⓕ Ⓖ Ⓗ Ⓘ
111. Ⓐ Ⓑ Ⓒ Ⓓ Ⓔ Ⓕ Ⓖ Ⓗ Ⓘ
112. Ⓐ Ⓑ Ⓒ Ⓓ Ⓔ Ⓕ Ⓖ Ⓗ Ⓘ
113. Ⓐ Ⓑ Ⓒ Ⓓ Ⓔ Ⓕ Ⓖ Ⓗ Ⓘ
114. Ⓐ Ⓑ Ⓒ Ⓓ Ⓔ Ⓕ Ⓖ Ⓗ Ⓘ
115. Ⓐ Ⓑ Ⓒ Ⓓ Ⓔ Ⓕ Ⓖ Ⓗ Ⓘ
116. Ⓐ Ⓑ Ⓒ Ⓓ Ⓔ Ⓕ Ⓖ Ⓗ Ⓘ
117. Ⓐ Ⓑ Ⓒ Ⓓ Ⓔ Ⓕ Ⓖ Ⓗ Ⓘ
118. Ⓐ Ⓑ Ⓒ Ⓓ Ⓔ Ⓕ Ⓖ Ⓗ Ⓘ
119. Ⓐ Ⓑ Ⓒ Ⓓ Ⓔ Ⓕ Ⓖ Ⓗ Ⓘ
120. Ⓐ Ⓑ Ⓒ Ⓓ Ⓔ Ⓕ Ⓖ Ⓗ Ⓘ
121. Ⓐ Ⓑ Ⓒ Ⓓ Ⓔ Ⓕ Ⓖ Ⓗ Ⓘ
122. Ⓐ Ⓑ Ⓒ Ⓓ Ⓔ Ⓕ Ⓖ Ⓗ Ⓘ
123. Ⓐ Ⓑ Ⓒ Ⓓ Ⓔ Ⓕ Ⓖ Ⓗ Ⓘ
124. Ⓐ Ⓑ Ⓒ Ⓓ Ⓔ Ⓕ Ⓖ Ⓗ Ⓘ
125. Ⓐ Ⓑ Ⓒ Ⓓ Ⓔ Ⓕ Ⓖ Ⓗ Ⓘ
126. Ⓐ Ⓑ Ⓒ Ⓓ Ⓔ Ⓕ Ⓖ Ⓗ Ⓘ
127. Ⓐ Ⓑ Ⓒ Ⓓ Ⓔ Ⓕ Ⓖ Ⓗ Ⓘ
128. Ⓐ Ⓑ Ⓒ Ⓓ Ⓔ Ⓕ Ⓖ Ⓗ Ⓘ
129. Ⓐ Ⓑ Ⓒ Ⓓ Ⓔ Ⓕ Ⓖ Ⓗ Ⓘ
130. Ⓐ Ⓑ Ⓒ Ⓓ Ⓔ Ⓕ Ⓖ Ⓗ Ⓘ
131. Ⓐ Ⓑ Ⓒ Ⓓ Ⓔ Ⓕ Ⓖ Ⓗ Ⓘ
132. Ⓐ Ⓑ Ⓒ Ⓓ Ⓔ Ⓕ Ⓖ Ⓗ Ⓘ
133. Ⓐ Ⓑ Ⓒ Ⓓ Ⓔ Ⓕ Ⓖ Ⓗ Ⓘ
134. Ⓐ Ⓑ Ⓒ Ⓓ Ⓔ Ⓕ Ⓖ Ⓗ Ⓘ
135. Ⓐ Ⓑ Ⓒ Ⓓ Ⓔ Ⓕ Ⓖ Ⓗ Ⓘ
136. Ⓐ Ⓑ Ⓒ Ⓓ Ⓔ Ⓕ Ⓖ Ⓗ Ⓘ
137. Ⓐ Ⓑ Ⓒ Ⓓ Ⓔ Ⓕ Ⓖ Ⓗ Ⓘ
138. Ⓐ Ⓑ Ⓒ Ⓓ Ⓔ Ⓕ Ⓖ Ⓗ Ⓘ
139. Ⓐ Ⓑ Ⓒ Ⓓ Ⓔ Ⓕ Ⓖ Ⓗ Ⓘ
140. Ⓐ Ⓑ Ⓒ Ⓓ Ⓔ Ⓕ Ⓖ Ⓗ Ⓘ

141. Ⓐ Ⓑ Ⓒ Ⓓ Ⓔ Ⓕ Ⓖ Ⓗ Ⓘ
142. Ⓐ Ⓑ Ⓒ Ⓓ Ⓔ Ⓕ Ⓖ Ⓗ Ⓘ
143. Ⓐ Ⓑ Ⓒ Ⓓ Ⓔ Ⓕ Ⓖ Ⓗ Ⓘ
144. Ⓐ Ⓑ Ⓒ Ⓓ Ⓔ Ⓕ Ⓖ Ⓗ Ⓘ
145. Ⓐ Ⓑ Ⓒ Ⓓ Ⓔ Ⓕ Ⓖ Ⓗ Ⓘ
146. Ⓐ Ⓑ Ⓒ Ⓓ Ⓔ Ⓕ Ⓖ Ⓗ Ⓘ
147. Ⓐ Ⓑ Ⓒ Ⓓ Ⓔ Ⓕ Ⓖ Ⓗ Ⓘ
148. Ⓐ Ⓑ Ⓒ Ⓓ Ⓔ Ⓕ Ⓖ Ⓗ Ⓘ
149. Ⓐ Ⓑ Ⓒ Ⓓ Ⓔ Ⓕ Ⓖ Ⓗ Ⓘ
150. Ⓐ Ⓑ Ⓒ Ⓓ Ⓔ Ⓕ Ⓖ Ⓗ Ⓘ
151. Ⓐ Ⓑ Ⓒ Ⓓ Ⓔ Ⓕ Ⓖ Ⓗ Ⓘ
152. Ⓐ Ⓑ Ⓒ Ⓓ Ⓔ Ⓕ Ⓖ Ⓗ Ⓘ
153. Ⓐ Ⓑ Ⓒ Ⓓ Ⓔ Ⓕ Ⓖ Ⓗ Ⓘ
154. Ⓐ Ⓑ Ⓒ Ⓓ Ⓔ Ⓕ Ⓖ Ⓗ Ⓘ
155. Ⓐ Ⓑ Ⓒ Ⓓ Ⓔ Ⓕ Ⓖ Ⓗ Ⓘ
156. Ⓐ Ⓑ Ⓒ Ⓓ Ⓔ Ⓕ Ⓖ Ⓗ Ⓘ
157. Ⓐ Ⓑ Ⓒ Ⓓ Ⓔ Ⓕ Ⓖ Ⓗ Ⓘ
158. Ⓐ Ⓑ Ⓒ Ⓓ Ⓔ Ⓕ Ⓖ Ⓗ Ⓘ
159. Ⓐ Ⓑ Ⓒ Ⓓ Ⓔ Ⓕ Ⓖ Ⓗ Ⓘ
160. Ⓐ Ⓑ Ⓒ Ⓓ Ⓔ Ⓕ Ⓖ Ⓗ Ⓘ
161. Ⓐ Ⓑ Ⓒ Ⓓ Ⓔ Ⓕ Ⓖ Ⓗ Ⓘ
162. Ⓐ Ⓑ Ⓒ Ⓓ Ⓔ Ⓕ Ⓖ Ⓗ Ⓘ
163. Ⓐ Ⓑ Ⓒ Ⓓ Ⓔ Ⓕ Ⓖ Ⓗ Ⓘ
164. Ⓐ Ⓑ Ⓒ Ⓓ Ⓔ Ⓕ Ⓖ Ⓗ Ⓘ
165. Ⓐ Ⓑ Ⓒ Ⓓ Ⓔ Ⓕ Ⓖ Ⓗ Ⓘ
166. Ⓐ Ⓑ Ⓒ Ⓓ Ⓔ Ⓕ Ⓖ Ⓗ Ⓘ
167. Ⓐ Ⓑ Ⓒ Ⓓ Ⓔ Ⓕ Ⓖ Ⓗ Ⓘ
168. Ⓐ Ⓑ Ⓒ Ⓓ Ⓔ Ⓕ Ⓖ Ⓗ Ⓘ
169. Ⓐ Ⓑ Ⓒ Ⓓ Ⓔ Ⓕ Ⓖ Ⓗ Ⓘ
170. Ⓐ Ⓑ Ⓒ Ⓓ Ⓔ Ⓕ Ⓖ Ⓗ Ⓘ
171. Ⓐ Ⓑ Ⓒ Ⓓ Ⓔ Ⓕ Ⓖ Ⓗ Ⓘ
172. Ⓐ Ⓑ Ⓒ Ⓓ Ⓔ Ⓕ Ⓖ Ⓗ Ⓘ
173. Ⓐ Ⓑ Ⓒ Ⓓ Ⓔ Ⓕ Ⓖ Ⓗ Ⓘ
174. Ⓐ Ⓑ Ⓒ Ⓓ Ⓔ Ⓕ Ⓖ Ⓗ Ⓘ
175. Ⓐ Ⓑ Ⓒ Ⓓ Ⓔ Ⓕ Ⓖ Ⓗ Ⓘ

176. Ⓐ Ⓑ Ⓒ Ⓓ Ⓔ Ⓕ Ⓖ Ⓗ Ⓘ
177. Ⓐ Ⓑ Ⓒ Ⓓ Ⓔ Ⓕ Ⓖ Ⓗ Ⓘ
178. Ⓐ Ⓑ Ⓒ Ⓓ Ⓔ Ⓕ Ⓖ Ⓗ Ⓘ
179. Ⓐ Ⓑ Ⓒ Ⓓ Ⓔ Ⓕ Ⓖ Ⓗ Ⓘ
180. Ⓐ Ⓑ Ⓒ Ⓓ Ⓔ Ⓕ Ⓖ Ⓗ Ⓘ
181. Ⓐ Ⓑ Ⓒ Ⓓ Ⓔ Ⓕ Ⓖ Ⓗ Ⓘ
182. Ⓐ Ⓑ Ⓒ Ⓓ Ⓔ Ⓕ Ⓖ Ⓗ Ⓘ
183. Ⓐ Ⓑ Ⓒ Ⓓ Ⓔ Ⓕ Ⓖ Ⓗ Ⓘ
184. Ⓐ Ⓑ Ⓒ Ⓓ Ⓔ Ⓕ Ⓖ Ⓗ Ⓘ
185. Ⓐ Ⓑ Ⓒ Ⓓ Ⓔ Ⓕ Ⓖ Ⓗ Ⓘ
186. Ⓐ Ⓑ Ⓒ Ⓓ Ⓔ Ⓕ Ⓖ Ⓗ Ⓘ
187. Ⓐ Ⓑ Ⓒ Ⓓ Ⓔ Ⓕ Ⓖ Ⓗ Ⓘ
188. Ⓐ Ⓑ Ⓒ Ⓓ Ⓔ Ⓕ Ⓖ Ⓗ Ⓘ
189. Ⓐ Ⓑ Ⓒ Ⓓ Ⓔ Ⓕ Ⓖ Ⓗ Ⓘ
190. Ⓐ Ⓑ Ⓒ Ⓓ Ⓔ Ⓕ Ⓖ Ⓗ Ⓘ
191. Ⓐ Ⓑ Ⓒ Ⓓ Ⓔ Ⓕ Ⓖ Ⓗ Ⓘ
192. Ⓐ Ⓑ Ⓒ Ⓓ Ⓔ Ⓕ Ⓖ Ⓗ Ⓘ
193. Ⓐ Ⓑ Ⓒ Ⓓ Ⓔ Ⓕ Ⓖ Ⓗ Ⓘ
194. Ⓐ Ⓑ Ⓒ Ⓓ Ⓔ Ⓕ Ⓖ Ⓗ Ⓘ
195. Ⓐ Ⓑ Ⓒ Ⓓ Ⓔ Ⓕ Ⓖ Ⓗ Ⓘ
196. Ⓐ Ⓑ Ⓒ Ⓓ Ⓔ Ⓕ Ⓖ Ⓗ Ⓘ
197. Ⓐ Ⓑ Ⓒ Ⓓ Ⓔ Ⓕ Ⓖ Ⓗ Ⓘ
198. Ⓐ Ⓑ Ⓒ Ⓓ Ⓔ Ⓕ Ⓖ Ⓗ Ⓘ
199. Ⓐ Ⓑ Ⓒ Ⓓ Ⓔ Ⓕ Ⓖ Ⓗ Ⓘ
200. Ⓐ Ⓑ Ⓒ Ⓓ Ⓔ Ⓕ Ⓖ Ⓗ Ⓘ
201. Ⓐ Ⓑ Ⓒ Ⓓ Ⓔ Ⓕ Ⓖ Ⓗ Ⓘ
202. Ⓐ Ⓑ Ⓒ Ⓓ Ⓔ Ⓕ Ⓖ Ⓗ Ⓘ
203. Ⓐ Ⓑ Ⓒ Ⓓ Ⓔ Ⓕ Ⓖ Ⓗ Ⓘ
204. Ⓐ Ⓑ Ⓒ Ⓓ Ⓔ Ⓕ Ⓖ Ⓗ Ⓘ
205. Ⓐ Ⓑ Ⓒ Ⓓ Ⓔ Ⓕ Ⓖ Ⓗ Ⓘ
206. Ⓐ Ⓑ Ⓒ Ⓓ Ⓔ Ⓕ Ⓖ Ⓗ Ⓘ
207. Ⓐ Ⓑ Ⓒ Ⓓ Ⓔ Ⓕ Ⓖ Ⓗ Ⓘ
208. Ⓐ Ⓑ Ⓒ Ⓓ Ⓔ Ⓕ Ⓖ Ⓗ Ⓘ
209. Ⓐ Ⓑ Ⓒ Ⓓ Ⓔ Ⓕ Ⓖ Ⓗ Ⓘ
210. Ⓐ Ⓑ Ⓒ Ⓓ Ⓔ Ⓕ Ⓖ Ⓗ Ⓘ

211. Ⓐ Ⓑ Ⓒ Ⓓ Ⓔ Ⓕ Ⓖ Ⓗ Ⓘ
212. Ⓐ Ⓑ Ⓒ Ⓓ Ⓔ Ⓕ Ⓖ Ⓗ Ⓘ
213. Ⓐ Ⓑ Ⓒ Ⓓ Ⓔ Ⓕ Ⓖ Ⓗ Ⓘ
214. Ⓐ Ⓑ Ⓒ Ⓓ Ⓔ Ⓕ Ⓖ Ⓗ Ⓘ
215. Ⓐ Ⓑ Ⓒ Ⓓ Ⓔ Ⓕ Ⓖ Ⓗ Ⓘ
216. Ⓐ Ⓑ Ⓒ Ⓓ Ⓔ Ⓕ Ⓖ Ⓗ Ⓘ
217. Ⓐ Ⓑ Ⓒ Ⓓ Ⓔ Ⓕ Ⓖ Ⓗ Ⓘ
218. Ⓐ Ⓑ Ⓒ Ⓓ Ⓔ Ⓕ Ⓖ Ⓗ Ⓘ
219. Ⓐ Ⓑ Ⓒ Ⓓ Ⓔ Ⓕ Ⓖ Ⓗ Ⓘ

220. Ⓐ Ⓑ Ⓒ Ⓓ Ⓔ Ⓕ Ⓖ Ⓗ Ⓘ
221. Ⓐ Ⓑ Ⓒ Ⓓ Ⓔ Ⓕ Ⓖ Ⓗ Ⓘ
222. Ⓐ Ⓑ Ⓒ Ⓓ Ⓔ Ⓕ Ⓖ Ⓗ Ⓘ
223. Ⓐ Ⓑ Ⓒ Ⓓ Ⓔ Ⓕ Ⓖ Ⓗ Ⓘ
224. Ⓐ Ⓑ Ⓒ Ⓓ Ⓔ Ⓕ Ⓖ Ⓗ Ⓘ
225. Ⓐ Ⓑ Ⓒ Ⓓ Ⓔ Ⓕ Ⓖ Ⓗ Ⓘ
226. Ⓐ Ⓑ Ⓒ Ⓓ Ⓔ Ⓕ Ⓖ Ⓗ Ⓘ
227. Ⓐ Ⓑ Ⓒ Ⓓ Ⓔ Ⓕ Ⓖ Ⓗ Ⓘ
228. Ⓐ Ⓑ Ⓒ Ⓓ Ⓔ Ⓕ Ⓖ Ⓗ Ⓘ

229. Ⓐ Ⓑ Ⓒ Ⓓ Ⓔ Ⓕ Ⓖ Ⓗ Ⓘ
230. Ⓐ Ⓑ Ⓒ Ⓓ Ⓔ Ⓕ Ⓖ Ⓗ Ⓘ
231. Ⓐ Ⓑ Ⓒ Ⓓ Ⓔ Ⓕ Ⓖ Ⓗ Ⓘ
232. Ⓐ Ⓑ Ⓒ Ⓓ Ⓔ Ⓕ Ⓖ Ⓗ Ⓘ
233. Ⓐ Ⓑ Ⓒ Ⓓ Ⓔ Ⓕ Ⓖ Ⓗ Ⓘ
234. Ⓐ Ⓑ Ⓒ Ⓓ Ⓔ Ⓕ Ⓖ Ⓗ Ⓘ
235. Ⓐ Ⓑ Ⓒ Ⓓ Ⓔ Ⓕ Ⓖ Ⓗ Ⓘ
236. Ⓐ Ⓑ Ⓒ Ⓓ Ⓔ Ⓕ Ⓖ Ⓗ Ⓘ

Part A: Address Checking

60 QUESTIONS • 6 MINUTES

> **Directions:** Compare the **List to be Checked** with the **Correct List.** Decide if there are **(A) NO ERRORS,** an error in the **(B) ADDRESS ONLY,** an error in the **(C) ZIP CODE ONLY,** or an error in **(D) BOTH** the address and ZIP Code. Record your answers on the answer sheet.

	Correct List		List to be Checked	
	Address	*ZIP Code*	*Address*	*ZIP Code*
1.	462 Midland Avenue Wappinger Falls, NY	12590	462 Midland Avenue Wappinger Falls, NY	12590
2.	2319 Sherry Drive Worcester, MA	01610	3219 Sherry Drive Worcester, ME	01610
3.	1015 Kimball Avenue Miami Beach, FL	33139	1015 Kimball Avenue Miami Beach, FL	33193
4.	1255 North Avenue Palm Springs, CA	92262	1225 North Avenue Palm Springs, CA	92262
5.	1826 Tibbets Road Buffalo, NY	42113	1826 Tibetts Road Buffulo, NY	42113
6.	603 N. Division Street Watertown, MA	02172	603 N. Division Street Watertown, MA	02172
7.	2304 Manhattan Avenue West Chester, PA	19380	2034 Manhattan Avenue West Chester, PA	19830
8.	1186 Vernon Drive Sunrise, FL	33313	186 Vernon Drive Sunrise, FL	33133
9.	209 Peter Bont Road Dover, DE	19901	209 Peter Bent Road Dover, DL	19901
10.	1100 West Avenue Purchase, NY	10577	1100 East Avenue Purchase, NY	10577
11.	2063 Winyah Terrace Elmhurst, NY	11373	2036 Winyah Terrace Elmherst, NY	11373
12.	3483 Suncrest Avenue Wilmington, DE	19810	3483 Suncrest Drive Wilmington, DE	19810

13. 234 Rochambeau Road
     Bronxville, NY   10708

     234 Roshambeau Road
     Bronxville, NJ   10708

14. 306 N. Terrace Boulevard
     Baltimore, MD   21215

     306 N. Terrace Boulevard
     Baltimore, MD   21215

15. 1632 Paine Street
     Miami Beach, FL   33179

     1632 Pain Street
     Miami, FL   33179

16. 286 Marietta Avenue
     Indianapolis, IN   46260

     286 Marrietta Avenue
     Indianapolis, IN   46260

17. 2445 Pigott Road
     Jamaica, NY   11435

     2445 Pigott Road
     Jamiaca, NY   11435

18. 2204 PineBrook Boulevard
     Kew Gardens, NY   11415

     2204 Pinebrook Boulevard
     Kew Garden, NY   11415

19. 487 Warburton Avenue
     Bronx, NY   10475

     487 Warburton Avenue
     Bronx, NY   10475

20. 9386 North Street
     Darien, CT   06820

     9386 North Avenue
     Darien, CT   06820

21. 2272 Glandale Road
     Ontarioville, IL   60103

     2772 Glandale Road
     Ontarioville, IL   60103

22. 9236 Puritan Drive
     Quickley, MA   09821

     9236 Puritan Place
     Quickley, ME   09821

23. 7803 Kimball Avenue
     Walden, CO   80480

     7803 Kimbal Avenue
     Waldon, CO   08480

24. 1362 Colonial Parkway
     Muscle Shoals, AL   35660

     1362 Colonial Parkway
     Muscle Shoals, AL   35660

25. 115 Rolling Hills Road
     Daytona Beach, Fla   32016

     115 Rolling Hills Road
     Daytona Beach, FL   32016

26. 218 Rockledge Road
     Hammond, GA   31785

     2181 Rockledge Road
     Hammond, GA   31785

27. 8346 N. Broadnax Street
     Francisco, WY   82636

     8346 W. Broadnax Street
     Francisco, WY   82636

28. 9224 Highland Way
     Centralville, MT   08869

     9244 Highland Way
     Centralville, MT   08869

29. 8383 Mamaroneck Avenue
     Quenemo, KS   66528

     8383 Mamaroneck Avenue
     Quenemo, KS   66528

30.	276 Furnace Dock Road Wilburnum, MS	65566	276 Furnace Dock Road Vilburnum, MS	65566	
31.	4137 Loockerman Street Ware, MA	08215	4137 Lockerman Street Ware, MA	08215	
32.	532 Broadhollow Road Scarsdale, NY	10583	532 Broadhollow Road Scarsdale, NY	10583	
33.	148 Cortlandt Road Milwaukee, WI	53202	148 Cortland Road Milwaukee, WI	53202	
34.	5951 W. Hartsdale Road Portland, OR	97208	5951 W. Hartsdale Avenue Portland, OR	97208	
35.	5231 Alta Vista Circle Omaha, NE	68127	5321 Alta Vista Circle Omaha, NE	68127	
36.	6459 Chippewa Road Dallas, TX	75234	6459 Chippewa Road Dallas, TX	75224	
37.	1171 S. Highland Road San Francisco, CA	94108	1771 S. Highland Road San Francisco, CA	94108	
38.	2363 Old Farm Lane Westport, CT	06880	2363 Old Farm Lane Westport, CT	06888	
39.	1001 Hemingway Drive Noquochoke, MA	02790	1001 Hemmingway Drive Noquochoke, MA	02790	
40.	1555 Morningside Avenue Kingsfield, ME	04947	1555 Morningslide Avenue Kingsfield, ME	04947	
41.	1189 E. 9th Street Seattle, WA	98102	1189 E. 9th Street Seattle, WY	98102	
42.	168 Old Lyme Road Boiceville, NY	12412	186 Old Lyme Road Boiceville, NY	12412	
43.	106 Notingham Road New Orleans, LA	70153	106 Nottingham Road New Orleans, LA	70153	
44.	1428 Midland Avenue Charlotte, VT	05445	1428 Midland Avenue Charlotte, VA	05445	
45.	1450 West Chester Pike Havertown, PA	19083	1450 West Chester Pike Havertown, PA	19883	
46.	3357 Main Street Freeport, ME	04033	3357 Main Street Freeport, NE	04033	

47.	5062 Marietta Avenue Natick, MA	01760	5062 Marrietta Avenue Natick, MA	01760
48.	1890 3rd Court Irvington, NY	10533	1980 3rd Court Irvington, NY	10533
49.	1075 Park Avenue Sea Island, GA	31561	1075 W. Park Avenue Sea Inland, GA	31561
50.	672 Bacon Hill Road Providence, RI	02903	672 Beacon Hill Road Providence, RI	02903
51.	1725 W. 17th Street Arundel, ME	04046	1725 W. 17th Street Anurdel, ME	04046
52.	2066 Old Wilmot Road Oakland, CA	94604	2066 Old Wilmont Road Oakland, CA	94604
53.	3333 State Road Philadelphia, PA	19124	3333 State Road Philadelphia, PN	19124
54.	1483 Meritoria Drive Essex, CT	06426	1438 Meritoria Drive Essex, CT	06426
55.	2327 E. 23rd Street Alamo, TX	78516	2327 E. 27th Street Alamo, TX	78516
56.	137 Clarence Road Los Angeles, CA	90013	137 Claremont Road Los Angeles, CA	90018
57.	3516 N. Ely Avenue New York, NY	10016	3516 N. Ely Avenue New York, NY	10016
58.	111 Beechwood Street Gainesville, FL	43611	1111 Beechwood Street Gainsville, FL	32611
59.	143 N. Highland Avenue Onoro, ME	04473	143 N. Highland Avenue Orono, ME	04473
60.	6430 Spring Mill Road Des Moines, IA	50311	6340 Spring Mill Road Des Moines, IA	50311

Part B: Forms Completion

30 QUESTIONS • 15 MINUTES

> **Directions:** Read each form and answer the items based on the information provided. Mark your answers on the answer sheet.

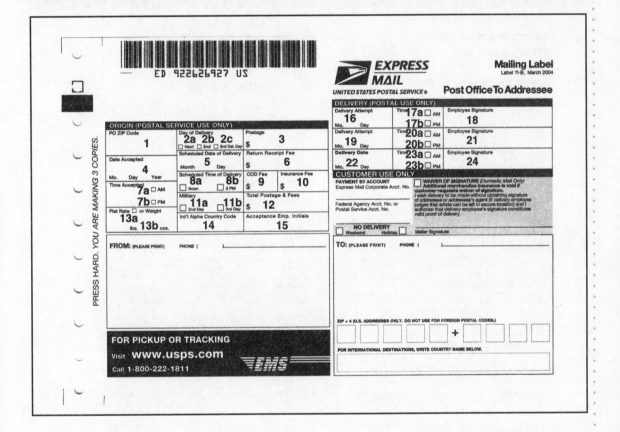

1. Which of these would be a correct entry for Box 5?
   - **(A)** A check mark
   - **(B)** $13.85
   - **(C)** 12 and 20
   - **(D)** 08530

2. Where would you enter the insurance fee?
   - **(A)** Box 3
   - **(B)** Box 6
   - **(C)** Box 10
   - **(D)** Box 12

3. A check mark would be the correct entry for every box EXCEPT
   - **(A)** Box 6
   - **(B)** Box 7a
   - **(C)** Box 8a
   - **(D)** Box 11b

4. Where would you indicate that the package was delivered?
   - **(A)** Box 16
   - **(B)** Box 18
   - **(C)** Box 19
   - **(D)** Box 22

5. All of the following boxes indicate employee signatures are needed EXCEPT

   (A) Box 4
   (B) Box 18
   (C) Box 21
   (D) Box 24

6. Which of these would be a correct entry for Box 13b?

   (A) A check mark
   (B) 3 lbs. 6 oz.
   (C) 4/11
   (D) $13.85

7. Which box would you check to show 2nd day delivery to the military?

   (A) Box 2a
   (B) Box 2b
   (C) Box 8a
   (D) Box 11a

8. The country code for mail being sent out of the United States is entered in which box?

   (A) Box 1
   (B) Box 14
   (C) Box 15
   (D) Box 16

9. Which of these would be the correct entry for Box 15?

   (A) A check mark
   (B) $1.60
   (C) Initials
   (D) 6/12/05

	1a	1b	1c	1d	1e	1f

Item Description (Nature de l'envoi)	Registered □ Article (Envoi recommandé)	□ Letter (Lettre)	Printed □ Matter (Imprimé)	□ Other (Autre)	Recorded Delivery □ (Envoi à livraison attestée)	Express □ Mail International

Completed by the office of origin. (A remplir par le bureau d'origine.)

Insured Parcel 2 □ (Colis avec valeur déclarée)	Insured Value (Valeur déclarée) 3	Article Number 4
Office of Mailing (Bureau de dépôt) 5		Date of Posting (Date de dépôt) 6

Addressee Name or Firm (Nom ou raison sociale du destinataire) 7

Street and No. (Rue et No.) 8

Place and Country (Localité et pays) 9

Completed at destination. (A compléter à destination.)

This receipt must be signed by: (1) the addressee; or, (2) a person authorized to sign under the regulations of the country of destination; or, (3) if those regulations so provide, by the employee of the office of destination. This signed form will be returned to the sender by the first mail.

(Cet avis doit être signé par le destinataire ou par une personne y autorisée en vertu des règlements du pays de destination, ou, si ces règlements le comportent, par l'agent du bureau de destination, et renvoyé par le premier courrier directement à expéditeur.)

Postmark of the office of destination (Timbre du bureau de destination) 14

□ The article mentioned above was duly delivered. (L'envoi mentionné ci-dessus a été dûment livré.) 10   Date 11

Signature of Addressee (Signature du destinataire) 12	Office of Destination Employee Signature (Signature de l'agent du bureau du destination) 13

PS Form 2865, February 1997 (Reverse)

10. Which of these would be a correct entry for Box 9?

    (A) Paris, France
    (B) Ms. Marie Hrouda
    (C) 10/21/06
    (D) $100

11. Where would you indicate that the item is Express Mail International?

    (A) Box 1a
    (B) Box 1b
    (C) Box 1c
    (D) Box 1f

12. Which of these would be a correct entry for Box 7?
    - **(A)** A check mark
    - **(B)** Computer Programmers World-wide
    - **(C)** 14 Piccadilly Lane
    - **(D)** 9/30/06

13. How would you indicate that the piece of mail was a letter?
    - **(A)** Check Box 1a
    - **(B)** Check Box 1b
    - **(C)** Write the word in Box 3
    - **(D)** Write the word in Box 5

14. Where would you enter the Article Number?
    - **(A)** Box 2
    - **(B)** Box 3
    - **(C)** Box 4
    - **(D)** Box 6

15. Which of these would be the correct entry for Box 3?
    - **(A)** A check mark
    - **(B)** Peoria, IL
    - **(C)** London, England
    - **(D)** $250

16. Where would you enter the check number for the COD package?
    - **(A)** Box 2
    - **(B)** Box 3
    - **(C)** Box 4
    - **(D)** Box 5

17. Which of the following would be a correct entry for Box 2?
    - **(A)** 2/22/06
    - **(B)** A check mark
    - **(C)** #2345
    - **(D)** Mr. Steve Krasowski

18. You could enter a date in each of the following boxes EXCEPT
    - **(A)** Box 1
    - **(B)** Box 4
    - **(C)** Box 5
    - **(D)** Box 6

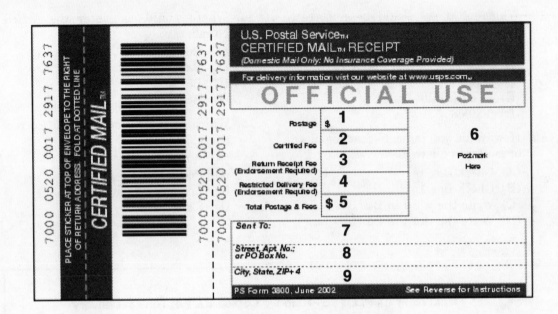

19. Which of these would be a correct entry for Box 7?
- **(A)** A check mark
- **(B)** $1,000
- **(C)** Ms. Dy Anne Going
- **(D)** 3/22/06

20. Where would you stamp the receipt?
- **(A)** Box 1
- **(B)** Box 2
- **(C)** Box 6
- **(D)** Box 9

21. Where would you indicate that the item is being sent to Boston?
- **(A)** Box 2
- **(B)** Box 4
- **(C)** Box 6
- **(D)** Box 9

Authorization to Hold Mail
NOTE: *Complete and give to your letter carrier or mail to the post office that delivers your mail.*

We can hold your mail for a minimum of **3**, but not for more than **30 days.**

Postmaster: Please hold mail for:

Name(s)

☐ **A.** Please deliver all accumulated mail and resume normal delivery on the ending date shown below.

Address *(Number, street, apt./suite no., city, state, ZIP + 4)*

☐ **B.** I will pick up all accumulated mail when I return and understand that mail delivery will not resume until I do.

Beginning Date	Ending Date *(May only be changed by the customer in writing)*	Customer Signature

For Post Office Use Only

Date Received **1.**		
Clerk **2.**	Bin Number **3.**	
Carrier **4.**	Route Number **5.**	

(Complete this section only if customer selected option B)

6. ☐ Accumulated mail has been picked up.	Resume Delivery of Mail *(Date)* **7.**	By **8.**

PS Form **8076,** April 2001

---

22. Which of these would be a correct entry for Box 5?
(A) Rural Route 5
(B) $1.60
(C) 6/5/06
(D) Tim Criswell

23. Where would you enter the mail carrier's name?
(A) Box 1
(B) Box 2
(C) Box 3
(D) Box 4

24. Which of these would be a correct answer for Box 6?
(A) A check mark
(B) 5/20/06
(C) 5/20/06 to 6/1/06
(D) Michelle McDermott

25. Which of these would be a correct answer for Box 7?
(A) A check mark
(B) 1/20/06
(C) 510 Crescent Boulevard
(D) 07046

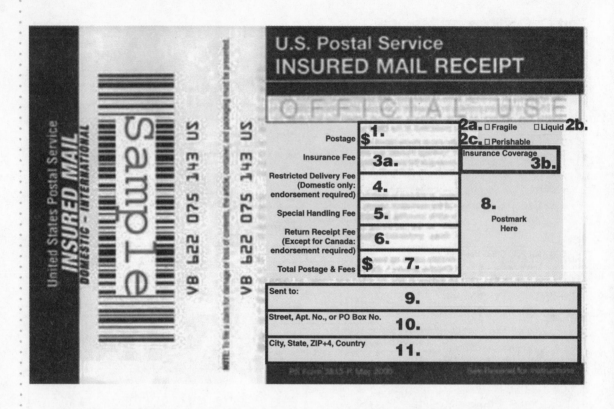

26. Where would you check that the item is perishable?
- **(A)** Box 2a
- **(B)** Box 2b
- **(C)** Box 2c
- **(D)** Box 3b

27. Where would you enter the total postage and fees?
- **(A)** Box 1
- **(B)** Box 3a
- **(C)** Box 5
- **(D)** Box 7

28. What would be the correct entry for Box 8?
- **(A)** A check mark
- **(B)** A postmark
- **(C)** $2.50
- **(D)** 12456

29. If the item was being mailed to a foreign country, which box could NOT be completed?
- **(A)** Box 1
- **(B)** Box 3b
- **(C)** Box 4
- **(D)** Box 5

30. You could enter fees in all of the following boxes EXCEPT
- **(A)** Box 1
- **(B)** Box 2a
- **(C)** Box 3a
- **(D)** Box 4

Part C: Coding and Memory

Section 1: Coding

36 QUESTIONS • 6 MINUTES

Directions: Work through items 1 through 36 assigning a code to each item based on the Coding Guide below. Mark your answers on the answer sheet. Work quickly and accurately.

CODING GUIDE

ADDRESS RANGE	DELIVERY ROUTE
100–199 N. Broad Avenue 50–250 E. 12th Street 10–25 E. Chestnut Street	A
200–500 N. Broad Avenue 26–70 E. Chestnut Street	B
20–35 Rural Route 2 7000–15000 S. Broad Avenue 300–1000 S. Chester Road	C
All mail that doesn't fall into one of the address ranges listed above.	D

Address	Delivery Route			
1. 105 N. Broad Avenue	A	B	C	D
2. 52 E. Chestnut Street	A	B	C	D
3. 220 N. Brook Street	A	B	C	D
4. 195 E. 12th Street	A	B	C	D
5. 68 E. Chestnut Street	A	B	C	D
6. 28 Rural Route 2	A	B	C	D
7. 7801 S. Broad Avenue	A	B	C	D
8. 10 Rural Route 2	A	B	C	D
9. 42 Rural Route 2	A	B	C	D
10. 72 E. 12th Street	A	B	C	D
11. 152 N. Brook Street	A	B	C	D
12. 9500 S. Broad Avenue	A	B	C	D
13. 900 S. Chester Road	A	B	C	D
14. 1000 N. Broad Avenue	A	B	C	D
15. 401 N. Broad Avenue	A	B	C	D

16. 76 E. Chestnut Street	A	B	C	D
17. 368 N. Broad Avenue	A	B	C	D
18. 8620 S. Broad Avenue	A	B	C	D
19. 1201 S. Clement Street	A	B	C	D
20. 14 Rural Route 2	A	B	C	D
21. 15 E. Chestnut Street	A	B	C	D
22. 1250 E. 12th Street	A	B	C	D
23. 59 W. Chestnut Street	A	B	C	D
24. 28 Rural Route 2	A	B	C	D
25. 1400 S. Broad Avenue	A	B	C	D
26. 305 S. Chester Road	A	B	C	D
27. 178 N. Broad Avenue	A	B	C	D
28. 15101 N. Broad Avenue	A	B	C	D
29. 59 E. Chestnut Street	A	B	C	D
30. 99 E. 12th Street	A	B	C	D
31. 7000 S. Brook Street	A	B	C	D
32. 249 N. Broad Avenue	A	B	C	D
33. 30 Rural Route 2	A	B	C	D
34. 1049 S. Chester Road	A	B	C	D
35. 19 E. Chestnut Street	A	B	C	D
36. 1000 S. Broad Avenue	A	B	C	D

Section 2: Memory

36 QUESTIONS • 7 MINUTES

> **Directions:** Take 3 minutes to memorize the Coding Guide on page 122. Work through
> items 1 through 36 assigning a code based on your memory of the Coding Guide. Mark
> your answers on the answer sheet. Work quickly and accurately.
>
> • You may NOT write down any addresses during the memorization period.
> • You may NOT look at the codes when answering the items.

Address		Delivery Route		
1. 250 E. 12th Street	A	B	C	D
2. 12501 S. Broad Avenue	A	B	C	D
3. 205 N. Broad Avenue	A	B	C	D
4. 601 N. Broad Avenue	A	B	C	D
5. 20 Rural Route 10	A	B	C	D
6. 30 Rural Route 2	A	B	C	D
7. 51 E. 12th Street	A	B	C	D
8. 25 E. 12th Street	A	B	C	D
9. 36 Belmont Lane	A	B	C	D
10. 300 E. 12th Street	A	B	C	D
11. 137 N. Broad Avenue	A	B	C	D
12. 301 N. Broad Avenue	A	B	C	D
13. 400 E. 12th Street	A	B	C	D
14. 900 S. Chester Road	A	B	C	D
15. 13040 S. Broad Street	A	B	C	D
16. 406 S. Chester Road	A	B	C	D.
17. 6700 S. Broad Avenue	A	B	C	D
18. 48 E. 14th Street	A	B	C	D
19. 51 E. Chestnut Street	A	B	C	D
20. 15 E. Chestnut Street	A	B	C	D
21. 115 E. 12th Street	A	B	C	D
22. 1000 S. Brook Street	A	B	C	D
23. 210 E. 12th Street	A	B	C	D
24. 105 N. Broad Avenue	A	B	C	D
25. 15 Rural Route 2	A	B	C	D

26. 68 E. Chestnut Street   A   B   C   D

27. 28 Rural Route 2   A   B   C   D

28. 325 N. Broad Avenue   A   B   C   D

29. 1000 E. Chestnut Street   A   B   C   D

30. 14 North Broad Avenue   A   B   C   D

31. 117 S. 12th Street   A   B   C   D

32. 717 S. Chester Road   A   B   C   D

33. 14 N. Broad Avenue   A   B   C   D

34. 25 Belmont Lane   A   B   C   D

35. 67 E. Chestnut Street   A   B   C   D

36. 608 S. Chester Road   A   B   C   D

Part D: Personal Characteristics and Experience Inventory

Section 1: Agree/Disagree

236 QUESTIONS • 90 MINUTES

> **Directions:** Read each item carefully. Decide which of the four responses ranging from **Strongly Agree** to **Strongly Disagree** fits you best. For some items, more than one response may describe you. Choose the best description and mark only that one answer on the answer sheet. It is important to answer each item, even if you are not certain which response is best for you. Also, try to work at a fairly rapid pace.

1. You like to work at a fast pace.
   - (A) Strongly Agree
   - (B) Agree
   - (C) Disagree
   - (D) Strongly Disagree

2. You like a job where you are in contact with people.
   - (A) Strongly Agree
   - (B) Agree
   - (C) Disagree
   - (D) Strongly Disagree

3. You like to have others give you directions about what to do.
   - (A) Strongly Agree
   - (B) Agree
   - (C) Disagree
   - (D) Strongly Disagree

4. You are very organized about your work and work area.
   - (A) Strongly Agree
   - (B) Agree
   - (C) Disagree
   - (D) Strongly Disagree

5. You believe in doing every task to the best of your ability.
   - (A) Strongly Agree
   - (B) Agree
   - (C) Disagree
   - (D) Strongly Disagree

6. You like looking for answers to problems.
   - (A) Strongly Agree
   - (B) Agree
   - (C) Disagree
   - (D) Strongly Disagree

7. You do not like to vary how you do a task.
   - (A) Strongly Agree
   - (B) Agree
   - (C) Disagree
   - (D) Strongly Disagree

8. You like to help others when they are having difficulty doing a task.
   - (A) Strongly Agree
   - (B) Agree
   - (C) Disagree
   - (D) Strongly Disagree

9. You never like change in the beginning but adapt to it in time.
   - (A) Strongly Agree
   - (B) Agree
   - (C) Disagree
   - (D) Strongly Disagree

10. Because all jobs are stressful, you have figured out how to manage stress.
    - (A) Strongly Agree
    - (B) Agree
    - (C) Disagree
    - (D) Strongly Disagree

11. You take on new tasks at work enthusiastically.
    - (A) Strongly Agree
    - (B) Agree
    - (C) Disagree
    - (D) Strongly Disagree

12. You need quiet to work effectively.
    (A) Strongly Agree
    (B) Agree
    (C) Disagree
    (D) Strongly Disagree

13. You find details boring.
    (A) Strongly Agree
    (B) Agree
    (C) Disagree
    (D) Strongly Disagree

14. You follow through on whatever tasks you take on.
    (A) Strongly Agree
    (B) Agree
    (C) Disagree
    (D) Strongly Disagree

15. You put other people at ease.
    (A) Strongly Agree
    (B) Agree
    (C) Disagree
    (D) Strongly Disagree

16. You find change exciting.
    (A) Strongly Agree
    (B) Agree
    (C) Disagree
    (D) Strongly Disagree

17. Details are the most important part of a task.
    (A) Strongly Agree
    (B) Agree
    (C) Disagree
    (D) Strongly Disagree

18. You enjoy the feeling of a job well done.
    (A) Strongly Agree
    (B) Agree
    (C) Disagree
    (D) Strongly Disagree

19. You do not like having to ask for additional information to do a task.
    (A) Strongly Agree
    (B) Agree
    (C) Disagree
    (D) Strongly Disagree

20. You never stop until a task is finished to the best of your ability.
    (A) Strongly Agree
    (B) Agree
    (C) Disagree
    (D) Strongly Disagree

21. You like to move around in your job.
    (A) Strongly Agree
    (B) Agree
    (C) Disagree
    (D) Strongly Disagree

22. You like helping other people solve a problem.
    (A) Strongly Agree
    (B) Agree
    (C) Disagree
    (D) Strongly Disagree

23. You like a job that involves physical activity such as lifting or moving things.
    (A) Strongly Agree
    (B) Agree
    (C) Disagree
    (D) Strongly Disagree

24. You like a job that has a number of different tasks.
    (A) Strongly Agree
    (B) Agree
    (C) Disagree
    (D) Strongly Disagree

25. You are very organized in how you do your work.
    (A) Strongly Agree
    (B) Agree
    (C) Disagree
    (D) Strongly Disagree

26. You can explain procedures easily to others.
    (A) Strongly Agree
    (B) Agree
    (C) Disagree
    (D) Strongly Disagree

27. The more complicated a task is the better you like doing it.
    (A) Strongly Agree
    (B) Agree
    (C) Disagree
    (D) Strongly Disagree

28. You do not like having to make decisions about how to get your job done.
    (A) Strongly Agree
    (B) Agree
    (C) Disagree
    (D) Strongly Disagree

29. You find criticism difficult to accept.
    (A) Strongly Agree
    (B) Agree
    (C) Disagree
    (D) Strongly Disagree

30. You like jobs that start early in the morning.
    (A) Strongly Agree
    (B) Agree
    (C) Disagree
    (D) Strongly Disagree

31. You like to work in a place with a lot of other people around.
    (A) Strongly Agree
    (B) Agree
    (C) Disagree
    (D) Strongly Disagree

32. You are comfortable with routine.
    (A) Strongly Agree
    (B) Agree
    (C) Disagree
    (D) Strongly Disagree

33. You like to set your own pace at work.
    (A) Strongly Agree
    (B) Agree
    (C) Disagree
    (D) Strongly Disagree

34. You enjoy finding different ways to accomplish tasks.
    (A) Strongly Agree
    (B) Agree
    (C) Disagree
    (D) Strongly Disagree

35. A leadership role makes you uncomfortable.
    (A) Strongly Agree
    (B) Agree
    (C) Disagree
    (D) Strongly Disagree

36. You like to figure out why something is not working.
    (A) Strongly Agree
    (B) Agree
    (C) Disagree
    (D) Strongly Disagree

37. You find change challenging, but manageable.
    (A) Strongly Agree
    (B) Agree
    (C) Disagree
    (D) Strongly Disagree

38. You always do what you say you will.
    (A) Strongly Agree
    (B) Agree
    (C) Disagree
    (D) Strongly Disagree

39. You prefer to work with a small number of people.
    (A) Strongly Agree
    (B) Agree
    (C) Disagree
    (D) Strongly Disagree

40. Repeating tasks is boring.
    (A) Strongly Agree
    (B) Agree
    (C) Disagree
    (D) Strongly Disagree

41. You worry whether you did a task as well as you could have.
    (A) Strongly Agree
    (B) Agree
    (C) Disagree
    (D) Strongly Disagree

42. You would rather have someone else in charge.
    (A) Strongly Agree
    (B) Agree
    (C) Disagree
    (D) Strongly Disagree

43. You like to work behind the scenes to get things done.
    (A) Strongly Agree
    (B) Agree
    (C) Disagree
    (D) Strongly Disagree

practice test

44. Work-related stress does not bother you.
- **(A)** Strongly Agree
- **(B)** Agree
- **(C)** Disagree
- **(D)** Strongly Disagree

45. You could be better organized about how you manage your time.
- **(A)** Strongly Agree
- **(B)** Agree
- **(C)** Disagree
- **(D)** Strongly Disagree

46. You prefer to work alone.
- **(A)** Strongly Agree
- **(B)** Agree
- **(C)** Disagree
- **(D)** Strongly Disagree

47. You do not mind sitting for long periods of time when you work.
- **(A)** Strongly Agree
- **(B)** Agree
- **(C)** Disagree
- **(D)** Strongly Disagree

48. You like a job with a number of tasks to complete.
- **(A)** Strongly Agree
- **(B)** Agree
- **(C)** Disagree
- **(D)** Strongly Disagree

49. You do not find it easy to explain things to others.
- **(A)** Strongly Agree
- **(B)** Agree
- **(C)** Disagree
- **(D)** Strongly Disagree

50. You like interaction with large numbers of coworkers.
- **(A)** Strongly Agree
- **(B)** Agree
- **(C)** Disagree
- **(D)** Strongly Disagree

51. A job with a great deal of routine would be boring.
- **(A)** Strongly Agree
- **(B)** Agree
- **(C)** Disagree
- **(D)** Strongly Disagree

52. You do not mind asking for help when you do not know how to do something.
- **(A)** Strongly Agree
- **(B)** Agree
- **(C)** Disagree
- **(D)** Strongly Disagree

53. Job satisfaction is not important to you.
- **(A)** Strongly Agree
- **(B)** Agree
- **(C)** Disagree
- **(D)** Strongly Disagree

54. You like to move from one task to another during a workday.
- **(A)** Strongly Agree
- **(B)** Agree
- **(C)** Disagree
- **(D)** Strongly Disagree

55. You work well late in the day when others begin to fade.
- **(A)** Strongly Agree
- **(B)** Agree
- **(C)** Disagree
- **(D)** Strongly Disagree

56. You would rather work past quitting time than ask for help to finish a job.
- **(A)** Strongly Agree
- **(B)** Agree
- **(C)** Disagree
- **(D)** Strongly Disagree

57. You can pick up the pace if the amount of work increases during certain periods.
- **(A)** Strongly Agree
- **(B)** Agree
- **(C)** Disagree
- **(D)** Strongly Disagree

58. You leave troubleshooting problems to someone else.
- **(A)** Strongly Agree
- **(B)** Agree
- **(C)** Disagree
- **(D)** Strongly Disagree

59. You enjoy trying new tasks.
- **(A)** Strongly Agree
- **(B)** Agree
- **(C)** Disagree
- **(D)** Strongly Disagree

60. You tend to take on too many respon-
    sibilities.
    (A) Strongly Agree
    (B) Agree
    (C) Disagree
    (D) Strongly Disagree

61. Feeling productive and appreciated at
    work is important to you.
    (A) Strongly Agree
    (B) Agree
    (C) Disagree
    (D) Strongly Disagree

62. You find the details of a job
    uninteresting.
    (A) Strongly Agree
    (B) Agree
    (C) Disagree
    (D) Strongly Disagree

63. You like someone else to set the pace
    at work.
    (A) Strongly Agree
    (B) Agree
    (C) Disagree
    (D) Strongly Disagree

64. You like to make decisions about how
    you get your work done.
    (A) Strongly Agree
    (B) Agree
    (C) Disagree
    (D) Strongly Disagree

65. You learn from criticism.
    (A) Strongly Agree
    (B) Agree
    (C) Disagree
    (D) Strongly Disagree

66. You do not like having to stand for a
    long time when you work.
    (A) Strongly Agree
    (B) Agree
    (C) Disagree
    (D) Strongly Disagree

67. Doing your best is your number-one
    work priority.
    (A) Strongly Agree
    (B) Agree
    (C) Disagree
    (D) Strongly Disagree

68. You make decisions only when you
    have all the facts.
    (A) Strongly Agree
    (B) Agree
    (C) Disagree
    (D) Strongly Disagree

69. You find out as much information as
    you can before you begin a new task.
    (A) Strongly Agree
    (B) Agree
    (C) Disagree
    (D) Strongly Disagree

70. Speed results in errors.
    (A) Strongly Agree
    (B) Agree
    (C) Disagree
    (D) Strongly Disagree

71. You always finish what you start.
    (A) Strongly Agree
    (B) Agree
    (C) Disagree
    (D) Strongly Disagree

72. You prefer jobs where you do not have
    to interact with a number of people.
    (A) Strongly Agree
    (B) Agree
    (C) Disagree
    (D) Strongly Disagree

73. You become tense when working un-
    der the pressure of a deadline.
    (A) Strongly Agree
    (B) Agree
    (C) Disagree
    (D) Strongly Disagree

74. You find it difficult to stop and start
    tasks because of interruptions.
    (A) Strongly Agree
    (B) Agree
    (C) Disagree
    (D) Strongly Disagree

75. You do not like having to deal with
    angry or frustrated people.
    (A) Strongly Agree
    (B) Agree
    (C) Disagree
    (D) Strongly Disagree

practice test

76. You appreciate it when a coworker puts a new person at ease.
    (A) Strongly Agree
    (B) Agree
    (C) Disagree
    (D) Strongly Disagree

77. You are very good at details.
    (A) Strongly Agree
    (B) Agree
    (C) Disagree
    (D) Strongly Disagree

78. You can always find something in the way a task is done that needs improving.
    (A) Strongly Agree
    (B) Agree
    (C) Disagree
    (D) Strongly Disagree

79. You find it difficult to ask for help when you do not know how to do something.
    (A) Strongly Agree
    (B) Agree
    (C) Disagree
    (D) Strongly Disagree

80. You find it easy to shift from one task to another.
    (A) Strongly Agree
    (B) Agree
    (C) Disagree
    (D) Strongly Disagree

81. You like being challenged in your job to find new ways of doing things.
    (A) Strongly Agree
    (B) Agree
    (C) Disagree
    (D) Strongly Disagree

82. Working at a fast pace is difficult and uncomfortable for you.
    (A) Strongly Agree
    (B) Agree
    (C) Disagree
    (D) Strongly Disagree

83. You like routine in your job.
    (A) Strongly Agree
    (B) Agree
    (C) Disagree
    (D) Strongly Disagree

84. You become bored if you have to repeat the same tasks.
    (A) Strongly Agree
    (B) Agree
    (C) Disagree
    (D) Strongly Disagree

85. You find working with a large group makes a job easier to do.
    (A) Strongly Agree
    (B) Agree
    (C) Disagree
    (D) Strongly Disagree

86. You enjoy working at difficult tasks.
    (A) Strongly Agree
    (B) Agree
    (C) Disagree
    (D) Strongly Disagree

87. You find it easy to deal with people.
    (A) Strongly Agree
    (B) Agree
    (C) Disagree
    (D) Strongly Disagree

88. You try to make the best of less than perfect situations.
    (A) Strongly Agree
    (B) Agree
    (C) Disagree
    (D) Strongly Disagree

89. When asked to do a new task, you ask very practical questions about how to do it.
    (A) Strongly Agree
    (B) Agree
    (C) Disagree
    (D) Strongly Disagree

90. You prefer doing many tasks at once rather than one after another.
    (A) Strongly Agree
    (B) Agree
    (C) Disagree
    (D) Strongly Disagree

91. You figure out how to accomplish your tasks more quickly and efficiently than others.
    (A) Strongly Agree
    (B) Agree
    (C) Disagree
    (D) Strongly Disagree

92. You adapt easily to changes in how things are done.
    (A) Strongly Agree
    (B) Agree
    (C) Disagree
    (D) Strongly Disagree

93. You are an accurate judge of how long tasks will take you.
    (A) Strongly Agree
    (B) Agree
    (C) Disagree
    (D) Strongly Disagree

94. When your ideas do not work, you can easily admit it.
    (A) Strongly Agree
    (B) Agree
    (C) Disagree
    (D) Strongly Disagree

95. You work well with people on a one-to-one basis.
    (A) Strongly Agree
    (B) Agree
    (C) Disagree
    (D) Strongly Disagree

96. You work against the clock, not against other people.
    (A) Strongly Agree
    (B) Agree
    (C) Disagree
    (D) Strongly Disagree

97. You reexamine how things are done from time to time to see if you can improve on them.
    (A) Strongly Agree
    (B) Agree
    (C) Disagree
    (D) Strongly Disagree

98. A slow, steady pace gets the job done.
    (A) Strongly Agree
    (B) Agree
    (C) Disagree
    (D) Strongly Disagree

99. You concentrate on one task at a time even if you have several to work on at the same time.
    (A) Strongly Agree
    (B) Agree
    (C) Disagree
    (D) Strongly Disagree

100. Most things that go wrong on a job are beyond your control.
    (A) Strongly Agree
    (B) Agree
    (C) Disagree
    (D) Strongly Disagree

101. Unclear instructions are the cause of most of your problems on the job.
    (A) Strongly Agree
    (B) Agree
    (C) Disagree
    (D) Strongly Disagree

102. The biggest problem on a job is the unrealistic expectations of a supervisor.
    (A) Strongly Agree
    (B) Agree
    (C) Disagree
    (D) Strongly Disagree

Section 2: Frequency

Directions: Read each item carefully. Decide which of the four responses ranging from **Very Often** to **Rarely** fits you best. For some items, more than one response may describe you. Choose the best description and mark only that one answer on the answer sheet. It is important to answer each item, even if you are not certain which response is best for you. Also, try to work at a fairly rapid pace.

103. You think things through carefully before making a decision.
    (A) Very often
    (B) Often
    (C) Sometimes
    (D) Rarely

104. Whatever you start, you finish.
    (A) Very often
    (B) Often
    (C) Sometimes
    (D) Rarely

105. You find it easy to pick up a task if you are interrupted.
    (A) Very often
    (B) Often
    (C) Sometimes
    (D) Rarely

106. You put others at ease.
    (A) Very often
    (B) Often
    (C) Sometimes
    (D) Rarely

107. You put off making decisions hoping that the problem will solve itself.
    (A) Very often
    (B) Often
    (C) Sometimes
    (D) Rarely

108. You accomplish tasks more quickly than coworkers.
    (A) Very often
    (B) Often
    (C) Sometimes
    (D) Rarely

109. You ask questions in meetings if you do not understand something.
    (A) Very often
    (B) Often
    (C) Sometimes
    (D) Rarely

110. You are the person who sets the pace at work.
    (A) Very often
    (B) Often
    (C) Sometimes
    (D) Rarely

111. You find criticism helpful in improving your job performance.
    (A) Very often
    (B) Often
    (C) Sometimes
    (D) Rarely

112. Deadlines create stress for you.
    (A) Very often
    (B) Often
    (C) Sometimes
    (D) Rarely

113. You are willing to explain something several times if a person does not understand.
    (A) Very often
    (B) Often
    (C) Sometimes
    (D) Rarely

114. You consider others' points of view in making decisions.
    (A) Very often
    (B) Often
    (C) Sometimes
    (D) Rarely

115. You lose track of the details of a task.
    (A) Very often
    (B) Often
    (C) Sometimes
    (D) Rarely

116. You restate instructions to make sure that you understand what to do.
    (A) Very often
    (B) Often
    (C) Sometimes
    (D) Rarely

117. You carry work stress into your outside life.
    (A) Very often
    (B) Often
    (C) Sometimes
    (D) Rarely

118. You wait for someone else to offer suggestions about how to complete a task.
    (A) Very often
    (B) Often
    (C) Sometimes
    (D) Rarely

119. You become impatient with people who want to do something the same way all the time.
    (A) Very often
    (B) Often
    (C) Sometimes
    (D) Rarely

120. You compliment others on a job well done.
    (A) Very often
    (B) Often
    (C) Sometimes
    (D) Rarely

121. When shown that another way would work better, you stick with the original way.
    (A) Very often
    (B) Often
    (C) Sometimes
    (D) Rarely

122. You shift from task to task without slowing your work pace.
    (A) Very often
    (B) Often
    (C) Sometimes
    (D) Rarely

123. You become impatient with people who make small talk about family and friends during work time.
    (A) Very often
    (B) Often
    (C) Sometimes
    (D) Rarely

124. You take criticism personally.
    (A) Very often
    (B) Often
    (C) Sometimes
    (D) Rarely

125. You overpromise what you can reasonably accomplish in a given period of time.
    (A) Very often
    (B) Often
    (C) Sometimes
    (D) Rarely

126. You ask for help if you cannot finish a task by the deadline.
    (A) Very often
    (B) Often
    (C) Sometimes
    (D) Rarely

127. You lose interest in what you are doing if the task is going well.
    (A) Very often
    (B) Often
    (C) Sometimes
    (D) Rarely

128. You can figure out the problem when others cannot.
    (A) Very often
    (B) Often
    (C) Sometimes
    (D) Rarely

129. You become impatient with others when you are rushing to finish a task.
    (A) Very often
    (B) Often
    (C) Sometimes
    (D) Rarely

130. You become tense when dealing with angry or frustrated people.
    (A) Very often
    (B) Often
    (C) Sometimes
    (D) Rarely

131. If you speed up doing tasks, you make errors.
    (A) Very often
    (B) Often
    (C) Sometimes
    (D) Rarely

132. Without being asked, you offer criticism of coworkers' job performance.
    (A) Very often
    (B) Often
    (C) Sometimes
    (D) Rarely

133. You are the leader in a group.
    (A) Very often
    (B) Often
    (C) Sometimes
    (D) Rarely

134. You worry about your work even after you leave the job.
    (A) Very often
    (B) Often
    (C) Sometimes
    (D) Rarely

135. You become impatient if others do not understand something as quickly as you do.
    (A) Very often
    (B) Often
    (C) Sometimes
    (D) Rarely

136. You try to calm the situation if conflicts develop.
    (A) Very often
    (B) Often
    (C) Sometimes
    (D) Rarely

137. You ask for help if you cannot finish a task by the deadline.
    (A) Very often
    (B) Often
    (C) Sometimes
    (D) Rarely

138. You plan ahead so that you do not miss any details.
    (A) Very often
    (B) Often
    (C) Sometimes
    (D) Rarely

139. You change routines to fit you rather than follow the established process.
    (A) Very often
    (B) Often
    (C) Sometimes
    (D) Rarely

140. You let others try new tasks before you yourself try them.
    (A) Very often
    (B) Often
    (C) Sometimes
    (D) Rarely

141. You become sidetracked by the details of a task.
    (A) Very often
    (B) Often
    (C) Sometimes
    (D) Rarely

142. You ignore conflict when it develops.
    (A) Very often
    (B) Often
    (C) Sometimes
    (D) Rarely

143. You are the first to notice when someone is having a bad day.
    (A) Very often
    (B) Often
    (C) Sometimes
    (D) Rarely

144. You step in to help coworkers solve problems.
    (A) Very often
    (B) Often
    (C) Sometimes
    (D) Rarely

145. You seek out complicated tasks to do.
    (A) Very often
    (B) Often
    (C) Sometimes
    (D) Rarely

146. You figure out for yourself how to accomplish a task rather than follow someone else's directions.
    (A) Very often
    (B) Often
    (C) Sometimes
    (D) Rarely

147. You encourage others to do their best at their jobs.
    (A) Very often
    (B) Often
    (C) Sometimes
    (D) Rarely

148. You lose focus on what you are doing if you do the same thing for a long period of time.
    (A) Very often
    (B) Often
    (C) Sometimes
    (D) Rarely

149. You are the one whom others ask to explain something they do not understand.
    (A) Very often
    (B) Often
    (C) Sometimes
    (D) Rarely

150. You do a job exactly as your supervisor explains the process.
    (A) Very often
    (B) Often
    (C) Sometimes
    (D) Rarely

151. You become frustrated if you cannot do a task.
    (A) Very often
    (B) Often
    (C) Sometimes
    (D) Rarely

152. Your work area is disorganized.
    (A) Very often
    (B) Often
    (C) Sometimes
    (D) Rarely

153. You see the practical issues involved in getting a task done.
    (A) Very often
    (B) Often
    (C) Sometimes
    (D) Rarely

154. You complete tasks to the best of your ability.
    (A) Very often
    (B) Often
    (C) Sometimes
    (D) Rarely

155. You are one of the crowd rather than the leader.
    (A) Very often
    (B) Often
    (C) Sometimes
    (D) Rarely

156. You take on tasks that allow you to work on your own.
    (A) Very often
    (B) Often
    (C) Sometimes
    (D) Rarely

157. You increase the pace of your work to outdo your coworkers.
    (A) Very often
    (B) Often
    (C) Sometimes
    (D) Rarely

158. You find it difficult to keep up a steady, rapid pace at tasks.
    (A) Very often
    (B) Often
    (C) Sometimes
    (D) Rarely

159. You become tense because of stress on the job.
    (A) Very often
    (B) Often
    (C) Sometimes
    (D) Rarely

practice test

160. You are the first to suggest changes in routines.
- **(A)** Very often
- **(B)** Often
- **(C)** Sometimes
- **(D)** Rarely

161. You get into arguments.
- **(A)** Very often
- **(B)** Often
- **(C)** Sometimes
- **(D)** Rarely

162. You troubleshoot problems rather than ask someone else what is wrong.
- **(A)** Very often
- **(B)** Often
- **(C)** Sometimes
- **(D)** Rarely

163. You accept others' suggestions about how a task can be done.
- **(A)** Very often
- **(B)** Often
- **(C)** Sometimes
- **(D)** Rarely

164. You set goals for yourself to accomplish certain things each day.
- **(A)** Very often
- **(B)** Often
- **(C)** Sometimes
- **(D)** Rarely

165. You offer help when someone is having difficulty with a task.
- **(A)** Very often
- **(B)** Often
- **(C)** Sometimes
- **(D)** Rarely

166. You worry whether you did a task as well as you could have.
- **(A)** Very often
- **(B)** Often
- **(C)** Sometimes
- **(D)** Rarely

167. You anticipate problems that may arise in doing a task.
- **(A)** Very often
- **(B)** Often
- **(C)** Sometimes
- **(D)** Rarely

168. You tell others how to do their jobs without their asking.
- **(A)** Very often
- **(B)** Often
- **(C)** Sometimes
- **(D)** Rarely

169. You volunteer to try out new ways of doing things.
- **(A)** Very often
- **(B)** Often
- **(C)** Sometimes
- **(D)** Rarely

170. You lose track of what you are doing if you are interrupted while you work.
- **(A)** Very often
- **(B)** Often
- **(C)** Sometimes
- **(D)** Rarely

171. You make decisions quickly rather than wait for complete information.
- **(A)** Very often
- **(B)** Often
- **(C)** Sometimes
- **(D)** Rarely

172. You confront conflict when it occurs rather than let it grow.
- **(A)** Very often
- **(B)** Often
- **(C)** Sometimes
- **(D)** Rarely

173. The details of a task can seem overwhelming to you at times.
- **(A)** Very often
- **(B)** Often
- **(C)** Sometimes
- **(D)** Rarely

174. You encourage others to try new ways of doing things.
- **(A)** Very often
- **(B)** Often
- **(C)** Sometimes
- **(D)** Rarely

175. You become impatient if others do not understand your explanation of something.
    (A) Very often
    (B) Often
    (C) Sometimes
    (D) Rarely

176. You are the one whom others turn to for help on the job.
    (A) Very often
    (B) Often
    (C) Sometimes
    (D) Rarely

177. You vary the way you accomplish tasks.
    (A) Very often
    (B) Often
    (C) Sometimes
    (D) Rarely

178. You are not satisfied with how you do your job.
    (A) Very often
    (B) Often
    (C) Sometimes
    (D) Rarely

179. You make sure that you follow through on whatever task you take on.
    (A) Very often
    (B) Often
    (C) Sometimes
    (D) Rarely

180. You ask for help if you do not understand how to do something.
    (A) Very often
    (B) Often
    (C) Sometimes
    (D) Rarely

181. You take on more responsibilities than you can handle comfortably.
    (A) Very often
    (B) Often
    (C) Sometimes
    (D) Rarely

182. You push to get your point of view across in a group.
    (A) Very often
    (B) Often
    (C) Sometimes
    (D) Rarely

183. You become angry if coworkers interrupt your work.
    (A) Very often
    (B) Often
    (C) Sometimes
    (D) Rarely

184. You find alternate ways for completing tasks.
    (A) Very often
    (B) Often
    (C) Sometimes
    (D) Rarely

185. You misjudge how long it will take to accomplish tasks.
    (A) Very often
    (B) Often
    (C) Sometimes
    (D) Rarely

186. You let others ask questions for you.
    (A) Very often
    (B) Often
    (C) Sometimes
    (D) Rarely

Section 3: Experience

Directions: Read each item carefully. Decide which response best describes your experience. For some items, more than one response may describe you. Choose the best description and mark only that one answer on the answer sheet. It is important to answer each item, even if you are not certain which response is best for you. Also, **try to work at a fairly rapid pace.**

187. Where do you like to work the most?
    (A) Outdoors most of the time
    (B) Outdoors all the time
    (C) Indoors most of the time
    (D) Indoors all the time
    (E) Splitting time about equally between indoor and outdoor work
    (F) Splitting time so that you work outdoors more than indoors
    (G) Splitting time so that you work indoors more than outdoors
    (H) Would not mind doing any of these

188. Most of your contact with customers has included which of the following?
    (A) Answering customers' questions
    (B) Explaining information to customers
    (C) Selling items to customers
    (D) Do not interact directly with customers
    (E) Not sure

189. Which of the following types of contact do you like the least in the work environment?
    (A) Dealing with customers
    (B) Dealing with other workers
    (C) Dealing with supervisors
    (D) Would not mind any of these
    (E) Not sure

190. Which of the following pattern of work is the most difficult for you?
    (A) Working on one task at a time
    (B) Working on several tasks at once
    (C) Shifting from task to task during a workday
    (D) Being interrupted while you work
    (E) Do not mind any of these

191. With which type of job do you have the most experience?
    (A) Operating machinery
    (B) Customer contact
    (C) Lifting and moving heavy loads of up to 70 pounds
    (D) Lifting and moving lighter loads
    (E) Handling money
    (F) Clerical work
    (G) Driving and making deliveries
    (H) Have no experience

192. When is the best time of day for you to work?
    (A) Early morning
    (B) Day
    (C) Evening
    (D) Night
    (E) Would not mind working any of these
    (F) Not sure

193. What type of work do you like the least?
    (A) Walking around throughout the work day
    (B) Driving for several hours a day
    (C) Standing or sitting in place for hours
    (D) Operating machinery all day
    (E) Lifting and moving loads
    (F) Would not mind any of these
    (G) Not sure

194. Which type of work pace do you like the most?
    (A) Fast pace
    (B) Slow pace
    (C) Steady pace: fast or slow
    (D) Moderate pace
    (E) Not sure

195. What kind of decision making do you want the most in your job?
    (A) Making all the decisions about how you do your work
    (B) Making no decisions about how you do your work
    (C) Making some decisions about how you do your work
    (D) Being asked for suggestions about how your work should be done
    (E) Would not mind any of these

196. In dealing with customers, you are best at which of the following?
    (A) Answering questions
    (B) Explaining instructions
    (C) Making change
    (D) Not sure

197. One of your greatest strengths working with people is which of the following?
    (A) Ignoring conflict
    (B) Calming angry or frustrated co-workers
    (C) Calming angry or frustrated customers
    (D) Confronting a situation before it turns into conflict
    (E) Not sure

198. Which of the following describes how you feel about working with numbers?
    (A) Not something you like to do
    (B) Something you can do but would rather not
    (C) Something you like to do
    (D) Not sure

199. Which of the following types of problem solving do you like the most?
    (A) Troubleshooting problems with machines
    (B) Helping customers with problems
    (C) Figuring out ways to get tasks done
    (D) Prioritizing your workload
    (E) Not sure

200. Which of the following is the best type of supervision for you?
    (A) Be able to set priorities with minimal supervision
    (B) Be able to set work routines with minimal supervision
    (C) Have supervisor set work routines
    (D) Have supervisor set priorities
    (E) Have freedom to change work routines to fit work flow as needed
    (F) Have freedom to change work priorities to fit work flow as needed
    (G) Not sure

201. Which of the following is the least important to you in a work environment?
    (A) Quiet
    (B) A lot of activity around you
    (C) A large number of coworkers
    (D) A small number of coworkers
    (E) Lack of pressure
    (F) Would not mind any of these
    (G) Not sure

202. Which of the following types of work do you find the most difficult to do all day?
    (A) Sit in one place
    (B) Stand in one place
    (C) Drive
    (D) Move and lift loads
    (E) Operate machinery
    (F) Deal with customers
    (G) Walk
    (H) Do not mind any of these
    (I) Not sure

203. Which of the following types of responsibility do you like the least?
    (A) Handling and being accountable for money
    (B) Explaining instructions
    (C) Answering questions
    (D) Operating machinery
    (E) Driving a vehicle
    (F) Routing shipments
    (G) Making work-related decisions
    (H) Would not mind any of these
    (I) Not sure

204. Which of the following would you like the least?
   (A) Being out in all kinds of weather
   (B) Taking the same route every day
   (C) Driving in all kinds of weather
   (D) Working on weekends
   (E) Starting early in the morning
   (F) Walking all day
   (G) Carrying loads
   (H) Would not mind any of these
   (I) Not sure

205. Which of the following tasks do you like the least?
   (A) Handling money
   (B) Dealing with customers
   (C) Memorizing information
   (D) Operating machines
   (E) Working with details
   (F) Sorting items
   (G) Would not mind any of these
   (H) Not sure

206. What amount of responsibility do you like to have in a job?
   (A) Little responsibility
   (B) Moderate amount of responsibility
   (C) Great deal of responsibility
   (D) Does not matter
   (E) Not sure

207. Most of your experience with technology has been with which of the following?
   (A) Cash registers
   (B) Data entry
   (C) Applications of databases
   (D) Word processing
   (E) Spreadsheets
   (F) Internet
   (G) Calculator
   (H) Have no experience with technology

208. How important is physical activity to you in a job?
   (A) No importance
   (B) Little importance
   (C) Moderate importance
   (D) Great importance
   (E) Not sure

209. Most of your experience with motor vehicles has been driving which of the following?
   (A) Cars
   (B) Vans
   (C) Pick-up trucks
   (D) Small trucks
   (E) Tractor-trailers
   (F) Have no experience with motor vehicles

210. Which type of work do you like the most?
   (A) Driving and making deliveries
   (B) Standing or sitting in one place
   (C) Walking around throughout the day
   (D) Operating machinery
   (E) Lifting and moving loads
   (F) Would not mind any of these
   (G) Not sure

211. Which of the following characteristics of a machine-based job do you like the least?
   (A) Working under pressure
   (B) Focusing on a machine all day
   (C) Feeding materials through a machine
   (D) Moving material to and from machines
   (E) Troubleshooting machinery problems
   (F) Machinery noise
   (G) Lack of coworker interaction
   (H) Would not mind any of these
   (I) Not sure

212. Which type of pressure do you like the least?
   (A) Working under a deadline
   (B) Working under a quota system
   (C) Competition from coworkers
   (D) Solving a problem for an angry or frustrated customer
   (E) Troubleshooting a machine problem
   (F) Would not mind any of these
   (G) Not sure

213. Which type of physical activity do you like the least?

(A) Stretching, reaching, bending

(B) Lifting and moving heavy loads up to 70 pounds

(C) Lifting and moving lighter loads

(D) Packing shipments

(E) Pushing a handtruck

(F) Loading goods onto trucks

(G) Would not mind any of these

(H) Not sure

214. Which of the following do you like the least about working with numbers?

(A) Remembering numbers

(B) Entering data with numbers and letters

(C) Comparing information that includes numbers

(D) Handling money

(E) Coding using numbers and letters

(F) Have no experience

215. With which of the following do you have the least experience?

(A) Operating office machines

(B) Using databases

(C) Dealing with customers

(D) Working independently

(E) Have none of this experience

216. You have most experience working in which of the following situations?

(A) Working independently without direct day-to-day supervision

(B) Working as part of a small work team or work group

(C) Working as one of many workers in a department

(D) Supervising others

(E) Not sure

217. What is the perfect size for a work group?

(A) Alone

(B) Between 2 and 10

(C) Between 11 and 25

(D) More than 25

(E) Number does not matter

(F) Not sure

218. Which of the following tasks could you do best under pressure?

(A) Repetitive tasks

(B) Operate machinery

(C) Enter data in a database

(D) Retrieve information from a database

(E) Deal with customers

(F) Could do all of these

(G) Not sure

219. Which of the following tasks related to instructions do you like the least?

(A) Reading written instructions

(B) Following written instructions

(C) Remembering oral instructions

(D) Following oral instructions

(E) Giving oral instructions to others

(F) Writing instructions for others

(G) Would not mind any of these

(H) Not sure

220. Which of the following would you like least about a job?

(A) Pressure to work quickly

(B) Working on weekends

(C) Working at night

(D) Standing in one place for long periods of time

(E) Bending, stretching, reaching, lifting, and moving loads

(F) Troubleshooting problems with machines

(G) Would not mind any of these

(H) Not sure

221. Which of the following is the most difficult type of work for you?

(A) Working with numbers

(B) Working with details

(C) Memorizing information

(D) Dealing with people

(E) Repeating the same task over and over

(F) Doing a variety of tasks

(G) Working quickly

(H) Not sure

222. Which of the following describes the amount of people contact that you like the least?

(A) Interacting with the same people on a daily basis

(B) Interacting with many people daily—customers and coworkers

(C) Having long periods of time during a day when you work alone

(D) Always working around and with other people

(E) Would not mind any of these

(F) Not sure

223. Which work pattern do you like the most?

(A) Varying my routine often during the day

(B) Following the same routine every day

(C) Having an occasional change in routine during the day

(D) Would not mind any of these

224. Which of the following is the most likely to create tension for you?

(A) Deadlines

(B) Amount of work to be completed within a period of time

(C) Supervisor's expectations

(D) Competition from coworkers

(E) Angry or frustrated customers

(F) Angry coworkers

(G) Mechanical problems with machinery

(H) None of these

225. Which of the following best describes your experience with machines?

(A) Operate heavy machinery

(B) Operate light machinery

(C) Use a computer

(D) Troubleshoot mechanical problems

(E) Drive a truck

(F) Have no experience with machines

226. With which type of work do you have the least experience?

(A) Customer contact

(B) Handling money

(C) Clerical work

(D) Driving and making deliveries

(E) Operating machinery

(F) Lifting and moving heavy loads of up to 70 pounds

(G) Lifting and moving lighter loads

(H) Have none of these experiences

227. Which is the most difficult time for you to work?

(A) Early morning

(B) Day

(C) Evening

(D) Night

228. Which type of work situation do you like the most?

(A) Interacting only with coworkers

(B) Dealing with the public

(C) Interacting with coworkers and the public

(D) Would not mind any of these

(E) Not sure

229. Which of the following is the least important to you in a job?

(A) Steady work pace

(B) Mix of fast and slow periods

(C) Steady routine

(D) Variety of tasks to accomplish

(E) Only a few tasks to accomplish

(F) Not sure

230. Which of the following skills is your strongest?

(A) Working with numbers

(B) Working with details

(C) Dealing with people

(D) Doing repetitive tasks without becoming bored

(E) Not sure

231. In which type of work environment would you like least to work?

(A) Loading dock

(B) Open area with many machines going all day

(C) Sales counter

(D) Outdoors in all kinds of weather

(E) Small work area

(F) Would not mind any of these

(G) Not sure

232. Which of the following types of responsibility for doing your job is most important to you?

(A) Responsibility for setting your priorities

(B) Responsibility for how you set up your work routine

(C) Responsibility for how much you accomplish each day

(D) Responsibility for how long it takes you to do tasks during the day

(E) Does not matter

(F) Not sure

233. Which of the following describes how you feel about handling money and making change?

(A) Not something you like to do

(B) One of your strengths

(C) Something you can do but would rather not

(D) Not sure

234. What type of physical work do you like the least?

(A) Sitting or standing in one place all day

(B) Driving and making deliveries

(C) Walking

(D) Operating machines

(E) Lifting and moving loads

(F) Would not mind any of these

(G) Not sure

235. How do you prefer to get your job done?

(A) Following a routine set by someone else

(B) Making your own routine

(C) Not having a regular routine in a job

(D) Would not mind any of these

236. In how large a group do you prefer to work?

(A) Alone

(B) With a small group of people

(C) With a large group of people

(D) With a small group within a larger group

(E) Would not mind any of these

(F) Not sure

practice test

ANSWER KEY AND EXPLANATIONS

Address Checking

1. A	13. B	25. B	37. A	49. B
2. B	14. A	26. B	38. C	50. A
3. C	15. B	27. B	39. B	51. B
4. B	16. B	28. A	40. B	52. B
5. B	17. A	29. A	41. B	53. B
6. A	18. B	30. B	42. A	54. A
7. D	19. A	31. B	43. B	55. B
8. D	20. B	32. A	44. B	56. D
9. B	21. B	33. B	45. C	57. A
10. B	22. B	34. B	46. B	58. D
11. B	23. D	35. A	47. B	59. B
12. B	24. A	36. C	48. B	60. B

Forms Completion

1. C	7. D	13. B	19. C	25. B
2. C	8. B	14. C	20. C	26. C
3. A	9. C	15. D	21. D	27. D
4. D	10. A	16. B	22. A	28. B
5. A	11. D	17. A	23. D	29. C
6. B	12. B	18. D	24. A	30. B

1. **The correct answer is (C).** Box 5 requires a date (Month/Day). Therefore, the correct answer is (C), 12 and 20.

2. **The correct answer is (C).** Box 10 is labeled Insurance Fee. Therefore, the correct answer is (C), Box 10.

3. **The correct answer is (A).** Box 6 is labeled Return Receipt Fee. Boxes 7a, 8a, and 11b all have boxes to be checked. Therefore, the correct answer is (A), Box 6.

4. **The correct answer is (D).** Box 22 is labeled Delivery Date. Therefore, the correct answer is (D), Box 22.

5. **The correct answer is (A).** Box 4 is labeled Date Accepted. Boxes 18, 21, and 24 are all labeled Employee Signature. Therefore, the correct answer is (A), Box 4.

6. **The correct answer is (B).** Box 13b is labeled lbs and ozs. Therefore, the correct answer is (B), 3 lbs 6 oz.

7. **The correct answer is (D).** Box 11a is labeled Military 2nd Day. Therefore, the correct answer is (D), Box 11a.

8. **The correct answer is (B).** Box 14 is labeled Int'l Alpha Country Code. Therefore, the correct answer is (B), Box 14.

9. **The correct answer is (C).** Box 15 is labeled Acceptance Emp. Initials. Therefore, the correct answer is (C), Initials.

10. **The correct answer is (A).** Box 9 is labeled Place and Country. Therefore, the correct answer is (A), Paris, France.

11. **The correct answer is (D).** Box 1f is labeled Express Mail International.

Therefore, the correct answer is (D), Express Mail International.

12. **The correct answer is (B).** Box 7 is labeled Addressee Name or Firm. Therefore, the correct answer is (B), Computer Programmers Worldwide.

13. **The correct answer is (B).** Box 1b is labeled Letter. Therefore, the correct answer is (B), Check Box 1b.

14. **The correct answer is (C).** Box 4 is labeled Article Number. Therefore, the correct answer is (C), Box 4.

15. **The correct answer is (D).** Box 3 is labeled Insured Value. Therefore, the correct answer is (D), $250.

16. **The correct answer is (B).** Box 3 is labeled Check Number. Therefore, the correct answer is (B), Box 3.

17. **The correct answer is (A).** Box 2 is labeled Date Delivered. Therefore, the correct answer is (A), 2/22/06.

18. **The correct answer is (D).** Box 6 is labeled MO Number(s). Boxes 1, 4, and 5 are require dates. Therefore, the correct answer is (D), Box 6.

19. **The correct answer is (C).** Box 7 is labeled Sent To. Therefore, the correct answer is (C), Ms. Dy Anne Going.

20. **The correct answer is (C).** Box 6 is labeled Postmark Here. Therefore, the correct answer is (C), Box 6.

21. **The correct answer is (D).** Box 9 is labeled City, State, Zip+4. Therefore, the correct answer is (D), Box 9.

22. **The correct answer is (A).** Box 5 is labeled Route Number. Therefore, the correct answer is (A), Rural Route 5.

23. **The correct answer is (D).** Box 4 is labeled Carrier. Therefore, the correct answer is (D), Box 4.

24. **The correct answer is (A).** Box 6 is completed by making a check mark. Therefore, the correct answer is (A), A check mark.

25. **The correct answer is (B).** Box 7 is labeled Resume Delivery of Mail (Date). Therefore, the correct answer is (B), 1/20/06.

26. **The correct answer is (C).** Box 2c is labeled Perishable. Therefore, the correct answer is (C), Box 2c.

27. **The correct answer is (D).** Box 7 is labeled Total Postage and Fees. Therefore, the correct answer is (D), Box 7.

28. **The correct answer is (B).** Box 8 is labeled Postmark Here. Therefore, the correct answer is (B), Box 8.

29. **The correct answer is (C).** Box 4 is labeled Restricted Delivery Fee (Domestic only: endorsement required). Therefore, the correct answer is (C), Box 4.

30. **The correct answer is (B).** Box 2a is labeled Fragile. Therefore, the correct answer is (B), Box 2a.

answers

Coding

1. A	9. D	16. D	23. D	30. A
2. B	10. A	17. B	24. C	31. D
3. D	11. D	18. C	25. D	32. B
4. A	12. C	19. D	26. C	33. C
5. B	13. C	20. D	27. A	34. D
6. C	14. D	21. A	28. D	35. A
7. C	15. B	22. D	29. B	36. D
8. D				

1. **The correct answer is (A).** The address 105 N. Broad Avenue falls in one of the address ranges in the same row as Delivery Route A.

2. **The correct answer is (B).** The address 52 E. Chestnut Street falls in one of the address ranges in the same row as Delivery Route B.

3. **The correct answer is (D).** The address 220 N. Brook Street does not fall into any of the address ranges for Delivery Routes A, B, or C.

4. **The correct answer is (A).** The address 195 E. 12th Street falls in one of the address ranges in the same row as Delivery Route A.

5. **The correct answer is (B).** The address 68 E. Chestnut Street falls in one of the address ranges in the same row as Delivery Route B.

6. **The correct answer is (C).** The address 28 Rural Route 2 falls in one of the address ranges in the same row as Delivery Route C.

7. **The correct answer is (C).** The address 7801 S. Broad Avenue falls in one of the address ranges in the same row as Delivery Route C.

8. **The correct answer is (D).** The address 10 Rural Route 2 does not fall into any of the address ranges for Delivery Routes A, B, or C.

9. **The correct answer is (D).** The address 42 Rural Route 2 does not fall into any of the address ranges for Delivery Routes A, B, or C.

10. **The correct answer is (A).** The address 72 E. 12th Street falls in one of the address ranges in the same row as Delivery Route A.

11. **The correct answer is (D).** The address 152 N. Brook Street does not fall into any of the address ranges for Delivery Routes A, B, or C.

12. **The correct answer is (C).** The address 9500 South Broad Avenue falls in one of the address ranges in the same row as Delivery Route C.

13. **The correct answer is (C).** The address 900 S. Chester Road falls in one of the address ranges in the same row as Delivery Route C.

14. **The correct answer is (D).** The address 1000 N. Broad Avenue does not fall into any of the address ranges for Delivery Routes A, B, or C.

15. **The correct answer is (B).** The address 401 N. Broad Avenue falls in one of the address ranges in the same row as Delivery Route B.

16. **The correct answer is (D).** The address 76 E. Chestnut Street does not fall into any of the address ranges for Delivery Routes A, B, or C.

17. **The correct answer is (B).** The address 368 N. Broad Avenue falls in one of the address ranges in the same row as Delivery Route B.

18. **The correct answer is (C).** The address 8620 S. Broad Avenue falls in one of the address ranges in the same row as Delivery Route C.

19. **The correct answer is (D).** The address 1201 S. Clement Street does not

fall into any of the address ranges for Delivery Routes A, B, or C.

20. **The correct answer is (D).** The address 14 Rural Route 2 does not fall into any of the address ranges for Delivery Routes A, B, or C.

21. **The correct address is (A).** The address 15 E. Chestnut Street falls in one of the address ranges in the same row as Delivery Route A.

22. **The correct answer is (D).** The address 1250 E. 12th Street does not fall into any of the address ranges for Delivery Routes A, B, or C.

23. **The correct answer is (D).** The address 59 W. Chestnut Street does not fall into any of the address ranges for Delivery Routes A, B, or C.

24. **The correct address is (C).** The address 28 Rural Route 2 falls in one of the address ranges in the same row as Delivery Route C.

25. **The correct answer is (D).** The address 1400 S. Broad Avenue does not fall into any of the address ranges for Delivery Routes A, B, or C.

26. **The correct answer is (C).** The address 305 S. Chester Road falls in one of the address ranges in the same row as Delivery Route C.

27. **The correct answer is (A).** The address 178 N. Broad Avenue falls in one of the address ranges in the same row as Delivery Route A.

28. **The correct answer is (D).** The address 15101 N. Broad Avenue does not fall into any of the address ranges for Delivery Routes A, B, or C.

29. **The correct answer is (B).** The address 59 E. Chestnut Street falls in one of the address ranges in the same row as Delivery Route B.

30. **The correct answer is (A).** The address 99 E. 12th Street falls in one of the address ranges in the same row as Delivery Route A.

31. **The correct answer is (D).** The address 7000 S. Brook Avenue does not fall into any of the address ranges for Delivery Routes A, B, or C.

32. **The correct answer is (B).** The address 249 N. Broad Avenue falls in one of the address ranges in the same row as Delivery Route B.

33. **The correct answer is (C).** The address 30 Rural Route 2 falls in one of the address ranges in the same row as Delivery Route C.

34. **The correct answer is (D).** The address 1049 S. Chester Road does not fall into any of the address ranges for Delivery Routes A, B, or C.

35. **The correct answer is (A).** The address 19 E. Chestnut Street falls in one of the address ranges in the same row as Delivery Route A.

36. **The correct answer is (D).** The address 1000 S. Broad Avenue does not fall into any of the address ranges for Delivery Routes A, B, or C.

Memory

1. A	9. D	16. C	23. A	30. D
2. C	10. D	17. D	24. A	31. A
3. B	11. A	18. D	25. D	32. C
4. D	12. B	19. B	26. B	33. D
5. D	13. D	20. A	27. C	34. D
6. C	14. C	21. A	28. B	35. B
7. A	15. C	22. D	29. D	36. C
8. D				

1. **The correct answer is (A).** The address 250 E. 12th Street falls in one of the address ranges in the same row as Delivery Route A.

2. **The correct answer is (C).** The address 12501 S. Broad Avenue falls in one of the address ranges in the same row as Delivery Route C.

3. **The correct answer is (B).** The address 205 N. Broad Avenue falls in one of the address ranges in the same row as Delivery Route B.

4. **The correct answer is (D).** The address 601 N. Broad Avenue does not fall into any of the address ranges for Delivery Routes A, B, or C.

5. **The correct answer is (D).** The address 20 Rural Route 10 does not fall into any of the address ranges for Delivery Routes A, B, or C.

6. **The correct answer is (C).** The address 30 Rural Route 2 falls in one of the address ranges in the same row as Delivery Route C.

7. **The correct answer is (A).** The address 51 E. 12th Street falls in one of the address ranges in the same row as Delivery Route (A).

8. **The correct answer is (D).** The address 25 E. 12th Street does not fall into any of the address ranges for Delivery Routes A, B, or C.

9. **The correct answer is (D).** The address 36 Belmont Lane does not fall into any of the address ranges for Delivery Routes A, B, or C.

10. **The correct answer is (D).** The address 300 E. 12th Street does not fall into any of the address ranges for Delivery Routes A, B, or C.

11. **The correct answer is (A).** The address 137 N. Broad Avenue falls in one of the address ranges in the same row as Delivery Route A.

12. **The correct answer is (B).** The address 301 N. Broad Avenue falls in one of the address ranges in the same row as Delivery Route B.

13. **The correct answer is (D).** The address 400 E. 12th Street does not fall into any of the address ranges for Delivery Routes A, B, or C.

14. **The correct answer is (C).** The address 900 S. Chester Road falls in one of the address ranges in the same row as Delivery Route C.

15. **The correct answer is (C).** The address 13040 S. Broad Street falls in one of the address ranges in the same row as Delivery Route C.

16. **The correct answer is (C).** The address 406 S. Chester Road falls in one of the address ranges in the same row as Delivery Route C.

17. **The correct answer is (D).** The address 6700 S. Broad Avenue does not fall into any of the address ranges for Delivery Routes A, B, or C.

18. **The correct answer is (D).** The address 48 E. 14th Street does not fall into any of the address ranges for Delivery Routes A, B, or C.

19. **The correct answer is (B).** The address 51 E. Chestnut Street falls in one of the address ranges in the same row as Delivery Route B.

20. **The correct answer is (A).** The address 15 E. Chestnut Street falls in one of the address ranges in the same row as Delivery Route A.

21. **The correct answer is (A).** The address 115 E. 12th Street falls in one of the address ranges in the same row as Delivery Route A.

22. **The correct answer is (D).** The address 1000 S. Brook Street does not fall into any of the address ranges for Delivery Routes A, B, or C.

23. **The correct answer is (A).** The address 210 E. 12th Street falls in one of the address ranges in the same row as Delivery Route A.

24. **The correct answer is (A).** The address 105 N. Broad Avenue falls in one of the address ranges in the same row as Delivery Route A.

25. **The correct answer is (D).** The address 15 Rural Route 2 does not fall into any of the address ranges for Delivery Routes A, B, or C.

26. **The correct answer is (B).** The address 68 E. Chestnut Street falls in one of the address ranges in the same row as Delivery Route B.

27. **The correct answer is (C).** The address 28 Rural Route 2 falls in one of the address ranges in the same row as Delivery Route C.

28. **The correct answer is (B).** The address 325 N. Broad Avenue falls in one of the address ranges in the same row as Delivery Route B.

29. **The correct answer is (D).** The address 1000 E. Chestnut Street does not fall into any of the address ranges for Delivery Routes A, B, or C.

30. **The correct answer is (D).** The address 14 N. Broad Avenue does not fall into any of the address ranges for Delivery Routes A, B, or C.

31. **The correct answer is (A).** The address 117 S. 12th Street falls in one of the address ranges in the same row as Delivery Route A.

32. **The correct answer is (C).** The address 717 S. Chester Road falls in one of the address ranges in the same row as Delivery Route C.

33. **The correct answer is (D).** The address 14 N. Broad Avenue does not fall into any of the address ranges for Delivery Routes A, B, or C.

34. **The correct answer is (D).** The address 25 Belmont Lane does not fall into any of the address ranges for Delivery Routes A, B, or C.

35. **The correct answer is (B).** The address 67 E. Chestnut Street falls in one of the address ranges in the same row as Delivery Route B.

36. **The correct answer is (C).** The address 608 S. Chester Road falls in one of the address ranges in the same row as Delivery Route C.

Personal Characteristics and Experience Inventory

Answers will vary according to individual characteristics and experiences.

PRACTICE TEST 2: EXAM 710 AND EXAM 711 ANSWER SHEET

Part A: Clerical Ability

1. Ⓐ Ⓑ Ⓒ Ⓓ
2. Ⓐ Ⓑ Ⓒ Ⓓ
3. Ⓐ Ⓑ Ⓒ Ⓓ
4. Ⓐ Ⓑ Ⓒ Ⓓ
5. Ⓐ Ⓑ Ⓒ Ⓓ
6. Ⓐ Ⓑ Ⓒ Ⓓ
7. Ⓐ Ⓑ Ⓒ Ⓓ
8. Ⓐ Ⓑ Ⓒ Ⓓ
9. Ⓐ Ⓑ Ⓒ Ⓓ
10. Ⓐ Ⓑ Ⓒ Ⓓ
11. Ⓐ Ⓑ Ⓒ Ⓓ
12. Ⓐ Ⓑ Ⓒ Ⓓ
13. Ⓐ Ⓑ Ⓒ Ⓓ
14. Ⓐ Ⓑ Ⓒ Ⓓ
15. Ⓐ Ⓑ Ⓒ Ⓓ
16. Ⓐ Ⓑ Ⓒ Ⓓ
17. Ⓐ Ⓑ Ⓒ Ⓓ
18. Ⓐ Ⓑ Ⓒ Ⓓ
19. Ⓐ Ⓑ Ⓒ Ⓓ
20. Ⓐ Ⓑ Ⓒ Ⓓ
21. Ⓐ Ⓑ Ⓒ Ⓓ
22. Ⓐ Ⓑ Ⓒ Ⓓ

23. Ⓐ Ⓑ Ⓒ Ⓓ
24. Ⓐ Ⓑ Ⓒ Ⓓ
25. Ⓐ Ⓑ Ⓒ Ⓓ
26. Ⓐ Ⓑ Ⓒ Ⓓ
27. Ⓐ Ⓑ Ⓒ Ⓓ
28. Ⓐ Ⓑ Ⓒ Ⓓ
29. Ⓐ Ⓑ Ⓒ Ⓓ
30. Ⓐ Ⓑ Ⓒ Ⓓ
31. Ⓐ Ⓑ Ⓒ Ⓓ
32. Ⓐ Ⓑ Ⓒ Ⓓ
33. Ⓐ Ⓑ Ⓒ Ⓓ
34. Ⓐ Ⓑ Ⓒ Ⓓ
35. Ⓐ Ⓑ Ⓒ Ⓓ
36. Ⓐ Ⓑ Ⓒ Ⓓ
37. Ⓐ Ⓑ Ⓒ Ⓓ
38. Ⓐ Ⓑ Ⓒ Ⓓ
39. Ⓐ Ⓑ Ⓒ Ⓓ
40. Ⓐ Ⓑ Ⓒ Ⓓ
41. Ⓐ Ⓑ Ⓒ Ⓓ
42. Ⓐ Ⓑ Ⓒ Ⓓ
43. Ⓐ Ⓑ Ⓒ Ⓓ

44. Ⓐ Ⓑ Ⓒ Ⓓ
45. Ⓐ Ⓑ Ⓒ Ⓓ
46. Ⓐ Ⓑ Ⓒ Ⓓ
47. Ⓐ Ⓑ Ⓒ Ⓓ
48. Ⓐ Ⓑ Ⓒ Ⓓ
49. Ⓐ Ⓑ Ⓒ Ⓓ
50. Ⓐ Ⓑ Ⓒ Ⓓ
51. Ⓐ Ⓑ Ⓒ Ⓓ
52. Ⓐ Ⓑ Ⓒ Ⓓ
53. Ⓐ Ⓑ Ⓒ Ⓓ
54. Ⓐ Ⓑ Ⓒ Ⓓ
55. Ⓐ Ⓑ Ⓒ Ⓓ
56. Ⓐ Ⓑ Ⓒ Ⓓ
57. Ⓐ Ⓑ Ⓒ Ⓓ
58. Ⓐ Ⓑ Ⓒ Ⓓ
59. Ⓐ Ⓑ Ⓒ Ⓓ
60. Ⓐ Ⓑ Ⓒ Ⓓ
61. Ⓐ Ⓑ Ⓒ Ⓓ
62. Ⓐ Ⓑ Ⓒ Ⓓ
63. Ⓐ Ⓑ Ⓒ Ⓓ
64. Ⓐ Ⓑ Ⓒ Ⓓ

65. Ⓐ Ⓑ Ⓒ Ⓓ
66. Ⓐ Ⓑ Ⓒ Ⓓ
67. Ⓐ Ⓑ Ⓒ Ⓓ
68. Ⓐ Ⓑ Ⓒ Ⓓ
69. Ⓐ Ⓑ Ⓒ Ⓓ
70. Ⓐ Ⓑ Ⓒ Ⓓ
71. Ⓐ Ⓑ Ⓒ Ⓓ
72. Ⓐ Ⓑ Ⓒ Ⓓ
73. Ⓐ Ⓑ Ⓒ Ⓓ
74. Ⓐ Ⓑ Ⓒ Ⓓ
75. Ⓐ Ⓑ Ⓒ Ⓓ
76. Ⓐ Ⓑ Ⓒ Ⓓ
77. Ⓐ Ⓑ Ⓒ Ⓓ
78. Ⓐ Ⓑ Ⓒ Ⓓ
79. Ⓐ Ⓑ Ⓒ Ⓓ
80. Ⓐ Ⓑ Ⓒ Ⓓ
81. Ⓐ Ⓑ Ⓒ Ⓓ
82. Ⓐ Ⓑ Ⓒ Ⓓ
83. Ⓐ Ⓑ Ⓒ Ⓓ
84. Ⓐ Ⓑ Ⓒ Ⓓ
85. Ⓐ Ⓑ Ⓒ Ⓓ

Part B: Verbal Ability

1. Ⓐ Ⓑ Ⓒ Ⓓ   26. Ⓐ Ⓑ Ⓒ Ⓓ   51. Ⓐ Ⓑ Ⓒ Ⓓ   76. Ⓐ Ⓑ Ⓒ Ⓓ   101. Ⓐ Ⓑ Ⓒ Ⓓ
2. Ⓐ Ⓑ Ⓒ Ⓓ   27. Ⓐ Ⓑ Ⓒ Ⓓ   52. Ⓐ Ⓑ Ⓒ Ⓓ   77. Ⓐ Ⓑ Ⓒ Ⓓ   102. Ⓐ Ⓑ Ⓒ Ⓓ
3. Ⓐ Ⓑ Ⓒ Ⓓ   28. Ⓐ Ⓑ Ⓒ Ⓓ   53. Ⓐ Ⓑ Ⓒ Ⓓ   78. Ⓐ Ⓑ Ⓒ Ⓓ   103. Ⓐ Ⓑ Ⓒ Ⓓ
4. Ⓐ Ⓑ Ⓒ Ⓓ   29. Ⓐ Ⓑ Ⓒ Ⓓ   54. Ⓐ Ⓑ Ⓒ Ⓓ   79. Ⓐ Ⓑ Ⓒ Ⓓ   104. Ⓐ Ⓑ Ⓒ Ⓓ
5. Ⓐ Ⓑ Ⓒ Ⓓ   30. Ⓐ Ⓑ Ⓒ Ⓓ   55. Ⓐ Ⓑ Ⓒ Ⓓ   80. Ⓐ Ⓑ Ⓒ Ⓓ   105. Ⓐ Ⓑ Ⓒ Ⓓ
6. Ⓐ Ⓑ Ⓒ Ⓓ   31. Ⓐ Ⓑ Ⓒ Ⓓ   56. Ⓐ Ⓑ Ⓒ Ⓓ   81. Ⓐ Ⓑ Ⓒ Ⓓ   106. Ⓐ Ⓑ Ⓒ Ⓓ
7. Ⓐ Ⓑ Ⓒ Ⓓ   32. Ⓐ Ⓑ Ⓒ Ⓓ   57. Ⓐ Ⓑ Ⓒ Ⓓ   82. Ⓐ Ⓑ Ⓒ Ⓓ   107. Ⓐ Ⓑ Ⓒ Ⓓ
8. Ⓐ Ⓑ Ⓒ Ⓓ   33. Ⓐ Ⓑ Ⓒ Ⓓ   58. Ⓐ Ⓑ Ⓒ Ⓓ   83. Ⓐ Ⓑ Ⓒ Ⓓ   108. Ⓐ Ⓑ Ⓒ Ⓓ
9. Ⓐ Ⓑ Ⓒ Ⓓ   34. Ⓐ Ⓑ Ⓒ Ⓓ   59. Ⓐ Ⓑ Ⓒ Ⓓ   84. Ⓐ Ⓑ Ⓒ Ⓓ   109. Ⓐ Ⓑ Ⓒ Ⓓ
10. Ⓐ Ⓑ Ⓒ Ⓓ   35. Ⓐ Ⓑ Ⓒ Ⓓ   60. Ⓐ Ⓑ Ⓒ Ⓓ   85. Ⓐ Ⓑ Ⓒ Ⓓ   110. Ⓐ Ⓑ Ⓒ Ⓓ
11. Ⓐ Ⓑ Ⓒ Ⓓ   36. Ⓐ Ⓑ Ⓒ Ⓓ   61. Ⓐ Ⓑ Ⓒ Ⓓ   86. Ⓐ Ⓑ Ⓒ Ⓓ   111. Ⓐ Ⓑ Ⓒ Ⓓ
12. Ⓐ Ⓑ Ⓒ Ⓓ   37. Ⓐ Ⓑ Ⓒ Ⓓ   62. Ⓐ Ⓑ Ⓒ Ⓓ   87. Ⓐ Ⓑ Ⓒ Ⓓ   112. Ⓐ Ⓑ Ⓒ Ⓓ
13. Ⓐ Ⓑ Ⓒ Ⓓ   38. Ⓐ Ⓑ Ⓒ Ⓓ   63. Ⓐ Ⓑ Ⓒ Ⓓ   88. Ⓐ Ⓑ Ⓒ Ⓓ   113. Ⓐ Ⓑ Ⓒ Ⓓ
14. Ⓐ Ⓑ Ⓒ Ⓓ   39. Ⓐ Ⓑ Ⓒ Ⓓ   64. Ⓐ Ⓑ Ⓒ Ⓓ   89. Ⓐ Ⓑ Ⓒ Ⓓ   114. Ⓐ Ⓑ Ⓒ Ⓓ
15. Ⓐ Ⓑ Ⓒ Ⓓ   40. Ⓐ Ⓑ Ⓒ Ⓓ   65. Ⓐ Ⓑ Ⓒ Ⓓ   90. Ⓐ Ⓑ Ⓒ Ⓓ   115. Ⓐ Ⓑ Ⓒ Ⓓ
16. Ⓐ Ⓑ Ⓒ Ⓓ   41. Ⓐ Ⓑ Ⓒ Ⓓ   66. Ⓐ Ⓑ Ⓒ Ⓓ   91. Ⓐ Ⓑ Ⓒ Ⓓ   116. Ⓐ Ⓑ Ⓒ Ⓓ
17. Ⓐ Ⓑ Ⓒ Ⓓ   42. Ⓐ Ⓑ Ⓒ Ⓓ   67. Ⓐ Ⓑ Ⓒ Ⓓ   92. Ⓐ Ⓑ Ⓒ Ⓓ   117. Ⓐ Ⓑ Ⓒ Ⓓ
18. Ⓐ Ⓑ Ⓒ Ⓓ   43. Ⓐ Ⓑ Ⓒ Ⓓ   68. Ⓐ Ⓑ Ⓒ Ⓓ   93. Ⓐ Ⓑ Ⓒ Ⓓ   118. Ⓐ Ⓑ Ⓒ Ⓓ
19. Ⓐ Ⓑ Ⓒ Ⓓ   44. Ⓐ Ⓑ Ⓒ Ⓓ   69. Ⓐ Ⓑ Ⓒ Ⓓ   94. Ⓐ Ⓑ Ⓒ Ⓓ   119. Ⓐ Ⓑ Ⓒ Ⓓ
20. Ⓐ Ⓑ Ⓒ Ⓓ   45. Ⓐ Ⓑ Ⓒ Ⓓ   70. Ⓐ Ⓑ Ⓒ Ⓓ   95. Ⓐ Ⓑ Ⓒ Ⓓ   120. Ⓐ Ⓑ Ⓒ Ⓓ
21. Ⓐ Ⓑ Ⓒ Ⓓ   46. Ⓐ Ⓑ Ⓒ Ⓓ   71. Ⓐ Ⓑ Ⓒ Ⓓ   96. Ⓐ Ⓑ Ⓒ Ⓓ   121. Ⓐ Ⓑ Ⓒ Ⓓ
22. Ⓐ Ⓑ Ⓒ Ⓓ   47. Ⓐ Ⓑ Ⓒ Ⓓ   72. Ⓐ Ⓑ Ⓒ Ⓓ   97. Ⓐ Ⓑ Ⓒ Ⓓ   122. Ⓐ Ⓑ Ⓒ Ⓓ
23. Ⓐ Ⓑ Ⓒ Ⓓ   48. Ⓐ Ⓑ Ⓒ Ⓓ   73. Ⓐ Ⓑ Ⓒ Ⓓ   98. Ⓐ Ⓑ Ⓒ Ⓓ   123. Ⓐ Ⓑ Ⓒ Ⓓ
24. Ⓐ Ⓑ Ⓒ Ⓓ   49. Ⓐ Ⓑ Ⓒ Ⓓ   74. Ⓐ Ⓑ Ⓒ Ⓓ   99. Ⓐ Ⓑ Ⓒ Ⓓ   124. Ⓐ Ⓑ Ⓒ Ⓓ
25. Ⓐ Ⓑ Ⓒ Ⓓ   50. Ⓐ Ⓑ Ⓒ Ⓓ   75. Ⓐ Ⓑ Ⓒ Ⓓ   100. Ⓐ Ⓑ Ⓒ Ⓓ   125. Ⓐ Ⓑ Ⓒ Ⓓ

Part C: Stenography

1. Ⓐ Ⓑ Ⓒ Ⓓ	12. Ⓐ Ⓑ Ⓒ Ⓓ	23. Ⓐ Ⓑ Ⓒ Ⓓ	34. Ⓐ Ⓑ Ⓒ Ⓓ	45. Ⓐ Ⓑ Ⓒ Ⓓ
2. Ⓐ Ⓑ Ⓒ Ⓓ	13. Ⓐ Ⓑ Ⓒ Ⓓ	24. Ⓐ Ⓑ Ⓒ Ⓓ	35. Ⓐ Ⓑ Ⓒ Ⓓ	46. Ⓐ Ⓑ Ⓒ Ⓓ
3. Ⓐ Ⓑ Ⓒ Ⓓ	14. Ⓐ Ⓑ Ⓒ Ⓓ	25. Ⓐ Ⓑ Ⓒ Ⓓ	36. Ⓐ Ⓑ Ⓒ Ⓓ	47. Ⓐ Ⓑ Ⓒ Ⓓ
4. Ⓐ Ⓑ Ⓒ Ⓓ	15. Ⓐ Ⓑ Ⓒ Ⓓ	26. Ⓐ Ⓑ Ⓒ Ⓓ	37. Ⓐ Ⓑ Ⓒ Ⓓ	48. Ⓐ Ⓑ Ⓒ Ⓓ
5. Ⓐ Ⓑ Ⓒ Ⓓ	16. Ⓐ Ⓑ Ⓒ Ⓓ	27. Ⓐ Ⓑ Ⓒ Ⓓ	38. Ⓐ Ⓑ Ⓒ Ⓓ	49. Ⓐ Ⓑ Ⓒ Ⓓ
6. Ⓐ Ⓑ Ⓒ Ⓓ	17. Ⓐ Ⓑ Ⓒ Ⓓ	28. Ⓐ Ⓑ Ⓒ Ⓓ	39. Ⓐ Ⓑ Ⓒ Ⓓ	50. Ⓐ Ⓑ Ⓒ Ⓓ
7. Ⓐ Ⓑ Ⓒ Ⓓ	18. Ⓐ Ⓑ Ⓒ Ⓓ	29. Ⓐ Ⓑ Ⓒ Ⓓ	40. Ⓐ Ⓑ Ⓒ Ⓓ	51. Ⓐ Ⓑ Ⓒ Ⓓ
8. Ⓐ Ⓑ Ⓒ Ⓓ	19. Ⓐ Ⓑ Ⓒ Ⓓ	30. Ⓐ Ⓑ Ⓒ Ⓓ	41. Ⓐ Ⓑ Ⓒ Ⓓ	52. Ⓐ Ⓑ Ⓒ Ⓓ
9. Ⓐ Ⓑ Ⓒ Ⓓ	20. Ⓐ Ⓑ Ⓒ Ⓓ	31. Ⓐ Ⓑ Ⓒ Ⓓ	42. Ⓐ Ⓑ Ⓒ Ⓓ	53. Ⓐ Ⓑ Ⓒ Ⓓ
10. Ⓐ Ⓑ Ⓒ Ⓓ	21. Ⓐ Ⓑ Ⓒ Ⓓ	32. Ⓐ Ⓑ Ⓒ Ⓓ	43. Ⓐ Ⓑ Ⓒ Ⓓ	54. Ⓐ Ⓑ Ⓒ Ⓓ
11. Ⓐ Ⓑ Ⓒ Ⓓ	22. Ⓐ Ⓑ Ⓒ Ⓓ	33. Ⓐ Ⓑ Ⓒ Ⓓ	44. Ⓐ Ⓑ Ⓒ Ⓓ	55. Ⓐ Ⓑ Ⓒ Ⓓ

Part A: Clerical Ability

Sequencing

20 QUESTIONS • 3 MINUTES

> **Directions:** For each question there is a name, number, or code in a box at the left and four other names, numbers, or codes in alphabetical or numerical order at the right. Find the correct space for the boxed name or number so that it will be in alphabetical and/or numerical order with the others and mark the letter of that space on your answer sheet.

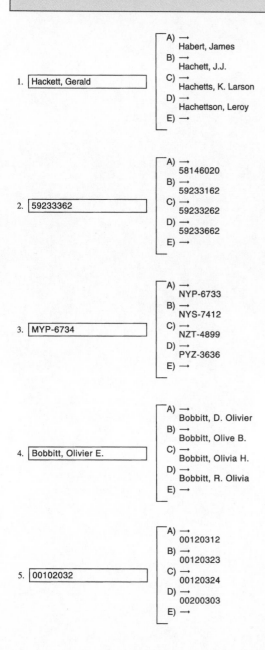

1. | Hackett, Gerald |

A) →
   Habert, James
B) →
   Hachett, J.J.
C) →
   Hachetts, K. Larson
D) →
   Hachettson, Leroy
E) →

2. | 59233362 |

A) →
   58146020
B) →
   59233162
C) →
   59233262
D) →
   59233662
E) →

3. | MYP-6734 |

A) →
   NYP-6733
B) →
   NYS-7412
C) →
   NZT-4899
D) →
   PYZ-3636
E) →

4. | Bobbitt, Olivier E. |

A) →
   Bobbitt, D. Olivier
B) →
   Bobbitt, Olive B.
C) →
   Bobbitt, Olivia H.
D) →
   Bobbitt, R. Olivia
E) →

5. | 00102032 |

A) →
   00120312
B) →
   00120323
C) →
   00120324
D) →
   00200303
E) →

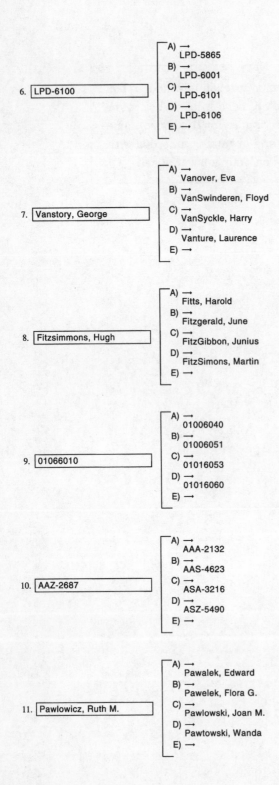

6. LPD-6100

A) →
LPD-5865
B) →
LPD-6001
C) →
LPD-6101
D) →
LPD-6106
E) →

7. Vanstory, George

A) →
Vanover, Eva
B) →
VanSwinderen, Floyd
C) →
VanSyckle, Harry
D) →
Vanture, Laurence
E) →

8. Fitzsimmons, Hugh

A) →
Fitts, Harold
B) →
Fitzgerald, June
C) →
FitzGibbon, Junius
D) →
FitzSimons, Martin
E) →

9. 01066010

A) →
01006040
B) →
01006051
C) →
01016053
D) →
01016060
E) →

10. AAZ-2687

A) →
AAA-2132
B) →
AAS-4623
C) →
ASA-3216
D) →
ASZ-5490
E) →

11. Pawlowicz, Ruth M.

A) →
Pawalek, Edward
B) →
Pawelek, Flora G.
C) →
Pawlowski, Joan M.
D) →
Pawtowski, Wanda
E) →

12. NCD-7834

A) →
   NBJ-4682
B) →
   NBT-5066
C) →
   NCD-7710
D) →
   NCD-7868
E) →

13. 36270013

A) →
   36260006
B) →
   36270000
C) →
   36270030
D) →
   36670012
E) →

14. Freedenburg, C. Erma

A) →
   Freedenberg, Emerson
B) →
   Freedenberg, Erma
C) →
   Freedenberg, Erma E.
D) →
   Freedinberg, Erma F.
E) →

15. Prouty, Martha

A) →
   Proutey, Margaret
B) →
   Proutey, Maude
C) →
   Prouty, Myra
D) →
   Prouty, Naomi
E) →

16. 58006021

A) →
   58006130
B) →
   58097222
C) →
   59000599
D) →
   59909000
E) →

practice test

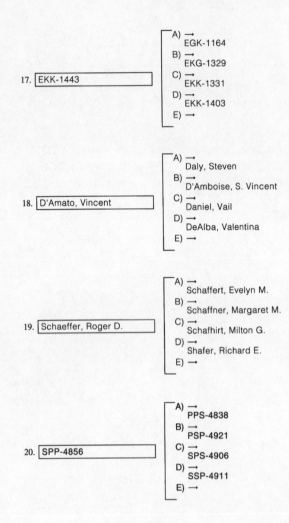

17. EKK-1443

A) →　EGK-1164
B) →　EKG-1329
C) →　EKK-1331
D) →　EKK-1403
E) →

18. D'Amato, Vincent

A) →　Daly, Steven
B) →　D'Amboise, S. Vincent
C) →　Daniel, Vail
D) →　DeAlba, Valentina
E) →

19. Schaeffer, Roger D.

A) →　Schaffert, Evelyn M.
B) →　Schaffner, Margaret M.
C) →　Schafhirt, Milton G.
D) →　Shafer, Richard E.
E) →

20. SPP-4856

A) →　PPS-4838
B) →　PSP-4921
C) →　SPS-4906
D) →　SSP-4911
E) →

Comparisons

30 QUESTIONS • 5 MINUTES

Directions: In each line across the page there are three names, addresses, or codes that are very much alike. Compare the three and decide which ones are EXACTLY alike. On your answer sheet, mark:
(A) if **ALL THREE** names, addresses, or codes are exactly **ALIKE**
(B) if only the **FIRST** and **SECOND** names, addresses, or codes are exactly **ALIKE**
(C) if only the **FIRST** and **THIRD** names, addresses, or codes are exactly **ALIKE**
(D) if only the **SECOND** and **THIRD** names, addresses, or codes are exactly **ALIKE**
(E) if **ALL THREE** names, addresses, or codes are **DIFFERENT**

21. Drusilla S. Ridgeley	Drusilla S. Ridgeley	Drusilla S. Ridgeley
22. Andrei I. Toumantzev	Andrei I. Tourmantzev	Andrei I. Toumantzov
23. 6-78912-e3e42	6-78912-3e3e42	6-78912-e3e42
24. 86529 Dunwoodie Drive	86529 Dunwoodie Drive	85629 Dunwoodie Drive
25. 1592514	1592574	1592574
26. Ella Burk Newham	Ella Burk Newnham	Elena Burk Newnham
27. 5416R-1952TZ-op	5416R-1952TZ-op	5416R-1952TZ-op
28. 60646 West Touhy Avenue	60646 West Touhy Avenue	60646 West Touhey Avenue
29. Mardikian & Moore, Inc.	Mardikian and Moore, Inc.	Mardikian & Moore, Inc.
30. 9670243	9670423	9670423
31. Eduardo Ingles	Eduardo Inglese	Eduardo Inglese
32. Roger T. DeAngelis	Roger T. D'Angelis	Roger T. DeAngeles
33. 7692138	7692138	7692138
34. 2695 East 3435 South	2695 East 3435 South	2695 East 3435 South
35. 63qs5-95YT3-001	63qs5-95YT3-001	63qs5-95YT3-001
36. 2789350	2789350	2798350
37. Helmut V. Lochner	Helmut V. Lockner	Helmut W. Lochner
38. 2454803	2548403	2454803
39. Lemberger, WA 28094-9182	Lemberger, VA 28094-9182	Lemberger, VA 28094-9182
40. 4168-GNP-78852	4168-GNP-78852	4168-GNP-78852
41. Yoshihito Saito	Yoshihito Saito	Yoshihito Saito
42. 5927681	5927861	5927681
43. O'Reilly Bay, LA 56212	O'Reillys Bay, LA 56212	O'Reilly Bay, LA 56212
44. Francis Ransdell	Frances Ramsdell	Francis Ramsdell
45. 5634-OotV5a-16867	5634-Ootv5a-16867	5634-Ootv5a-16867
46. Dolores Mollicone	Dolores Mollicone	Doloras Mollicone
47. David C. Routzon	David E. Routzon	David C. Routzron
48. 8932 Shimabui Hwy.	8932 Shimabui Hwy.	8932 Shimabui Hwy.
49. 6177396	6177936	6177396
50. A8987-B73245	A8987-B73245	A8987-B73245

Spelling

20 QUESTIONS • 3 MINUTES

Directions: Find the correct spelling of the word and darken the appropriate space on your answer sheet. If none of the spellings is correct, darken choice (D).

51. **(A)** anticipate
    (B) antisipate
    (C) anticapate
    (D) none of these

52. **(A)** similiar
    (B) simmilar
    (C) similar
    (D) none of these

53. **(A)** sufficiantly
    (B) suficeintly
    (C) sufficiently
    (D) none of these

54. **(A)** intelligence
    (B) inteligence
    (C) intellegence
    (D) none of these

55. **(A)** referance
    (B) referrence
    (C) referense
    (D) none of these

56. **(A)** conscious
    (B) consious
    (C) conscius
    (D) none of these

57. **(A)** paralell
    (B) parellel
    (C) parellell
    (D) none of these

58. **(A)** abundence
    (B) abundance
    (C) abundants
    (D) none of these

59. **(A)** corregated
    (B) corrigated
    (C) corrugated
    (D) none of these

60. **(A)** accumalation
    (B) accumulation
    (C) accumullation
    (D) none of these

61. **(A)** resonance
    (B) resonence
    (C) resonnance
    (D) none of these

62. **(A)** benaficial
    (B) benefitial
    (C) beneficial
    (D) none of these

63. **(A)** spesifically
    (B) specificially
    (C) specifically
    (D) none of these

64. **(A)** elemanate
    (B) elimenate
    (C) elliminate
    (D) none of these

65. **(A)** collosal
    (B) colosal
    (C) collossal
    (D) none of these

66. **(A)** auxillary
    (B) auxilliary
    (C) auxiliary
    (D) none of these

67. **(A)** inimitable
    (B) inimitible
    (C) inimatable
    (D) none of these

68. **(A)** disapearance
    (B) dissapearance
    (C) disappearence
    (D) none of these

69. **(A)** appelate
    (B) appellate
    (C) apellate
    (D) none of these

70. **(A)** esential
    (B) essential
    (C) essencial
    (D) none of these

Computations

15 QUESTIONS • 8 MINUTES

Directions: Perform the computation as indicated in the question and find the answer among the list of alternative responses. If the correct answer is not given among the choices, mark (E).

71.
$$\begin{array}{r} 83 \\ -\ 56 \end{array}$$

(A) 23
(B) 29
(C) 33
(D) 37
(E) none of these

72.
$$\begin{array}{r} 15 \\ +\ 17 \end{array}$$

(A) 22
(B) 32
(C) 39
(D) 42
(E) none of these

73.
$$\begin{array}{r} 32 \\ \times\ 7 \end{array}$$

(A) 224
(B) 234
(C) 324
(D) 334
(E) none of these

74.
$$\begin{array}{r} 39 \\ \times\ 2 \end{array}$$

(A) 77
(B) 78
(C) 79
(D) 81
(E) none of these

75.
$$\begin{array}{r} 43 \\ -\ 15 \end{array}$$

(A) 23
(B) 32
(C) 33
(D) 35
(E) none of these

76.
$$\begin{array}{r} 50 \\ +\ 49 \end{array}$$

(A) 89
(B) 90
(C) 99
(D) 109
(E) none of these

practice test

77. 6)366
- **(A)** 11
- **(B)** 31
- **(C)** 36
- **(D)** 66
- **(E)** none of these

78. 38 × 3
- **(A)** 111
- **(B)** 113
- **(C)** 115
- **(D)** 117
- **(E)** none of these

79. 19 + 21
- **(A)** 20
- **(B)** 30
- **(C)** 40
- **(D)** 50
- **(E)** none of these

80. 13 − 6
- **(A)** 5
- **(B)** 7
- **(C)** 9
- **(D)** 11
- **(E)** none of these

81. 6)180
- **(A)** 29
- **(B)** 31
- **(C)** 33
- **(D)** 39
- **(E)** none of these

82. 10 × 1
- **(A)** 0
- **(B)** 1
- **(C)** 10
- **(D)** 100
- **(E)** none of these

83. 7)287
- **(A)** 21
- **(B)** 27
- **(C)** 31
- **(D)** 37
- **(E)** none of these

84. 12 + 11
- **(A)** 21
- **(B)** 22
- **(C)** 23
- **(D)** 24
- **(E)** none of these

85. 85 − 64
- **(A)** 19
- **(B)** 21
- **(C)** 29
- **(D)** 31
- **(E)** none of these

Part B: Verbal Ability

55 QUESTIONS • 50 MINUTES

> **Directions:** Questions 1 through 20 test your ability to follow instructions. Each question directs you to mark a specific number and letter combination on your answer sheet. The questions require your total concentration because the answers that you are instructed to mark are, for the most part, NOT in numerical sequence (i.e., you would not use Number 1 on your answer sheet to answer Question 1; Number 2 for Question 2; etc.). Instead, you must mark the number and space specifically designated in each test question.

1. Look at the letters below. Draw a circle around the letter that comes first in the alphabet. Now, on your answer sheet, find Number 12 and darken the space for the letter you just circled.

    E G D Z B F

2. Draw a line under the odd number below that is more than 5 but less than 10. Find this number on your answer sheet and darken choice (E).

    8 10 5 6 11 9

3. Divide the number 16 by 4 and write your answer on the line below. Now find this number on your answer sheet and darken choice (A).

    _____

4. Write the letter C on the line next to the left-hand number below. Now, on your answer sheet, darken the space for the number-letter combination you see.

    5_____   19_____   7_____

5. If in any week Wednesday comes before Tuesday, write the number 15 on the line below. If not, write the number 18. Now, on your answer sheet, darken choice (A) for the number you just wrote.

    _____

6. Count the number of Bs in the line below and write that number at the end of the line. Now, on your answer sheet, darken choice (D) for the number you wrote.

    A D A E B D C A_____

7. Write the letter B on the line with the highest number. Now, on your answer sheet, darken the number-letter combination that appears on that line.

    16_____   9_____   20_____   11_____

8. If the product of 6 × 4 is greater than the product of 8 × 3, write the letter E on the line below. If not, write the letter C. Now, on your answer sheet find number 8 and darken the space for the letter you just wrote.

    _____

9. Write the number 2 in the larger circle below. Now, on your answer sheet, darken the space for the number-letter combination in that circle.

10. Write the letter D on the line next to the number that is the sum of 7 + 4 + 4. Now, on your answer sheet, darken the space for that number-letter combination.

      13_____ 14_____ 15_____ 16_____ 17_____

11. If 5 × 5 equals 25 and 5 + 5 equals 10, write the number 17 on the line below. If not, write the number 10. Now, on your answer sheet, darken choice (E) for the number you just wrote.

      _____

12. Circle the second letter below. On the line beside that letter write the number that represents the number of days in a week. Now, on your answer sheet, darken the space for that number-letter combination.

      _____C _____D _____B _____E

13. If a triangle has more angles than a rectangle, write the number 13 in the circle below. If not, write the number 14 in the square. Now, on your answer sheet, darken the space for the number-letter combination in the figure that you just wrote in.

14. Count the number of Bs below and write that number at the end of the line. Subtract 2 from that number. Now, on your answer sheet, darken choice (E) for the number that represents 2 less than the number of Bs in the line.

      B E A D E C C B B B A E B D_____

15. The numbers below represent morning pick-up times from neighborhood letter boxes. Draw a line under the number that represents the latest pick-up time. Now, on your answer sheet, darken choice (D) for the number that is the same as the "minutes" of the time that you underlined.

      9:19 10:16 10:10

16. If a person who is 6 feet tall is taller than a person who is 5 feet tall and if a pillow is softer than a rock, darken choice 11(A) on your answer sheet. If not, darken choice 6(B).

17. Write the fourth letter of the alphabet on the line next to the third number below. Now, on your answer sheet, darken that number-letter combination.

      10_____ 19_____ 13_____ 4_____

18. Write the letter B in the box containing the next to smallest number. On your answer sheet, darken the space for that number-letter combination.

| 10_____ | 19_____ | 11_____ | 6_____ |

19. Directly below you will see three boxes and three words. Write the third letter of the first word on the line in the second box. Now, on your answer sheet, darken the space for that number-letter combination.

| 6_____ | 19_____ | 12_____ | BAD   DRAB   ALE

20. Count the number of points on the figure below. If there are five or more points, darken choice 6(E) on your answer sheet. If there are fewer than five points, darken choice 6(A).

Directions: Each question from 21 through 40 consists of a sentence written in four different ways. Choose the sentence that is most appropriate with respect to grammar, usage, and punctuation, so as to be suitable for a business letter or report and darken its letter on your answer sheet. Answer each question in the answer space with the corresponding number.

---

21. **(A)** Double parking is when you park your car alongside one that is already having been parked.
   (B) When one double parks, you park your car alongside one that is already parked.
   (C) Double parking is parking alongside a car already parked.
   (D) To double park is alongside a car already parked.

22. **(A)** This is entirely among you and he.
   (B) This is completely among him and you.
   (C) This is between you and him.
   (D) This is between he and you.

23. **(A)** As I said, "neither of them are guilty."
   (B) As I said, "neither of them are guilty".
   (C) As I said, "neither of them is guilty."
   (D) As I said, neither of them is guilty.

24. **(A)** I think that they will promote whoever has the best record.
   (B) The firm would have liked to have promoted all employees with good records.
   (C) Such of them that have the best records have excellent prospects of promotion.
   (D) I feel sure they will give the promotion to whomever has the best record.

25. **(A)** The receptionist must answer courteously the questions of all them callers.
    (B) The receptionist must answer courteously the questions what are asked by the callers.
    (C) There would have been no trouble if the receptionist had have always answered courteously.
    (D) The receptionist should answer courteously the questions of all callers.

26. **(A)** Since the report lacked the needed information, it was of no use to them.
    (B) This report was useless to them because there were no needed information in it.
    (C) Since the report did not contain the needed information, it was not real useful to them.
    (D) Being that the report lacked the needed information, they could not use it.

27. **(A)** The company had hardly declared the dividend till the notices were prepared for mailing.
    (B) They had no sooner declared the dividend when they sent the notices to the stockholders.
    (C) No sooner had the dividend been declared than the notices were prepared for mailing.
    (D) Scarcely had the dividend been declared than the notices were sent out.

28. **(A)** The supervisors reprimanded the typists, whom she believed had made careless errors.
    (B) The typists would have corrected the errors had they of known that the supervisor would see the report.
    (C) The errors in the typed reports were so numerous that they could hardly be overlooked.
    (D) Many errors were found in the reports which they typed and could not disregard them.

29. **(A)** "Are you absolutely certain, she asked, that you are right?"
    (B) "Are you absolutely certain," she asked, "that you are right?"
    (C) "Are you absolutely certain," she asked, "That you are right"?
    (D) "Are you absolutely certain", she asked, "That you are right?"

30. **(A)** He goes only to church on Christmas and Easter.
    (B) He only goes to church on Christmas and Easter.
    (C) He goes to only church on Christmas and Easter.
    (D) He goes to church only on Christmas and Easter.

31. **(A)** Most all these statements have been supported by persons who are reliable and can be depended upon.
    (B) The persons which have guaranteed these statements are reliable.
    (C) Reliable persons guarantee the facts with regards to the truth of these statements.
    (D) These statements can be depended on, for their truth has been guaranteed by reliable persons.

32. **(A)** The success of the book pleased both the publisher and authors.
    (B) Both the publisher and they was pleased with the success of the book.
    (C) Neither they or their publisher was disappointed with the success of the book.
    (D) Their publisher was as pleased as they with the success of the book.

33. **(A)** In reviewing the typists' work reports, the job analyst found records of unusual typing speeds.
    (B) It says in the job analyst's report that some employees type with great speed.
    (C) The job analyst found that, in reviewing the typists' work reports, that some unusual typing speeds had been made.
    (D) In the reports of typists' speeds, the job analyst found some records that are kind of unusual.

34. **(A)** Every carrier should always have something to throw; not something to throw at the dog but something what will divert its attention.
    (B) Every carrier should have something to throw—not something to throw at the dog but something to divert its attention.
    (C) Every carrier should always carry something to throw not something to throw at the dog but something that will divert it's attention.
    (D) Every carrier should always carry something to throw, not something to throw at the dog, but, something that will divert its' attention.

35. **(A)** Brown's & Company employees have recently received increases in salary.
    (B) Brown & Company recently increased the salaries of all its employees.
    (C) Recently Brown & Company has increased their employees' salaries.
    (D) Brown & Company have recently increased the salaries of all its employees.

36. **(A)** If properly addressed, the letter will reach my mother and I.
    (B) The letter had been addressed to myself and my mother.
    (C) I believe the letter was addressed to either my mother or I.
    (D) My mother's name, as well as mine, was on the letter.

37. **(A)** One of us have to make the reply before tomorrow.
    (B) Making the reply before tomorrow will have to be done by one of us.
    (C) One of us has to reply before tomorrow.
    (D) Anyone has to reply before tomorrow.

38. **(A)** You have got to get rid of some of these people if you expect to have the quality of the work improve.
    (B) The quality of the work would improve if they would leave fewer people do it.
    (C) I believe it would be desirable to have fewer persons doing this work.
    (D) If you had planned on employing fewer people than this to do the work, this situation would not have arose.

39. **(A)** The paper we use for this purpose must be light, glossy, and stand hard usage as well.
    (B) Only a light and a glossy, but durable, paper must be used for this purpose.
    (C) For this purpose, we want a paper that is light, glossy, but that will stand hard wear.
    (D) For this purpose, paper that is light, glossy, and durable is essential.

40. **(A)** This letter, together with the reports, are to be sent to the postmaster.

    (B) The reports, together with this letter, is to be sent to the postmaster.

    (C) The reports and this letter is to be sent to the postmaster.

    (D) This letter, together with the reports, is to be sent to the postmaster.

Directions: Each question from 41 through 48 consists of a sentence containing a word in boldface type. Choose the best meaning for the word in boldface type and darken its letter on your answer sheet. Answer each question in the answer space with the corresponding number.

---

41. Please consult your office **manual** to learn the proper operation of our copying machine. **Manual** means most nearly

    (A) labor

    (B) handbook

    (C) typewriter

    (D) handle

42. There is a specified punishment for each **infraction** of the rules. **Infraction** means most nearly

    (A) violation

    (B) use

    (C) interpretation

    (D) part

43. The order was **rescinded** within the week. **Rescinded** means most nearly

    (A) revised

    (B) canceled

    (C) misinterpreted

    (D) confirmed

44. If you have a question, please raise your hand to **summon** the test proctor. **Summon** means most nearly

    (A) ticket

    (B) fine

    (C) give

    (D) call

45. We dared not prosecute the terrorist for fear of **reprisal**. **Reprisal** means most nearly

    (A) retaliation

    (B) advantage

    (C) warning

    (D) denial

46. The increased use of dictation machines has severely **reduced** the need for office stenographers. **Reduced** means most nearly

    (A) enlarged

    (B) cut out

    (C) lessened

    (D) expanded

47. Frequent use of marijuana may **impair** your judgment. **Impair** means most nearly

    (A) weaken

    (B) conceal

    (C) improve

    (D) expose

48. It is altogether **fitting** that the parent discipline the child. **Fitting** means most nearly

    (A) illegal

    (B) bad practice

    (C) appropriate

    (D) required

Directions: For questions 49 through 55, read each paragraph and answer the question that follows it by darkening the letter of the correct answer on your answer sheet. Answer each question in the answer space with the corresponding number.

49. A survey to determine the subjects that have helped students most in their jobs shows that typewriting leads all other subjects in the business group. It also leads among the subjects college students consider most valuable and would take again if they were to return to high school.

The paragraph best supports the statement that

(A) the ability to type is an asset in business and in school
(B) students who return to night school take typing
(C) students with a knowledge of typing do superior work in college
(D) success in business is assured those who can type

50. Telegrams should be clear, concise, and brief. Omit all unnecessary words. The parts of speech most often used in telegrams are nouns, verbs, adjectives, and adverbs. If possible, do pronouns, prepositions, articles, and copulative verbs. Use simple sentences, rather than complex and compound.

The paragraph best supports the statement that in writing telegrams one should always use

(A) common and simple words
(B) only nouns, verbs, adjectives, and adverbs
(C) incomplete sentences
(D) only words essential to the meaning

51. Since the government can spend only what it obtains from the people, and this amount is ultimately limited by their capacity and willingness to pay taxes, it is very important that people be given full information about the work of the government.

The paragraph best supports the statement that

(A) governmental employees should be trained not only in their own work, but also in how to perform the duties of other employees in their agency
(B) taxation by the government rests upon the consent of the people
(C) the release of full information on the work of the government will increase the efficiency of governmental operations
(D) the work of the government, in recent years, has been restricted because of reduced tax collections

52. Both the high school and the college should take the responsibility for preparing the student to get a job. Since the ability to write a good application letter is one of the first steps toward this goal, every teacher should be willing to do what he can to help the student learn to write such letters.

The paragraph best supports the statement that

(A) inability to write a good letter may reduce one's job prospects
(B) the major responsibility of the school is to obtain jobs for its students
(C) success is largely a matter of the kind of work the student applies for first
(D) every teacher should teach a course in the writing of application letters

53. Direct lighting is the least satisfactory lighting arrangement. The desk or ceiling light with a reflector that diffuses all the rays downward is sure to cause a glare on the working surface.

The paragraph best supports the statement that direct lighting is least satisfactory as a method of lighting chiefly because

(A) the light is diffused causing eye strain

(B) the shade on the individual desk lamp is not constructed along scientific lines

(C) the working surface is usually obscured by the glare

(D) direct lighting is injurious to the eyes

54. "White collar" is a term used to describe one of the largest groups of workers in American industry and trade. It distinguishes those who work with the pencil and the mind from those who depend on their hands and the machine. It suggests occupations in which physical exertion and handling of materials are not primary features of the job.

The paragraph best supports the statement that "white collar" workers are

(A) not so strong physically as those who work with their hands

(B) those who supervise workers handling materials

(C) all whose work is entirely indoors

(D) not likely to use machines as much as are other groups of workers

55. In large organizations some standardized, simple, inexpensive method of giving employees information about company policies and rules, as well as specific instructions regarding their duties, is practically essential. This is the purpose of all office manuals of whatever type.

The paragraph best supports the statement that office manuals

(A) are all about the same

(B) should be simple enough for the average employee to understand

(C) are necessary to large organizations

(D) act as constant reminders to the employee of his or her duties

Part C: Stenography

DICTATION TIME: 3 MINUTES

Exactly on a minute start dictating.	**Finish reading each two lines at the number of seconds indicated below.**
In recent years there has been a great increase in the need for capable stenographers,	10
not only in business offices but also in public service agencies, both	20
governmental and private. (Period) The high schools and business schools in many parts of	30
the country have tried to meet this need by offering complete commercial courses. (Period)	40
The increase in the number of persons who are enrolled in these courses shows that	50
students have become aware of the great demand for stenographers. (Period) A person	1 min.
who wishes to secure employment in this field must be able to take dictation	10
and to transcribe the notes with both speed and accuracy. (Period) The rate of	20
speed at which dictation is given in most offices is somewhat less than that of	30
ordinary speech. (Period) Thus, one who has had a thorough training in shorthand	40
should have little trouble in taking complete notes. (Period) Skill in taking dictation	50
at a rapid rate is of slight value if the stenographer cannot also type the notes	2 min.
in proper form. (Period) A manager sometimes dictates a rough draft of the ideas	10
he/she wishes to have included in a letter, and leaves to the stenographer the task	20
of putting them in good form. (Period) For this reason, knowledge of the essentials	30
of grammar and of composition is as important as the ability to take	40
dictation. (Period) In addition, a stenographer should be familiar with the sources of	50
general information that are most likely to be used in office work. (Period)	3 min.

Dictation Transcript

125 QUESTIONS • 30 MINUTES

ALPHABETIC WORD LIST

Write E if the answer is **not** listed.

also—A	offering—C
also in—C	officials—D
business—C	one—C
busy—D	only—B
capable—A	parts—A
commerce—C	private—C
commercial—D	public—D
county—B	recent—B
culpable—D	recurrent—A
decrease—A	school—C
governing—D	schools—B
governmental—C	servant—D
had been—B	stenographers—D
has been—D	stenos—A
many—A	their—D
most—D	there—B
need—C	tied—A
needy—D	to beat—C
offending—A	tried—B

TRANSCRIPT

In ___ years ___ ___ a great ___
    1   2   3   4

in the ___ for ___ ___ , not ___ in
     5   6   7   8

___ ___ but ___ in ___ ___
 9   10   11   12   13

agencies, both ___ and ___ . The
              14   15

high ___ and ___ schools in ___
     16   17   18

___ of the ___ have ___ this
 19   20   21 22

___ by ___ complete ___ courses.
23   24   25

Continue on the next page without waiting for a signal.

ALPHABETIC WORD LIST

Write E if the answer is **not** listed.

awake—C	in a—B
aware—B	in the—A
be able—A	increase—C
be able to—C	increment—A
became—B	notations—B
better—A	notes—C
both—D	number—C
courses—D	numbers—D
curses—C	people—A
demand—C	person—C
demean—A	seclude—C
dictation—B	secure—B
dictation notes—C	speech—C
employing—A	speed—B
employment—D	students—C
enrolled—B	studies—D
enroute—D	the—C
feel—A	this—A
felt—D	transcribe—C
grate—D	transcript—D
great—A	who desires—C

TRANSCRIPT (continued)

The _____ _____ _____ of _____ who are
    26   27   28   29

_____ in these _____ shows _____ _____
30   31   32   33

have _____ _____ of the _____ _____ for
     34   35   36   37

stenographers. A _____ _____ to _____
                 38   39   40

_____ in _____ _____ must _____ to take
41   42   43   44

_____ and to _____ the _____ with _____
45   46   47   48

_____ and _____ .
49   50

*Continue on the next page without waiting for
a signal.*

ALPHABETIC WORD LIST

Write E if the answer is **not** listed.

also—D	rampant—B
also can—B	rate—C
at a—A	ratio—D
at the—C	should—D
compete—B	should not—A
complete—D	sight—C
dictates—B	slight—B
dictation—D	somehow—D
firm—C	speech—A
form—D	speed—A
gained—A	stenographer—C
give—D	taking—C
has—C	that—D
have—B	thorough—C
less—B	through—B
less than—A	treble—D
many—A	trial—A
most—D	typed—D
note—C	typewriter—A
notes—B	valuate—A
offices—C	value—C
orderly—C	what—C
ordinary—D	which—B
proffer—C	who gets—A
proper—A	who had—C

TRANSCRIPT (continued)

The ___ of ___ at ___ dictation is
    51   52   53

___ in ___ ___ is ___ ___ than
54   55 56   57 58

___ of ___ ___ . Thus, one ___
59   60 61   62

had a ___ ___ in shorthand ___
      63 64   65

___ little ___ in ___ ___ ___ .
66   67   68 69 70

Skill in ___ ___ ___ ___ ___ is
      71 72 73 74 75

of ___ ___ if the ___ cannot ___
   76 77   78   79

___ the ___ in ___ ___ .
80   81   82 83

Continue on the next page without waiting for a signal.

ALPHABETIC WORD LIST

Write E if the answer is **not** listed.

ability—B	letter—D
adding—C	like—A
addition—A	likely—C
are—D	manager—A
as—A	management—B
composing—A	of the —D
composition—C	of these—A
dictates—B	office—A
essence—B	official—B
essentials—C	put in—D
form—A	putting—C
familial—C	reasoning—B
familiar—A	rough—A
general—C	roughly—D
generous—A	sauces—A
good—C	shall—D
grammatical—D	should—B
great—A	some times—A
had—A	somethings—D
have—B	source—D
ideals—C	stenographic—A
ideas—A	take—D
included—C	task—D
inclusive—A	this—A
information—D	to—A
important—B	to be—B
impotent—A	used—C
knowledge—B	useful—A
knowledgeable—C	wished—D
leaves—B	wishes—A
lets—C	with the—D

TRANSCRIPT (continued)

A ___ ___ ___ a ___ ___ ___
   84 85 86   87 88 89

___ s/he ___ to ___ ___ in a
90   91   92 93

___ , and ___ to the ___ the ___
94   95   96   97

of ___ them in ___ ___ . For ___
98   99 100   101

___ ___ ___ ___ of ___ and of
102 103 104 105 106

___ is ___ ___ ___ ___ to
107 108 109 110 111 112

dictation. In ___ ___ stenographer
        113 114

___ be ___ ___ ___ of ___ ___
115 116 117 118   119 120

that ___ most ___ ___ ___ in
    121   122 123 124

___ work.
125

You will now have ten minutes to transfer your answers to the Part C answer sheet.

ANSWER KEY AND EXPLANATIONS

Clerical Ability

1. E	18. B	35. A	52. C	69. B
2. D	19. A	36. B	53. C	70. B
3. A	20. C	37. E	54. A	71. E
4. D	21. A	38. C	55. D	72. B
5. A	22. E	39. D	56. A	73. A
6. C	23. C	40. A	57. D	74. B
7. B	24. B	41. A	58. B	75. E
8. D	25. D	42. C	59. C	76. C
9. E	26. E	43. C	60. B	77. E
10. C	27. A	44. E	61. A	78. E
11. C	28. B	45. D	62. C	79. C
12. D	29. C	46. B	63. C	80. B
13. C	30. D	47. E	64. D	81. E
14. D	31. D	48. A	65. D	82. C
15. C	32. E	49. C	66. C	83. E
16. A	33. A	50. A	67. A	84. C
17. E	34. A	51. A	68. D	85. B

1. **The correct answer is (E).** Hachettson; Hackett

2. **The correct answer is (D).** 59233262; 59233362

3. **The correct answer is (A).** MYP; NYP

4. **The correct answer is (D).** Olivia H.; Olivier E.; R. Olivia

5. **The correct answer is (A).** 0010; 0012

6. **The correct answer is (C).** 6001; 6100; 6101

7. **The correct answer is (B).** Vanover; Vanstory; VanSwinderen

8. **The correct answer is (D).** FitzGibbon; Fitzsimmons; FitzSimons

9. **The correct answer is (E).** 01016060; 01066010

10. **The correct answer is (C).** AAS; AAZ; ASA

11. **The correct answer is (C).** Pawelek; Pawlowicz; Pawlowski

12. **The correct answer is (D).** 7710; 7834; 7868

13. **The correct answer is (C).** 36270000; 36270013; 36270030

14. **The correct answer is (D).** Freedenberg; Freedenburg; Freedinberg

15. **The correct answer is (C).** Proutey; Prouty, Martha; Prouty, Myra

16. **The correct answer is (A).** 58006021; 58006130

17. **The correct answer is (E).** EKK-1403; EKK-1443

18. **The correct answer is (B).** Daly; D'Amato; D'Amboise

19. **The correct answer is (A).** Schaeffer; Schaffert

20. **The correct answer is (C).** PSP; SPP; SPS

21. **The correct answer is (A).**
Drusilla S. Ridgeley   Drusilla S. Ridgeley   Drusilla S. Ridgeley

22. **The correct answer is (E).**
Andrei I. Toumantzev   Andrei I. Tourmantzev   Andrei I. Toumantzov

23. **The correct answer is (C).**
6-78912-e3e42   6-78912-3e3e42   6-78912-e3e42

24. **The correct answer is (B).**
86529 Dunwoodie Drive   86529 Dunwoodie Drive   85629 Dunwoodie Drive

25. **The correct answer is (D).**
1592514   1592574   1592574

26. **The correct answer is (E).**
Ella Burk Newham   Ella Burk Newnham   Elena Burk Newnham

27. **The correct answer is (A).**
5416R-1952TZ-op   5416R-1952TZ-op   5416R-1952TZ-op

28. **The correct answer is (B).**
60646 West Touhy Avenue   60646 West Touhy Avenue   60646 West Touhey Avenue

29. **The correct answer is (C).**
Mardikian & Moore, Inc.   Mardikian and Moore, Inc.   Mardikian & Moore, Inc.

30. **The correct answer is (D).**
9670243   9670423   9670423

31. **The correct answer is (D).**
Eduardo Ingles_   Eduardo Inglese   Eduardo Inglese

32. **The correct answer is (E).**
Roger T. DeAngelis   Roger T. D'Angelis   Roger T. DeAngeles

33. **The correct answer is (A).**
7692138   7692138   7692138

34. **The correct answer is (A).**
2695 East 3435 South   2695 East 3435 South   2695 East 3435 South

35. **The correct answer is (A).**
63qs5-95YT3-001   63qs5-95YT3-001   63qs5-95YT3-001

36. **The correct answer is (B).**
2789350   2789350   2798350

37. **The correct answer is (E).**
Helmut V. Lochner   Helmut V. Lockner   Helmut W. Lochner

38. **The correct answer is (C).**
2454803   2548403   2454803

39. The correct answer is (D).
Lemberger, <u>WA</u> 28094-9182   Lemberger, VA 28094-9182   Lemberger, VA 28094-9182

40. The correct answer is (A).
4168-GNP-78852   4168-GNP-78852   4168-GNP-78852

41. The correct answer is (A).
Yoshihito Saito   Yoshihito Saito   Yoshihito Saito

42. The correct answer is (C).
5927681   59278<u>61</u>   5927681

43. The correct answer is (C).
O'Reilly Bay, LA 56212   O'Reilly<u>s</u> Bay, LA 56212   O'Reilly Bay, LA 56212

44. The correct answer is (E).
Francis Ran<u>s</u>dell   Franc<u>es</u> Ram<u>s</u>dell   Francis Ram<u>s</u>dell

45. The correct answer is (D).
5634-Oot<u>V</u>5a-16867   5634-Ootv5a-16867   5634-Ootv5a-16867

46. The correct answer is (B).
Dolores Mollicone   Dolores Mollicone   Dolor<u>as</u> Mollicone

47. The correct answer is (E).
David C. Routzon   David <u>E</u>. Routzon   David C. Routz<u>r</u>on

48. The correct answer is (A).
8932 Shimabui Hwy.   8932 Shimabui Hwy.   8932 Shimabui Hwy.

49. The correct answer is (C).
6177396   61779<u>36</u>   6177396

50. The correct answer is (A).
A8987-B73245   A8987-B73245   A8987-B73245

51. The correct answer is (A). anticipate
52. The correct answer is (C). similar
53. The correct answer is (C). sufficiently
54. The correct answer is (A). intelligence
55. The correct answer is (D). reference
56. The correct answer is (A). conscious
57. The correct answer is (D). parallel
58. The correct answer is (B). abundance
59. The correct answer is (C). corrugated
60. The correct answer is (B). accumulation
61. The correct answer is (A). resonance
62. The correct answer is (C). beneficial
63. The correct answer is (C). specifically
64. The correct answer is (D). eliminate
65. The correct answer is (D). colossal
66. The correct answer is (C). auxiliary
67. The correct answer is (A). inimitable
68. The correct answer is (D). disappearance
69. The correct answer is (B). appellate
70. The correct answer is (B). essential

71. The correct answer is (E).
$$\begin{array}{r} 83 \\ -\ 56 \\ \hline 27 \end{array}$$

72. The correct answer is (B).
$$\begin{array}{r} 15 \\ +\ 17 \\ \hline 32 \end{array}$$

73. The correct answer is (A).
$$\begin{array}{r} 32 \\ \times\ \ 7 \\ \hline 224 \end{array}$$

74. The correct answer is (B).
$$\begin{array}{r} 39 \\ \times\ \ 2 \\ \hline 78 \end{array}$$

75. The correct answer is (E).
$$\begin{array}{r} 43 \\ -\ 15 \\ \hline 28 \end{array}$$

76. The correct answer is (C).
$$\begin{array}{r} 50 \\ +\ 49 \\ \hline 99 \end{array}$$

77. The correct answer is (E). $6\overline{)366}$ with quotient 61

78. The correct answer is (E).
$$\begin{array}{r} 38 \\ \times\ \ 3 \\ \hline 114 \end{array}$$

79. The correct answer is (C).
$$\begin{array}{r} 19 \\ +\ 21 \\ \hline 40 \end{array}$$

80. The correct answer is (B).
$$\begin{array}{r} 13 \\ -\ \ 6 \\ \hline 7 \end{array}$$

81. The correct answer is (E). $6\overline{)180}$ with quotient 30

82. The correct answer is (C).
$$\begin{array}{r} 10 \\ \times\ \ 1 \\ \hline 10 \end{array}$$

83. The correct answer is (E). $7\overline{)287}$ with quotient 41

84. The correct answer is (C).
$$\begin{array}{r} 12 \\ +\ 11 \\ \hline 23 \end{array}$$

85. The correct answer is (B).
$$\begin{array}{r} 85 \\ -\ 64 \\ \hline 21 \end{array}$$

Verbal Ability

1. D	12. B	23. D	34. B	45. A
2. C	13. D	24. A	35. B	46. C
3. E	14. A	25. D	36. D	47. A
4. A	15. D	26. A	37. C	48. C
5. C	16. D	27. C	38. C	49. A
6. E	17. E	28. C	39. D	50. D
7. D	18. A	29. B	40. D	51. B
8. C	19. D	30. D	41. B	52. A
9. E	20. B	31. D	42. A	53. C
10. B	21. C	32. A	43. B	54. D
11. A	22. C	33. A	44. D	55. C

21. **The correct answer is (C).** Sentence (C) is the best expression of the idea. Sentence (A) has two grammatical errors: the use of *when* to introduce a definition and the unacceptable verb form is *already having been parked*. Sentence (B) incorrectly shifts subjects from *one* to *you*. Sentence (D) does not make sense.

22. **The correct answer is (C).** Choice (B) is incorrect because only two persons are involved in this statement. *Between* is used when there are only two, *among* is reserved for three or more. (A) makes a similar error. In addition, both (A) and (D) use the pronoun *he*. The object of a preposition, in this case *between,* must be in the objective case, hence *him*.

23. **The correct answer is (D).** Punctuation aside, both (A) and (B) incorrectly place the verb in the plural, *are*. *Neither* is a singular indefinite pronoun. It means *not one and not the other* and requires a singular verb. The choice between (C) and (D) is more difficult, but basically this is a simple statement and not a direct quote.

24. **The correct answer is (A).** *Whoever* is the subject of the phrase *whoever has the best record.* Hence (A) is the correct answer and (D) is wrong. Both (B) and (C) are wordy and awkward.

25. **The correct answer is (D).** All the other choices contain obvious errors.

26. **The correct answer is (A).** Choice (B) uses the plural verb *were* with the singular subject *report*. (C) and (D) are colloquial and incorrect even for informal speech. They have no place in business writing.

27. **The correct answer is (C).** Choices (A) and (B) use adverbs incorrectly; choice (D) is awkward and unidiomatic.

28. **The correct answer is (C).** Choices (B) and (D) are obviously incorrect. In (A), the pronoun *who* should be the subject of the phrase *who had made careless errors.*

29. **The correct answer is (B).** Only the quoted material should appear enclosed by quotation marks, so (A) is incorrect. Only the first word of a sentence should begin with a capital letter, so both (C) and (D) are wrong. In addition, only the quoted material itself is a question; the entire sentence is a statement. Therefore, the question mark must be placed inside the quotes.

30. **The correct answer is (D).** Choices (A) and (B) imply that he stays in church all day on Christmas and Easter and goes nowhere else. Choice (C) makes the same implication and in addition splits the infinitive awkwardly. In (D) the modifier *only* is correctly placed to tell us that the only times he goes to church are on Christmas and Easter.

31. The correct answer is (D). Choice (A) might state either *most* or *all* but not both; choice (B) should read *persons who;* choice (C) should read *with regard to....*

32. The correct answer is (A). Choice (A) is the clearest expression of the idea; choice (B) requires the plural verb *were;* choice (C) requires the correlative construction *neither ... nor;* choice (D) is awkward.

33. The correct answer is (A). Choices (C) and (D) are glaringly poor. Choice (B) is not incorrect, but choice (A) is far better.

34. The correct answer is (B). Choice (A) incorrectly uses a semicolon to separate a complete clause from a sentence fragment. Additionally, (A) incorrectly uses *what* in place of *that.* Choice (C) is a run-on sentence that also misuses an apostrophe: *It's* is the contraction for *it is,* not the possessive of *it.* Choice (D) uses commas indiscriminately; it also misuses the apostrophe.

35. The correct answer is (B). In choice (A) the placement of the apostrophe is inappropriate; choices (C) and (D) use the plural, but there is only one company.

36. The correct answer is (D). Choices (A) and (C) are incorrect in use of the subject form *I* instead of the object of the preposition *me.* Choice (B) incorrectly uses the reflexive *myself.* Only I can address a letter to myself.

37. The correct answer is (C). Choice (A) incorrectly uses the plural verb form *have* with the singular subject *one.* (B) is awkward and wordy. (D) incorrectly changes the subject from *one of us* to *anyone.*

38. The correct answer is (C). (A) is wordy. In (B), the correct verb should be *have* in place of *leave.* In (D), the word *arose* should be *arisen.*

39. The correct answer is (D). The first three sentences lack parallel construction. All the words that modify *paper* must appear in the same form.

40. The correct answer is (D). The phrase *together with...* is extra information and not a part of the subject; therefore, both (A) and (B) represent similar errors of agreement. Choice (C) also presents disagreement in number between subject and verb, but in this case the compound subject, indicated by the use of the conjunction *and* requires a plural verb.

41. The correct answer is (B). Even if you do not recognize the root *manu* meaning *hand* and relating directly to *handbook,* you should have no trouble getting this question right. If you substitute each of the choices in the sentence, you will readily see that only one makes sense.

42. The correct answer is (A). Within the context of the sentence, the thought of a specified punishment for use, interpretation, or an edition of the rules does not make too much sense. *Fraction* gives a hint of *part,* but you must also contend with the negative prefix *in.* Since it is reasonable to expect punishment for negative behavior with relation to the rules, *violation,* which is the meaning of INFRACTION, is the proper answer.

43. The correct answer is (B). The prefix should help you narrow your choices. The prefix *re* meaning *back* or *again* narrows the choices to (A) or (B). To RESCIND is to *take back* or to *cancel.*

44. The correct answer is (D). First eliminate (C) since it does not make sense in the sentence. Your experience with the word *summons* may be with relation to *tickets* and *fines,* but tickets and fines have nothing to do with asking questions while taking a test. Even if you are unfamiliar with the word SUMMON, you should be able to choose *call* as the best synonym in this context.

45. The correct answer is (A). REPRISAL means injury done for injury received or *retaliation.*

46. The correct answer is (C). To RE-DUCE is to *make smaller* or to *lessen.*

47. The correct answer is (A). To IM-PAIR is to *make worse,* to *injure,* or to *weaken.*

48. The correct answer is (C). FIT-TING in this context means *suitable* or *appropriate.*

49. The correct answer is (A). The survey showed that of all subjects typing has helped most in business. It was also considered valuable by college students in their schoolwork.

50. The correct answer is (D). See the second sentence.

51. The correct answer is (B). According to the paragraph, the government can spend only what it obtains from the people. The government obtains money from the people by taxation. If the people are unwilling to pay taxes, the government has no source of funds.

52. The correct answer is (A). Step one in the job application process is often the application letter. If the letter is not effective, the applicant will not move on to the next step and job prospects will be greatly lessened.

53. The correct answer is (C). The second sentence states that direct lighting causes glare on the working surface.

54. The correct answer is (D). While all the answer choices are likely to be true, the answer suggested by the paragraph is that "white collar" workers work with their pencils and their minds rather than with their hands and machines.

55. The correct answer is (C). All the paragraph says is that office manuals are a necessity in large organizations.

Stenography

1. B	26. C	51. C	76. B	101. A
2. B	27. A	52. A	77. C	102. E
3. D	28. C	53. B	78. C	103. B
4. E	29. E	54. E	79. D	104. D
5. C	30. B	55. D	80. E	105. C
6. A	31. D	56. C	81. B	106. E
7. D	32. E	57. E	82. A	107. C
8. B	33. C	58. B	83. D	108. A
9. C	34. E	59. D	84. A	109. B
10. E	35. B	60. D	85. E	110. E
11. A	36. A	61. A	86. B	111. B
12. D	37. C	62. E	87. A	112. D
13. E	38. C	63. C	88. E	113. A
14. C	39. E	64. E	89. D	114. E
15. C	40. B	65. D	90. A	115. B
16. B	41. D	66. B	91. A	116. A
17. C	42. A	67. E	92. B	117. D
18. A	43. E	68. C	93. C	118. E
19. A	44. A	69. D	94. D	119. C
20. E	45. B	70. B	95. B	120. D
21. E	46. C	71. C	96. E	121. D
22. E	47. C	72. D	97. D	122. C
23. C	48. D	73. A	98. C	123. B
24. C	49. B	74. E	99. C	124. C
25. D	50. E	75. C	100. A	125. A

answers

Correctly Filled Transcript

In B/1 years B/2 D/3 a great E/4 in the C/5 for A/6 D/7 , not B/8 in C/9 E/10 but A/11 in D/12 E/13 agencies, both C/14 and C/15 . The high B/16 and C/17 schools in A/18 A/19 of the E/20 have E/21 E/22 this C/23 by C/24 complete D/25 courses. The C/26 A/27 C/28 of E/29 who are B/30 in these D/31 shows E/32 C/33 have E/34 B/35 of the A/36 C/37 for stenographers. A/38 C/39 E/40 to B/41 D/41 in A/42 E/43 must A/44 to take B/45 and to C/46 the C/47 with D/48 B/49 and E/50 .

The C/51 of A/52 at B/53 dictation is E/54 in D/55 C/56 is E/57 B/58 than D/59 of D/60 A/61 .

Thus, one E/62 had a C/63 E/64 in short-hand D/65 B/66 little E/67 in C/68 D/69 B/70 .

Skill in C/71 D/72 A/73 E/74 C/75 is of B/76 C/77 if the C/78 cannot D/79 E/80 the B/81 in A/82 D/83 .

A/84 A/85 E/86 B/87 a A/88 E/89 D/90 A/90 s/he A/91 to B/92 C/93 in a D/94 , and B/95 to the E/96 the D/97 of C/98 them in C/99 A/100 . For A/101 E/102 B/103 D/104 C/105 of E/106 and of C/107 is A/108 B/109 E/110 B/111 to D/112 dictation. In A/113 E/114 stenographer B/115 be B/116 D/117 E/118 of C/119 D/120 that D/121 most C/122 B/123 C/124 in A/125 work.

PRACTICE TEST 3: EXAM 911 ANSWER SHEET

1. Ⓐ Ⓑ Ⓒ Ⓓ Ⓔ	23. Ⓐ Ⓑ Ⓒ Ⓓ Ⓔ	45. Ⓐ Ⓑ Ⓒ Ⓓ Ⓔ	67. Ⓐ Ⓑ Ⓒ Ⓓ Ⓔ
2. Ⓐ Ⓑ Ⓒ Ⓓ Ⓔ	24. Ⓐ Ⓑ Ⓒ Ⓓ Ⓔ	46. Ⓐ Ⓑ Ⓒ Ⓓ Ⓔ	68. Ⓐ Ⓑ Ⓒ Ⓓ Ⓔ
3. Ⓐ Ⓑ Ⓒ Ⓓ Ⓔ	25. Ⓐ Ⓑ Ⓒ Ⓓ Ⓔ	47. Ⓐ Ⓑ Ⓒ Ⓓ Ⓔ	69. Ⓐ Ⓑ Ⓒ Ⓓ Ⓔ
4. Ⓐ Ⓑ Ⓒ Ⓓ Ⓔ	26. Ⓐ Ⓑ Ⓒ Ⓓ Ⓔ	48. Ⓐ Ⓑ Ⓒ Ⓓ Ⓔ	70. Ⓐ Ⓑ Ⓒ Ⓓ Ⓔ
5. Ⓐ Ⓑ Ⓒ Ⓓ Ⓔ	27. Ⓐ Ⓑ Ⓒ Ⓓ Ⓔ	49. Ⓐ Ⓑ Ⓒ Ⓓ Ⓔ	71. Ⓐ Ⓑ Ⓒ Ⓓ Ⓔ
6. Ⓐ Ⓑ Ⓒ Ⓓ Ⓔ	28. Ⓐ Ⓑ Ⓒ Ⓓ Ⓔ	50. Ⓐ Ⓑ Ⓒ Ⓓ Ⓔ	72. Ⓐ Ⓑ Ⓒ Ⓓ Ⓔ
7. Ⓐ Ⓑ Ⓒ Ⓓ Ⓔ	29. Ⓐ Ⓑ Ⓒ Ⓓ Ⓔ	51. Ⓐ Ⓑ Ⓒ Ⓓ Ⓔ	73. Ⓐ Ⓑ Ⓒ Ⓓ Ⓔ
8. Ⓐ Ⓑ Ⓒ Ⓓ Ⓔ	30. Ⓐ Ⓑ Ⓒ Ⓓ Ⓔ	52. Ⓐ Ⓑ Ⓒ Ⓓ Ⓔ	74. Ⓐ Ⓑ Ⓒ Ⓓ Ⓔ
9. Ⓐ Ⓑ Ⓒ Ⓓ Ⓔ	31. Ⓐ Ⓑ Ⓒ Ⓓ Ⓔ	53. Ⓐ Ⓑ Ⓒ Ⓓ Ⓔ	75. Ⓐ Ⓑ Ⓒ Ⓓ Ⓔ
10. Ⓐ Ⓑ Ⓒ Ⓓ Ⓔ	32. Ⓐ Ⓑ Ⓒ Ⓓ Ⓔ	54. Ⓐ Ⓑ Ⓒ Ⓓ Ⓔ	76. Ⓐ Ⓑ Ⓒ Ⓓ Ⓔ
11. Ⓐ Ⓑ Ⓒ Ⓓ Ⓔ	33. Ⓐ Ⓑ Ⓒ Ⓓ Ⓔ	55. Ⓐ Ⓑ Ⓒ Ⓓ Ⓔ	77. Ⓐ Ⓑ Ⓒ Ⓓ Ⓔ
12. Ⓐ Ⓑ Ⓒ Ⓓ Ⓔ	34. Ⓐ Ⓑ Ⓒ Ⓓ Ⓔ	56. Ⓐ Ⓑ Ⓒ Ⓓ Ⓔ	78. Ⓐ Ⓑ Ⓒ Ⓓ Ⓔ
13. Ⓐ Ⓑ Ⓒ Ⓓ Ⓔ	35. Ⓐ Ⓑ Ⓒ Ⓓ Ⓔ	57. Ⓐ Ⓑ Ⓒ Ⓓ Ⓔ	79. Ⓐ Ⓑ Ⓒ Ⓓ Ⓔ
14. Ⓐ Ⓑ Ⓒ Ⓓ Ⓔ	36. Ⓐ Ⓑ Ⓒ Ⓓ Ⓔ	58. Ⓐ Ⓑ Ⓒ Ⓓ Ⓔ	80. Ⓐ Ⓑ Ⓒ Ⓓ Ⓔ
15. Ⓐ Ⓑ Ⓒ Ⓓ Ⓔ	37. Ⓐ Ⓑ Ⓒ Ⓓ Ⓔ	59. Ⓐ Ⓑ Ⓒ Ⓓ Ⓔ	81. Ⓐ Ⓑ Ⓒ Ⓓ Ⓔ
16. Ⓐ Ⓑ Ⓒ Ⓓ Ⓔ	38. Ⓐ Ⓑ Ⓒ Ⓓ Ⓔ	60. Ⓐ Ⓑ Ⓒ Ⓓ Ⓔ	82. Ⓐ Ⓑ Ⓒ Ⓓ Ⓔ
17. Ⓐ Ⓑ Ⓒ Ⓓ Ⓔ	39. Ⓐ Ⓑ Ⓒ Ⓓ Ⓔ	61. Ⓐ Ⓑ Ⓒ Ⓓ Ⓔ	83. Ⓐ Ⓑ Ⓒ Ⓓ Ⓔ
18. Ⓐ Ⓑ Ⓒ Ⓓ Ⓔ	40. Ⓐ Ⓑ Ⓒ Ⓓ Ⓔ	62. Ⓐ Ⓑ Ⓒ Ⓓ Ⓔ	84. Ⓐ Ⓑ Ⓒ Ⓓ Ⓔ
19. Ⓐ Ⓑ Ⓒ Ⓓ Ⓔ	41. Ⓐ Ⓑ Ⓒ Ⓓ Ⓔ	63. Ⓐ Ⓑ Ⓒ Ⓓ Ⓔ	85. Ⓐ Ⓑ Ⓒ Ⓓ Ⓔ
20. Ⓐ Ⓑ Ⓒ Ⓓ Ⓔ	42. Ⓐ Ⓑ Ⓒ Ⓓ Ⓔ	64. Ⓐ Ⓑ Ⓒ Ⓓ Ⓔ	86. Ⓐ Ⓑ Ⓒ Ⓓ Ⓔ
21. Ⓐ Ⓑ Ⓒ Ⓓ Ⓔ	43. Ⓐ Ⓑ Ⓒ Ⓓ Ⓔ	65. Ⓐ Ⓑ Ⓒ Ⓓ Ⓔ	87. Ⓐ Ⓑ Ⓒ Ⓓ Ⓔ
22. Ⓐ Ⓑ Ⓒ Ⓓ Ⓔ	44. Ⓐ Ⓑ Ⓒ Ⓓ Ⓔ	66. Ⓐ Ⓑ Ⓒ Ⓓ Ⓔ	88. Ⓐ Ⓑ Ⓒ Ⓓ Ⓔ

Following Oral Instructions

25 MINUTES

> **Directions:** Give the following instructions to a friend and have him or her read them aloud to you at the rate of 80 words per minute. (Do NOT read aloud the words in parentheses.) Do NOT read them to yourself. Your friend will need a watch with a second hand. Listen carefully and do exactly what your friend tells you to do with the worksheet and with the answer sheet. Your friend will tell you some things to do with each item on the worksheet. After each set of instructions, your friend will give you time to mark your answer by darkening a circle on the answer sheet. Since B and D sound very much alike, your friend should say "B as in baker" when he or she means B and "D as in dog" when he or she means D.

Before proceeding further, tear out the worksheet on page 193. Then hand this book to your friend.

To the Person Who Is to Read the Instructions: The instructions are to be read at the rate of 80 words per minute. Do not read aloud the material that is in parentheses. Once you have begun the test itself, do not repeat any instructions. The next three paragraphs consist of approximately 120 words. Read these three paragraphs aloud to the candidate in about one and one-half minutes. You may reread these three paragraphs as often as necessary to establish an 80-words-per-minute reading speed.

Read Aloud to the Candidate

On the job you will have to listen to directions and then do what you have been told to do. In this test, I will read instructions to you. Try to understand them as I read them; I cannot repeat them. Once we begin, you may not ask any questions until the end of the test.

On the job you won't have to deal with pictures, numbers, and letters like those in the test, but you will have to listen to instructions and follow them. We are using this test to see how well you can follow instructions.

You are to mark your test booklet according to the instructions that I'll read to you. After each set of instructions, I'll give you time to record your answers on the separate answer sheet.

The actual test begins now.

Look at line 1 on your worksheet. Each number represents a length of rope. (Pause slightly.) Draw two lines under the number that represents the longest length of rope. (Pause 2 seconds.) Now, on your answer sheet, find the number under which you just drew two lines and darken B as in baker for that number. (Pause 5 seconds.)

Look at line 1 again. (Pause slightly.) Find the number that represents the shortest length of rope and draw one wavy line above that number. (Pause 2 seconds.) Now, on your answer sheet, darken space A for the number over which you just drew the wavy line. (Pause 5 seconds.)

Look at line 2 on your worksheet. The number in each carton represents the number of boxes of soap powder in the carton. (Pause slightly.) Write the letter D as in dog in the carton that is closest to empty. (Pause 2 seconds.) Now, on your answer sheet, darken the space for the number-letter combination in the carton you just wrote in. (Pause 5 seconds.)

Look at line 3 on your worksheet. (Pause slightly.) If Christmas is always on a Thursday, write the letter C next to the first number on line 3; if not, write the letter E next to the second number. (Pause 5 seconds.) Now, on your answer sheet, darken the space for the number next to which you just wrote a letter. (Pause 5 seconds.)

Look at line 3 again. (Pause slightly.) Write the second letter of the alphabet next to the lowest number on line 3. (Pause 2 seconds.) Now, on your answer sheet, darken the space for the number-letter combination you just wrote. (Pause 5 seconds.)

Look at line 4 on your worksheet. (Pause slightly.) Count the number of letters in the word and write the number of letters at the end of line 4. (Pause 2 seconds.) Now, on your answer sheet, darken letter C for the number you just wrote. (Pause 5 seconds.)

Look at line 4 again. (Pause slightly.) Draw a circle around the fifth letter in the word. (Pause 2 seconds.) Now, on your answer sheet, find number 64 and darken the space for the letter you just circled. (Pause 5 seconds.)

Look at line 5 on your worksheet. The numbers represent days of the month. Floors are to be washed on odd-numbered days. (Pause slightly.) Draw one line under the number of each day on which floors should be washed. (Pause 5 seconds.) Now, on your answer sheet, darken letter D as in dog for each number under which you drew a line. (Pause 10 seconds.)

Look at line 6 on your worksheet. (Pause slightly.) Write the letter C on the line in the bucket with the highest number. (Pause 2 seconds.) Now, on your answer sheet, darken the space for the number-letter combination in that bucket. (Pause 5 seconds.)

Look at line 6 again. (Pause slightly.) Write the letter B as in baker on the line in the middle bucket. (Pause 2 seconds.) Now, on your answer sheet, darken the space for the number-letter combination in that bucket. (Pause 5 seconds.)

Look at line 7 on your worksheet. (Pause slightly.) Count the number of times the letter A appears on line 7 and write that number at the end of the line. (Pause 2 seconds.) Add 10 to the number you just wrote. Now, on your answer sheet, find the number that represents the sum of the number you wrote plus 10 and darken space E for that number. (Pause 10 seconds.)

Look at line 8 on your worksheet. Each item on line 8 represents a key code. Only keys with odd-numbered codes open the restroom doors in the post office. (Pause slightly.) Draw two lines under the code for each key that will open a restroom door. (Pause 5 seconds.) Now, on your answer sheet, darken each space that represents a key that will open a restroom. (Pause 15 seconds.)

Look at line 9 on your worksheet. Each box contains a different kind of screw. (Pause slightly.) The box with the higher number holds wood screws, and the box with the lower number holds sheet-metal screws. (Pause 2 seconds.) Write the letter A in the box that holds sheet-metal screws. (Pause 2 seconds.) Write the letter E in the box that holds wood screws. (Pause 2 seconds.) Now, on your answer sheet, darken the spaces for the number-letter combinations in the boxes. (Pause 10 seconds.)

Look at line 10 on your worksheet. (Pause slightly.) If brooms are used for sweeping floors, write B as in baker in the triangle. If not, write D as in dog in the square. (Pause 2 seconds.) Now, on your answer sheet, darken the space for the number-letter combination in the figure you just wrote in. (Pause 5 seconds.)

Look at line 10 again. (Pause slightly.) Write the letter C in every figure that has no angles. (Pause 5 seconds.) Now, on your answer sheet, darken the number-letter combination in each figure that you just wrote in. (Pause 10 seconds.)

Look at line 11 on your worksheet. (Pause slightly.) The third mailbox on line 11 has a broken lock and must be reported for repair. Write the letter D as in dog on the line in the broken mailbox. (Pause 2 seconds.) Now, on your answer sheet, darken the space for the number-letter combination in the mailbox with the broken lock. (Pause 5 seconds.)

Look at line 11 again. (Pause slightly.) The first mailbox belongs to Mr. and Mrs. Dana. Write the second letter of the Danas' name in their mailbox. (Pause 2 seconds.) Now, on your answer sheet, darken the space for the number-letter combination in the Danas' mailbox. (Pause 5 seconds.)

Look at line 12 on your worksheet. (Pause slightly.) Write the number of minutes in an hour next to the fourth letter of the alphabet. (Pause 2 seconds.) Now, on your answer sheet, darken the space for the number-letter combination you just wrote. (Pause 5 seconds.)

Look at the brooms on line 13 on your worksheet. (Pause slightly.) Write the first letter of the word "broom" on the line under the first broom. (Pause 2 seconds.) Now, on your answer sheet, darken the space for the number-letter combination under the broom. (Pause 5 seconds.)

Look at the brooms on line 13 again. (Pause slightly.) Write the letter E on the line under the broom that is different from the other brooms. (Pause 2 seconds.) Now, on your answer sheet, darken the space for the number-letter combination under the broom. (Pause 5 seconds.)

Worksheet

> **Directions:** Listen carefully to each set of instructions and mark each item on this worksheet as directed. Then complete each question by marking the answer sheet as directed. For each direction you will darken the space for a number-letter combination. Should you fall behind and miss an instruction, don't get excited. Let that one go and listen for the next one. If, when you start to darken a space for a number, you find that you have already darkened another space for that number, either erase the first mark and darken the space for the new combination or let the first mark stay and do not darken a space for the new combination. Write with a pencil that has a clean eraser. When you finish, you should have no more than one space darkened for each number. Correct answers are on pages 195–197.

1.   3ft.   5yds.   10 in.   7 yds.

2. | 6__ | | 2__ | | 12__ | | 3__ |

3.   51___   77___   46___

4.   I N F L A M M A B L E __

5.   19   24   25   26   27   30

6.   55__   87__   42__   18__   63__

7.   G A D A G G A A D __

8.   83A   50C   59E   37B   32C   69C

9.    50__   12__

10. 79__   73__   30__   19__   40__

11.   75__   69__   56__   28__
       •   •   •   •

12.   __D   __B   __A   __E   __C

13.
     53__   21__   33__   85__   46__

ANSWER KEY

Correctly Filled Worksheet

1.   3ft.   5yds.   10 in.   <u>7 yds.</u>

2. $\boxed{6\_\_}$ $\boxed{2\,D}$ $\boxed{12\_\_}$ $\boxed{3\_\_}$

3.   51___   77 *E*   46 *B*

4.   I N F L (A) M M A B L E   ⊔

5.   <u>19</u> 24 <u>25</u> 26 <u>27</u> 30

6.   55__   87 *C*   42 *B*   18__   63__

7.   G A D A G G A A D   <u>4</u>

8. <u>83A</u>   50C   <u>59E</u>   <u>37B</u>   32C   <u>69C</u>

9.

10.

11.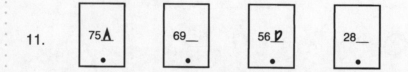

12. <u>**60**</u> D   ___B   ___A   ___E   ___C

13.

Correctly Filled Answer Sheet

1. Ⓐ Ⓑ Ⓒ Ⓓ Ⓔ
2. Ⓐ Ⓑ ● Ⓓ Ⓔ
3. Ⓐ Ⓑ Ⓒ Ⓓ Ⓔ
4. Ⓐ Ⓑ Ⓒ Ⓓ Ⓔ
5. Ⓐ Ⓑ Ⓒ Ⓓ Ⓔ
6. Ⓐ Ⓑ Ⓒ Ⓓ Ⓔ
7. Ⓐ ● Ⓒ Ⓓ Ⓔ
8. Ⓐ Ⓑ Ⓒ Ⓓ Ⓔ
9. Ⓐ Ⓑ Ⓒ Ⓓ Ⓔ
10. ● Ⓑ Ⓒ Ⓓ Ⓔ
11. Ⓐ Ⓑ ● Ⓓ Ⓔ
12. Ⓐ Ⓑ Ⓒ Ⓓ Ⓔ
13. Ⓐ Ⓑ Ⓒ Ⓓ Ⓔ
14. Ⓐ Ⓑ Ⓒ Ⓓ ●
15. Ⓐ Ⓑ Ⓒ Ⓓ Ⓔ
16. Ⓐ Ⓑ Ⓒ Ⓓ Ⓔ
17. Ⓐ Ⓑ Ⓒ Ⓓ Ⓔ
18. Ⓐ Ⓑ Ⓒ Ⓓ Ⓔ
19. Ⓐ Ⓑ Ⓒ ● Ⓔ
20. Ⓐ Ⓑ Ⓒ Ⓓ Ⓔ
21. Ⓐ Ⓑ Ⓒ Ⓓ Ⓔ
22. ● Ⓑ Ⓒ Ⓓ Ⓔ

23. Ⓐ Ⓑ Ⓒ Ⓓ Ⓔ
24. Ⓐ Ⓑ Ⓒ Ⓓ Ⓔ
25. Ⓐ Ⓑ Ⓒ ● Ⓔ
26. Ⓐ Ⓑ Ⓒ Ⓓ Ⓔ
27. Ⓐ Ⓑ Ⓒ ● Ⓔ
28. Ⓐ Ⓑ Ⓒ Ⓓ Ⓔ
29. Ⓐ Ⓑ Ⓒ Ⓓ Ⓔ
30. Ⓐ Ⓑ ● Ⓓ Ⓔ
31. Ⓐ Ⓑ Ⓒ Ⓓ Ⓔ
32. Ⓐ Ⓑ Ⓒ Ⓓ Ⓔ
33. Ⓐ Ⓑ Ⓒ Ⓓ ●
34. Ⓐ Ⓑ Ⓒ Ⓓ Ⓔ
35. Ⓐ Ⓑ Ⓒ Ⓓ Ⓔ
36. Ⓐ Ⓑ Ⓒ Ⓓ Ⓔ
37. Ⓐ ● Ⓒ Ⓓ Ⓔ
38. Ⓐ Ⓑ Ⓒ Ⓓ Ⓔ
39. Ⓐ Ⓑ Ⓒ Ⓓ Ⓔ
40. Ⓐ Ⓑ ● Ⓓ Ⓔ
41. Ⓐ Ⓑ Ⓒ Ⓓ Ⓔ
42. Ⓐ ● Ⓒ Ⓓ Ⓔ
43. Ⓐ Ⓑ Ⓒ Ⓓ Ⓔ
44. Ⓐ Ⓑ Ⓒ Ⓓ Ⓔ

45. Ⓐ Ⓑ Ⓒ Ⓓ Ⓔ
46. Ⓐ ● Ⓒ Ⓓ Ⓔ
47. Ⓐ Ⓑ Ⓒ Ⓓ Ⓔ
48. Ⓐ Ⓑ Ⓒ Ⓓ Ⓔ
49. Ⓐ Ⓑ Ⓒ Ⓓ Ⓔ
50. Ⓐ Ⓑ Ⓒ Ⓓ ●
51. Ⓐ Ⓑ Ⓒ Ⓓ Ⓔ
52. Ⓐ Ⓑ Ⓒ Ⓓ Ⓔ
53. Ⓐ ● Ⓒ Ⓓ Ⓔ
54. Ⓐ Ⓑ Ⓒ Ⓓ Ⓔ
55. Ⓐ Ⓑ Ⓒ Ⓓ Ⓔ
56. Ⓐ Ⓑ Ⓒ ● Ⓔ
57. Ⓐ Ⓑ Ⓒ Ⓓ Ⓔ
58. Ⓐ Ⓑ Ⓒ Ⓓ Ⓔ
59. Ⓐ Ⓑ Ⓒ Ⓓ ●
60. Ⓐ Ⓑ Ⓒ ● Ⓔ
61. Ⓐ Ⓑ Ⓒ Ⓓ Ⓔ
62. Ⓐ Ⓑ Ⓒ Ⓓ Ⓔ
63. Ⓐ Ⓑ Ⓒ Ⓓ Ⓔ
64. ● Ⓑ Ⓒ Ⓓ Ⓔ
65. Ⓐ Ⓑ Ⓒ Ⓓ Ⓔ
66. Ⓐ Ⓑ Ⓒ Ⓓ Ⓔ

67. Ⓐ Ⓑ Ⓒ Ⓓ Ⓔ
68. Ⓐ Ⓑ Ⓒ Ⓓ Ⓔ
69. Ⓐ Ⓑ ● Ⓓ Ⓔ
70. Ⓐ Ⓑ Ⓒ Ⓓ Ⓔ
71. Ⓐ Ⓑ Ⓒ Ⓓ Ⓔ
72. Ⓐ Ⓑ Ⓒ Ⓓ Ⓔ
73. Ⓐ ● Ⓒ Ⓓ Ⓔ
74. Ⓐ Ⓑ Ⓒ Ⓓ Ⓔ
75. ● Ⓑ Ⓒ Ⓓ Ⓔ
76. Ⓐ Ⓑ Ⓒ Ⓓ Ⓔ
77. Ⓐ Ⓑ Ⓒ Ⓓ ●
78. Ⓐ Ⓑ Ⓒ Ⓓ Ⓔ
79. Ⓐ Ⓑ ● Ⓓ Ⓔ
80. Ⓐ Ⓑ Ⓒ Ⓓ Ⓔ
81. Ⓐ Ⓑ Ⓒ Ⓓ Ⓔ
82. Ⓐ Ⓑ Ⓒ Ⓓ Ⓔ
83. ● Ⓑ Ⓒ Ⓓ Ⓔ
84. Ⓐ Ⓑ Ⓒ Ⓓ Ⓔ
85. Ⓐ Ⓑ Ⓒ Ⓓ Ⓔ
86. Ⓐ Ⓑ Ⓒ Ⓓ Ⓔ
87. Ⓐ Ⓑ ● Ⓓ Ⓔ
88. Ⓐ Ⓑ Ⓒ Ⓓ Ⓔ

answers

PRACTICE TEST 4: EXAM 91 ANSWER SHEET

Part A

1. _____

2. _____

   _____

3. _____

   _____

4. _____

   _____

5. _____

   _____

6. _____

   _____

7. _____

   _____

8. _____

   _____

9. _____

   _____

10.

11. _____

_____

12. _____

_____

13. _____

_____

14. _____

_____

15. _____

_____

16. _____

_____

17. _____

18. _____

19. _____

20. _____

21. _____

22. _____

CHART A

	Truck License Number	Kind of Service	Odometer Reading When Serviced
	835 XYZ	tune up	22,305
23.			
24.			

CHART B

	Driver ID Number	Truck License Number	Odometer Reading
	8723	997 IUP	88,141
25.			
26.			

CHART C

	Driver ID Number	Odometer Reading When Taken Out	Odometer Reading When Returned
	3406	12,562	12,591
27.			
28.			

CHART D

	Vehicle License Number	Kind of Service	Serviceperson ID Number
	592 TJD	grease job	8452
29.			
30.			

CHART E

	Truck License Number	Driver ID Number	Serviceperson ID Number
	042 RVB	5842	4307
31.			
32.			

33. _____

_____

34. _____

_____

35. _____

_____

36. _____

37. _____

38. _____

_____

39. _____

_____

40. _____

_____

Part B

41. Ⓐ Ⓑ Ⓒ Ⓓ Ⓔ	**49.** Ⓐ Ⓑ Ⓒ Ⓓ Ⓔ	**57.** Ⓐ Ⓑ Ⓒ Ⓓ Ⓔ	**65.** Ⓐ Ⓑ Ⓒ Ⓓ Ⓔ	**73.** Ⓐ Ⓑ Ⓒ Ⓓ Ⓔ
42. Ⓐ Ⓑ Ⓒ Ⓓ Ⓔ	**50.** Ⓐ Ⓑ Ⓒ Ⓓ Ⓔ	**58.** Ⓐ Ⓑ Ⓒ Ⓓ Ⓔ	**66.** Ⓐ Ⓑ Ⓒ Ⓓ Ⓔ	**74.** Ⓐ Ⓑ Ⓒ Ⓓ Ⓔ
43. Ⓐ Ⓑ Ⓒ Ⓓ Ⓔ	**51.** Ⓐ Ⓑ Ⓒ Ⓓ Ⓔ	**59.** Ⓐ Ⓑ Ⓒ Ⓓ Ⓔ	**67.** Ⓐ Ⓑ Ⓒ Ⓓ Ⓔ	**75.** Ⓐ Ⓑ Ⓒ Ⓓ Ⓔ
44. Ⓐ Ⓑ Ⓒ Ⓓ Ⓔ	**52.** Ⓐ Ⓑ Ⓒ Ⓓ Ⓔ	**60.** Ⓐ Ⓑ Ⓒ Ⓓ Ⓔ	**68.** Ⓐ Ⓑ Ⓒ Ⓓ Ⓔ	**76.** Ⓐ Ⓑ Ⓒ Ⓓ Ⓔ
45. Ⓐ Ⓑ Ⓒ Ⓓ Ⓔ	**53.** Ⓐ Ⓑ Ⓒ Ⓓ Ⓔ	**61.** Ⓐ Ⓑ Ⓒ Ⓓ Ⓔ	**69.** Ⓐ Ⓑ Ⓒ Ⓓ Ⓔ	**77.** Ⓐ Ⓑ Ⓒ Ⓓ Ⓔ
46. Ⓐ Ⓑ Ⓒ Ⓓ Ⓔ	**54.** Ⓐ Ⓑ Ⓒ Ⓓ Ⓔ	**62.** Ⓐ Ⓑ Ⓒ Ⓓ Ⓔ	**70.** Ⓐ Ⓑ Ⓒ Ⓓ Ⓔ	**78.** Ⓐ Ⓑ Ⓒ Ⓓ Ⓔ
47. Ⓐ Ⓑ Ⓒ Ⓓ Ⓔ	**55.** Ⓐ Ⓑ Ⓒ Ⓓ Ⓔ	**63.** Ⓐ Ⓑ Ⓒ Ⓓ Ⓔ	**71.** Ⓐ Ⓑ Ⓒ Ⓓ Ⓔ	**79.** Ⓐ Ⓑ Ⓒ Ⓓ Ⓔ
48. Ⓐ Ⓑ Ⓒ Ⓓ Ⓔ	**56.** Ⓐ Ⓑ Ⓒ Ⓓ Ⓔ	**64.** Ⓐ Ⓑ Ⓒ Ⓓ Ⓔ	**72.** Ⓐ Ⓑ Ⓒ Ⓓ Ⓔ	**80.** Ⓐ Ⓑ Ⓒ Ⓓ Ⓔ

Part A

40 QUESTIONS • 60 MINUTES

> **Directions:** Read the questions carefully. Be sure you know what the
> questions are about and then answer each question. Write or draw your
> answers on the separate answer sheet for Part A.

Picture 1

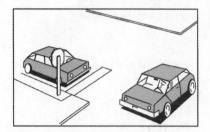

1. How many vehicles are shown in the picture?

2. What is happening in this picture?

Picture 2

3. What does the driver see in his rearview mirror? Be as complete as
   possible in your description. When you answer the questions in Part B,
   you may not look back at the pictures.

Picture 3

4. Describe the man on the left. Take special note of his seat belt.

5. Describe the man on the right.

Picture 4

6. If you come upon the scene shown in Picture 4 as you are driving along the road, what must you do?

Picture 5

7. What are the vehicles in picture 5 doing?

Picture 6

8. How is the sign on the left related to the vehicle on the right? What does it mean?

Picture 7

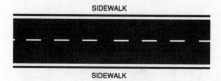

9. The roadway in Picture 7 is a

   (A) four-lane superhighway
   (B) no-passing zone
   (C) two-way street
   (D) single-lane street

10. On your answer sheet, draw arrows in the roadway indicating the direction of traffic flow.

Picture 8

11. Write as complete a description as you can of the objects and activities in Picture 8.

Picture 9

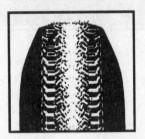

12. Describe the pattern of wear on this tire.

Picture 10

13. The meaning of this sign is

    (A) no parking
    (B) no truck parking
    (C) no trucks
    (D) trucks only

Picture 11

14. What should you look for when you see this sign?

Picture 12

15. What is the boy doing?

16. What else is happening in Picture 12?

Picture 13

17. The purpose of this sign is to caution you against

    (A) a winding road
    (B) drunk drivers
    (C) a road that may be slippery when wet
    (D) a steep hill

practice test

Picture 14

18. The words on this sign mean the same as

   (A) Dead End, No Exit
   (B) One Way Traffic
   (C) No U Turn, Keep Out
   (D) Special Parking Rules Today, Do Not Park Here

Picture 15

19. What is the vehicle in the picture?

20. Who are the passengers?

Question 21 is about words that might appear on a traffic sign. Decide which line—A, B, C, or D—means most nearly the same as the first line, and write the letter of that line on the answer sheet.

21. Bridge Freezes Before Roadway

   (A) Bridge May Be Icy
   (B) Detour—Bridge Under Repair
   (C) Yield to Road Maintenance Crews
   (D) Cold Weather Forecast for Tonight

Picture 16

22. The words on this sign mean that

(A) 500 people are working in the road

(B) for the next 1000 feet, people will be working in the road

(C) in 1000 feet, expect to find people working in the road

(D) please help the people working in the road for the next 1000 feet

Questions 23 and 24 have to do with filling in a chart. You are given the following information to put in Chart A.

Truck, license number 835 XZY, had a tune up at odometer reading 22,305.

Truck, license number 673 PUR, received a new fuel pump at odometer reading 67,422.

Truck, license number 441 RTG, had an oil change at odometer reading 46,098.

The information for the first truck has already been filled in. For question 23, write the information for the second truck in the proper columns in Chart A on the answer sheet. For question 24, write the information for the third truck in the proper columns in Chart A on the answer sheet.

Questions 25 and 26 have to do with filling in another chart. You are given the following information to put in Chart B.

Driver, ID number 8723, took truck license number 997 IUP at odometer reading 88,141.

Driver, ID number 6309, took truck license number 534 TRE at odometer reading 35,790.

Driver, ID number 7342, took truck license number 256 TAE at odometer reading 56,798.

The information for the first driver has already been filled in. For question 25, write the information for the second driver in the proper columns in Chart B on the answer sheet. For question 26, write the information for the third driver in the proper columns in Chart B on the answer sheet.

Questions 27 and 28 have to do with filling in another chart. You are given the following information to put in Chart C.

Driver, ID number 3406, took his Jeep at odometer reading 12,562 and returned it at odometer reading 12,591.

Driver, ID number 9845, took his Jeep at odometer reading 54,970 and returned it at odometer reading 54,997.

Driver, ID number 4785, took her Jeep at odometer reading 43,054 and returned it at odometer reading 43,086.

The information for the first driver has already been filled in. For question 27, write the information for the second driver in the proper columns in Chart C on the answer sheet. For question 28, write the information for the third driver in the proper columns in Chart C on the answer sheet.

Questions 29 and 30 have to do with filling in another chart. You are given the following information to put in Chart D.

Vehicle license number 592 TJD had a grease job by mechanic ID number 8452.

Vehicle license number 447 IKT had its carburetor adjusted by serviceperson ID number 7092.

Vehicle license number 837 PRE had a tire changed by serviceperson ID number 6052.

The information for the first vehicle has already been filled in. For question 29, write the information for the second vehicle in the proper columns in Chart D on the answer sheet. For question 30, write the information for the third vehicle in the proper columns in Chart D on the answer sheet.

Questions 31 and 32 have to do with filling in one more chart. You are given the following information to put in Chart E.

Truck license number 042 RVB is to be driven into the yard by driver ID number 5842 and turned over to serviceperson ID number 4307 for service.

Truck license number 759 YUX is to be driven into the yard by driver ID number 8372 and turned over to serviceperson ID number 3987 for service.

Truck license number 943 WCG is to be driven into the yard by driver ID number 6241 and turned over to serviceperson ID number 4273 for service.

The information for the first truck has already been filled in. For question 31, write the information for the second truck in the proper columns in Chart E on the answer sheet. For question 32, write the information for the third truck in the proper columns in Chart E on the answer sheet.

Questions 33 and 34 are about pictures of lane-control lights. Each picture has a letter. You are to tell what each picture shows by writing a short description of the picture on the answer sheet.

X

Y

33. What does Picture X show?

34. What does Picture Y show?

Picture 17

35. Describe Picture 17 in the space on the answer sheet.

Picture 18

36. The word on this sign means that the driver should

(A) stop
(B) turn around
(C) let merging traffic enter the roadway
(D) look carefully before proceeding

Picture 19

37. The meaning of this sign is

    (A) Right Turn Only
    (B) No Right Turn
    (C) No Left Turn
    (D) Left Turn Only

Picture 20

38. Describe what is happening in this picture.

Picture 21

39. What is happening in this picture? Write your description in the space on the answer sheet.

Picture 22

40. The driver who approaches this sign must

    (A) stop
    (B) slow down and look both ways
    (C) turn around
    (D) back up

Part B

40 QUESTIONS • 60 MINUTES

> **Directions:** To answer the questions in Part B, you must use the answers from Part A. Refer to your answer sheet for Part A to answer these questions. Mark the answers to questions 41 to 80 on the Part B answer sheet. You may not look back at the pictures while answering the questions in Part B.

Question 41 below is about question 1, and question 42 below is about question 2.

41. For number 41 on the answer sheet, mark space

   (A) if there are no vehicles in the picture
   (B) if there is one vehicle in the picture
   (C) if there are two vehicles in the picture
   (D) if there are three vehicles in the picture
   (E) if there are four vehicles in the picture

42. For number 42 on the answer sheet, mark space

   (A) if there is about to be a crash
   (B) if a vehicle just went through a stop sign
   (C) if a car is driving on the wrong side of the street
   (D) if there are no vehicles in the intersection
   (E) if one car has stopped at a stop sign

Question 43 is about question 3.

43. For number 43 on the answer sheet, mark space

   (A) if a motorcycle is passing a car
   (B) if a motorcycle is directly behind a car
   (C) if a truck is behind a car
   (D) if two motorcycles are in the left lane
   (E) if there is nothing in the rearview mirror

Question 44 below is about question 4, and question 45 below is about question 5.

44. For number 44 on the answer sheet, mark space

   (A) if the man is likely to suffer internal injuries in case of a crash
   (B) if the man is wearing his seat belt properly
   (C) if the man is well protected in case of an auto crash
   (D) if the man is wearing his seat belt across his right shoulder
   (E) if the man is likely to be thrown from the car in an accident

45. For number 45 on the answer sheet, mark space

   (A) if the man's shoulder strap goes under his tie
   (B) if the man's lap strap is unfastened
   (C) if the man is likely to be thrown through the windshield in a crash
   (D) if the man is wearing his seat belt and shoulder harness properly
   (E) if the man is wearing a jacket

Question 46 below is about question 6.

46. For number 46 on the answer sheet, mark space

   (A) if you should blow your horn
   (B) if you should get out of your car and move the barrier
   (C) if you should come to a full stop and wait
   (D) if you should accelerate and continue
   (E) if you should stop, look, and proceed

Question 47 below is about question 7.

47. For number 47 on the answer sheet, mark space

   (A) if a car is about to hit a pedestrian
   (B) if a person is jaywalking
   (C) if a police officer is directing traffic
   (D) if a cyclist is going the wrong way on a one-way street
   (E) if a woman and child are crossing in the crosswalk

Question 48 below is about question 8.

48. For number 48 on the answer sheet, mark space

   (A) if the sign should be blue and orange
   (B) if the sign signifies that this is a slow-moving vehicle
   (C) if the sign means "pass when safe"
   (D) if the sign should be worn on the driver's back
   (E) if the sign means that you should yield the right of way to the vehicle to which it is attached

For number 49 on the answer sheet, mark the space that has the same letter as the letter you wrote on the answer line for question 9.

Question 50 below is about question 10.

50. For number 50 on the answer sheet, mark space

   (A) if the arrow in one lane points in one direction and the arrow in the other lane points in the opposite direction
   (B) if the arrows in both lanes point to the right
   (C) if the arrows in both lanes point to the left
   (D) if there are arrows pointing in both directions in both lanes
   (E) if there is an arrow in only one lane

Question 51 below is about question 11.

51. For number 51 on the answer sheet, mark space

   (A) if it is raining
   (B) if there is one balloon on the ground
   (C) if there are four balloons
   (D) if there is heavy road traffic
   (E) if it would be wise for the motorist to pull over to the side of the road to watch the show

Question 52 below is about question 12.

52. For number 52 on the answer sheet, mark space

   (A) if the wear on the tire indicates the effect of overinflation
   (B) if the wear on the tire indicates the effect of excessive caster
   (C) if the wear on the tire indicates the effect of improper balance
   (D) if the wear on the tire indicates the effect of underinflation
   (E) if the wear on the tire indicates the effect of toe-out

For number 53 on the answer sheet, mark the space that has the same letter as the letter you wrote on the answer line for question 13.

Question 54 below is about question 14.

54. For number 54 on the answer sheet, mark space

   (A) if you should look for hitchhikers
   (B) if you should look for schoolchildren
   (C) if you should look for a garage sale
   (D) if you should watch out for a flagman
   (E) if you should watch for deaf pedestrians

Question 55 below is about question 15, and question 56 below is about question 16.

55. For number 55 on the answer sheet, mark space

   (A) if a little boy is running across the street
   (B) if a little boy is sleeping
   (C) if a little boy is helping an old lady cross the street
   (D) if a little boy is lying in the street
   (E) if a little boy is getting out of the car

56. For number 56 on the answer sheet, mark space

   (A) if an ambulance has just pulled up
   (B) if a person is getting out of the car
   (C) if there has been a hit-and-run accident
   (D) if a crowd is gathering around the little boy
   (E) if a woman is crying

For number 57 on the answer sheet, mark the space that has the same letter as the letter you wrote on the answer line for question 17.

For number 58 on the answer sheet, mark the space that has the same letter as the letter you wrote on the answer line for question 18.

Question 59 below is about question 19, and question 60 below is about question 20.

59. For number 59 on the answer sheet, mark space

   (A) if the vehicle is a taxicab
   (B) if the vehicle is a bus
   (C) if the vehicle is a tractor-trailer
   (D) if the vehicle is a farm tractor
   (E) if the vehicle is a Jeep

60. For number 60 on the answer sheet, mark space

   (A) if the passengers are schoolchildren
   (B) if the passengers are campers
   (C) if the passengers are farmers
   (D) if the passengers are military personnel
   (E) if the passengers are adults

For number 61 on the answer sheet, mark the space that has the same letter as the letter you wrote on the answer line for question 21.

For number 62 on the answer sheet, mark the space that has the same letter as the letter you wrote on the answer line for question 22.

practice test

Questions 63 and 64 below are about Chart A, which you filled in. Mark on the answer sheet the letter of the answer.

63. What is the license number of the truck that received a new fuel pump? Look at what you wrote on the chart. Do not try to answer from memory.

    (A) 673 PUR
    (B) 835 XZY
    (C) 441 RTG
    (D) 637 RUP

64. At what odometer reading did truck 441 RTG have its oil changed?

    (A) 46,908
    (B) 64,809
    (C) 46,098
    (D) 46,089

Questions 65 and 66 below are about Chart B, which you filled in. Look at what you wrote on the chart and mark the answer sheet with the letter of the correct answer.

65. What was the ID number of the driver who took truck license number 534 TRE?

    (A) 6390
    (B) 6309
    (C) 7342
    (D) 7243

66. At what odometer reading did driver number 7342 take out his truck?

    (A) 56,798
    (B) 88,141
    (C) 35,790
    (D) 65,798

Questions 67 and 68 below are about Chart C, which you filled in. Look at what you wrote on the chart and mark the answer sheet with the letter of the correct answer.

67. What was the odometer reading when driver number 9845 returned his Jeep?

    (A) 54,997
    (B) 54,970
    (C) 15,591
    (D) 43,086

68. What was the odometer reading when driver number 4785 took out her Jeep?

    (A) 12,562
    (B) 43,086
    (C) 54,970
    (D) 43,054

practice test

Questions 69 and 70 below are about Chart D, which you filled in. Look at what you wrote on the chart and mark the answer sheet with the letter of the correct answer.

69. What service was performed on vehicle license number 447 IKT?

(A) lubrication
(B) replacement of air hose
(C) carburetor adjustment
(D) tire change

70. What was the ID number of the serviceperson who changed a tire?

(A) 837 PRE
(B) 6052
(C) 6025
(D) 7092

Questions 71 and 72 below are about Chart E, which you filled in. Look at what you wrote on the chart and mark the answer sheet with the letter of the correct answer.

71. What was the ID number of the serviceperson to whom driver ID number 8372 turned over her truck?

(A) 3978
(B) 3987
(C) 3897
(D) 3879

72. What was the ID number of the driver who turned over her truck to serviceperson ID 4273?

(A) 943 WCG
(B) 5842
(C) 959 YUX
(D) 6241

Question 73 below is about question 33 under Picture X, and question 74 below is about question 34 under Picture Y.

73. For number 73 on the answer sheet, mark space

(A) if there are no lanes open in Picture X
(B) if there is only one lane open in Picture X
(C) if there are only two lanes open in Picture X
(D) if there are only three lanes open in Picture X
(E) if there is only one lane closed in Picture X

74. For number 74 on the answer sheet, mark space

(A) if there is only one lane closed in Picture Y
(B) if there are only two lanes closed in Picture Y
(C) if there are only three lanes closed in Picture Y
(D) if there are only four lanes closed in Picture Y
(E) if there are only five lanes closed in Picture Y

Question 75 below is about question 35.

75. For number 75 on the answer sheet, mark space

    (A) if drivers approaching from the right cannot see any traffic signals
    (B) if drivers approaching this light straight ahead have a green arrow pointing to the right
    (C) if drivers approaching from the left are guided by five different traffic signals
    (D) if drivers approaching this light straight ahead have a red arrow pointing to the left
    (E) if drivers approaching this light straight ahead have a green arrow pointing to the left

For number 76 on the answer sheet, mark the space that has the same letter as the letter you wrote on the answer line for question 36.

For number 77 on the answer sheet, mark the space that has the same letter as the letter you wrote on the answer line for question 37.

Question 78 below is about question 38.

78. For number 78 on the answer sheet, mark space

    (A) if a person is being pushed in a wheelchair
    (B) if there has been a traffic accident
    (C) if two men are putting a person into an ambulance
    (D) if a police officer is directing traffic
    (E) if a woman is wringing her hands in despair

Question 79 below is about question 39.

79. For number 79 on the answer sheet, mark space

    (A) if there is a mail truck in the picture
    (B) if a car is about to enter an intersection
    (C) if three people are walking abreast
    (D) if children are playing in the street
    (E) if a man is walking with a woman

For number 80 on the answer sheet, mark the space that has the same letter as the letter you wrote on the answer line for question 40.

ANSWER KEY AND EXPLANATIONS

Part A

1. Two
2. The car on the left has stopped at the stop sign; the car on the right is passing through the intersection.
3. In the rearview mirror, the driver sees that there is a motorcycle directly behind the car.
4. The man on the left is wearing his seat belt incorrectly. The shoulder strap is under his arm instead of across his shoulder.
5. The man on the right is wearing his seat belt correctly.
6. Stop and wait for the train to pass and the barrier to be lifted.
7. The vehicles have stopped for pedestrians in the crosswalk.
8. The sign on the left should be mounted on the tractor. The sign is a warning to other vehicles on the road that the vehicle upon which it is mounted is a slow-moving vehicle.
9. (C)
10.
11. There is one car on the road. There are three hot air balloons in the sky. The sun is peeking from behind some clouds.
12. The tire is worn right down the middle.
13. (C)
14. Look for a flagman.
15. The young boy is lying in the roadway.
16. A person is getting out of a car.
17. (C)
18. (B)
19. The vehicle is a bus.
20. The passengers are a group of well-dressed men and women, some with suitcases.
21. (A)
22. (C)

CHART A

	Truck License Number	Kind of Service	Odometer Reading When Serviced
	835 XYZ	tune up	22,305
23.	673 PUR	new fuel pump	67,422
24.	441 RTG	oil change	46,098

answers

CHART B

Driver ID Number	Truck License Number	Odometer Reading
8723	997 IUP	88,141
25. 6309	534 TRE	35,790
26. 7342	256 TAE	56,798

CHART C

Driver ID Number	Odometer Reading When Taken Out	Odometer Reading When Returned
3406	12,562	12,591
27. 9845	54,970	54,997
28. 4785	43,054	43,086

CHART D

Vehicle License Number	Kind of Service	Serviceperson ID Number
592 TJD	grease job	8452
29. 447 IKT	carburetor adjustment	7092
30. 837 PRE	tire change	6052

CHART E

Truck License Number	Driver ID Number	Serviceperson ID Number
042 RVB	5842	4307
31. 759 YUX	8372	3987
32. 943 WCG	6241	4273

33. Picture X shows the left lane is open to traffic (shown by arrow) and the two lanes to the right are closed to traffic (shown by Xs).
34. Picture Y shows six traffic lanes. Starting from the left, lanes 1 and 2 are open to traffic, lanes 3 and 4 are closed to traffic, lane 5 is open, and lane 6 is closed.
35. There is a signal light at a three- or four-way intersection. Cars coming straight at the signal light can have a red, yellow, or green light, or a green arrow pointing left. Cars coming from left and right probably have only a red, yellow, or green light.
36. (C)
37. (B)
38. Two men are putting a person on a stretcher into an ambulance.
39. A man and a woman are walking together.
40. (A)

Part B

41. C	49. C	57. C	65. B	73. B
42. E	50. A	58. B	66. A	74. C
43. B	51. E	59. B	67. A	75. E
44. A	52. A	60. E	68. D	76. C
45. D	53. C	61. A	69. C	77. B
46. C	54. D	62. C	70. B	78. C
47. E	55. D	63. A	71. B	79. E
48. B	56. B	64. C	72. D	80. A

PRACTICE TEST 5: EXAM 630 ANSWER SHEET

Part A: Name and Number Comparisons

1. Ⓐ Ⓑ Ⓒ Ⓓ Ⓔ	11. Ⓐ Ⓑ Ⓒ Ⓓ Ⓔ	21. Ⓐ Ⓑ Ⓒ Ⓓ Ⓔ	31. Ⓐ Ⓑ Ⓒ Ⓓ Ⓔ	41. Ⓐ Ⓑ Ⓒ Ⓓ Ⓔ
2. Ⓐ Ⓑ Ⓒ Ⓓ Ⓔ	12. Ⓐ Ⓑ Ⓒ Ⓓ Ⓔ	22. Ⓐ Ⓑ Ⓒ Ⓓ Ⓔ	32. Ⓐ Ⓑ Ⓒ Ⓓ Ⓔ	42. Ⓐ Ⓑ Ⓒ Ⓓ Ⓔ
3. Ⓐ Ⓑ Ⓒ Ⓓ Ⓔ	13. Ⓐ Ⓑ Ⓒ Ⓓ Ⓔ	23. Ⓐ Ⓑ Ⓒ Ⓓ Ⓔ	33. Ⓐ Ⓑ Ⓒ Ⓓ Ⓔ	43. Ⓐ Ⓑ Ⓒ Ⓓ Ⓔ
4. Ⓐ Ⓑ Ⓒ Ⓓ Ⓔ	14. Ⓐ Ⓑ Ⓒ Ⓓ Ⓔ	24. Ⓐ Ⓑ Ⓒ Ⓓ Ⓔ	34. Ⓐ Ⓑ Ⓒ Ⓓ Ⓔ	44. Ⓐ Ⓑ Ⓒ Ⓓ Ⓔ
5. Ⓐ Ⓑ Ⓒ Ⓓ Ⓔ	15. Ⓐ Ⓑ Ⓒ Ⓓ Ⓔ	25. Ⓐ Ⓑ Ⓒ Ⓓ Ⓔ	35. Ⓐ Ⓑ Ⓒ Ⓓ Ⓔ	45. Ⓐ Ⓑ Ⓒ Ⓓ Ⓔ
6. Ⓐ Ⓑ Ⓒ Ⓓ Ⓔ	16. Ⓐ Ⓑ Ⓒ Ⓓ Ⓔ	26. Ⓐ Ⓑ Ⓒ Ⓓ Ⓔ	36. Ⓐ Ⓑ Ⓒ Ⓓ Ⓔ	46. Ⓐ Ⓑ Ⓒ Ⓓ Ⓔ
7. Ⓐ Ⓑ Ⓒ Ⓓ Ⓔ	17. Ⓐ Ⓑ Ⓒ Ⓓ Ⓔ	27. Ⓐ Ⓑ Ⓒ Ⓓ Ⓔ	37. Ⓐ Ⓑ Ⓒ Ⓓ Ⓔ	47. Ⓐ Ⓑ Ⓒ Ⓓ Ⓔ
8. Ⓐ Ⓑ Ⓒ Ⓓ Ⓔ	18. Ⓐ Ⓑ Ⓒ Ⓓ Ⓔ	28. Ⓐ Ⓑ Ⓒ Ⓓ Ⓔ	38. Ⓐ Ⓑ Ⓒ Ⓓ Ⓔ	48. Ⓐ Ⓑ Ⓒ Ⓓ Ⓔ
9. Ⓐ Ⓑ Ⓒ Ⓓ Ⓔ	19. Ⓐ Ⓑ Ⓒ Ⓓ Ⓔ	29. Ⓐ Ⓑ Ⓒ Ⓓ Ⓔ	39. Ⓐ Ⓑ Ⓒ Ⓓ Ⓔ	49. Ⓐ Ⓑ Ⓒ Ⓓ Ⓔ
10. Ⓐ Ⓑ Ⓒ Ⓓ Ⓔ	20. Ⓐ Ⓑ Ⓒ Ⓓ Ⓔ	30. Ⓐ Ⓑ Ⓒ Ⓓ Ⓔ	40. Ⓐ Ⓑ Ⓒ Ⓓ Ⓔ	50. Ⓐ Ⓑ Ⓒ Ⓓ Ⓔ

Part B: Reading Comprehension

1. Ⓐ Ⓑ Ⓒ Ⓓ Ⓔ	7. Ⓐ Ⓑ Ⓒ Ⓓ Ⓔ	13. Ⓐ Ⓑ Ⓒ Ⓓ Ⓔ	19. Ⓐ Ⓑ Ⓒ Ⓓ Ⓔ	25. Ⓐ Ⓑ Ⓒ Ⓓ Ⓔ
2. Ⓐ Ⓑ Ⓒ Ⓓ Ⓔ	8. Ⓐ Ⓑ Ⓒ Ⓓ Ⓔ	14. Ⓐ Ⓑ Ⓒ Ⓓ Ⓔ	20. Ⓐ Ⓑ Ⓒ Ⓓ Ⓔ	26. Ⓐ Ⓑ Ⓒ Ⓓ Ⓔ
3. Ⓐ Ⓑ Ⓒ Ⓓ Ⓔ	9. Ⓐ Ⓑ Ⓒ Ⓓ Ⓔ	15. Ⓐ Ⓑ Ⓒ Ⓓ Ⓔ	21. Ⓐ Ⓑ Ⓒ Ⓓ Ⓔ	27. Ⓐ Ⓑ Ⓒ Ⓓ Ⓔ
4. Ⓐ Ⓑ Ⓒ Ⓓ Ⓔ	10. Ⓐ Ⓑ Ⓒ Ⓓ Ⓔ	16. Ⓐ Ⓑ Ⓒ Ⓓ Ⓔ	22. Ⓐ Ⓑ Ⓒ Ⓓ Ⓔ	28. Ⓐ Ⓑ Ⓒ Ⓓ Ⓔ
5. Ⓐ Ⓑ Ⓒ Ⓓ Ⓔ	11. Ⓐ Ⓑ Ⓒ Ⓓ Ⓔ	17. Ⓐ Ⓑ Ⓒ Ⓓ Ⓔ	23. Ⓐ Ⓑ Ⓒ Ⓓ Ⓔ	29. Ⓐ Ⓑ Ⓒ Ⓓ Ⓔ
6. Ⓐ Ⓑ Ⓒ Ⓓ Ⓔ	12. Ⓐ Ⓑ Ⓒ Ⓓ Ⓔ	18. Ⓐ Ⓑ Ⓒ Ⓓ Ⓔ	24. Ⓐ Ⓑ Ⓒ Ⓓ Ⓔ	30. Ⓐ Ⓑ Ⓒ Ⓓ Ⓔ

Part C: Arithmetic Reasoning

1. Ⓐ Ⓑ Ⓒ Ⓓ Ⓔ	5. Ⓐ Ⓑ Ⓒ Ⓓ Ⓔ	9. Ⓐ Ⓑ Ⓒ Ⓓ Ⓔ	13. Ⓐ Ⓑ Ⓒ Ⓓ Ⓔ	17. Ⓐ Ⓑ Ⓒ Ⓓ Ⓔ
2. Ⓐ Ⓑ Ⓒ Ⓓ Ⓔ	6. Ⓐ Ⓑ Ⓒ Ⓓ Ⓔ	10. Ⓐ Ⓑ Ⓒ Ⓓ Ⓔ	14. Ⓐ Ⓑ Ⓒ Ⓓ Ⓔ	18. Ⓐ Ⓑ Ⓒ Ⓓ Ⓔ
3. Ⓐ Ⓑ Ⓒ Ⓓ Ⓔ	7. Ⓐ Ⓑ Ⓒ Ⓓ Ⓔ	11. Ⓐ Ⓑ Ⓒ Ⓓ Ⓔ	15. Ⓐ Ⓑ Ⓒ Ⓓ Ⓔ	19. Ⓐ Ⓑ Ⓒ Ⓓ Ⓔ
4. Ⓐ Ⓑ Ⓒ Ⓓ Ⓔ	8. Ⓐ Ⓑ Ⓒ Ⓓ Ⓔ	12. Ⓐ Ⓑ Ⓒ Ⓓ Ⓔ	16. Ⓐ Ⓑ Ⓒ Ⓓ Ⓔ	20. Ⓐ Ⓑ Ⓒ Ⓓ Ⓔ

PRACTICE TEST 5: EXAM 630

Part A: Name and Number Comparisons

50 QUESTIONS • 8 MINUTES

> **Directions:** For each question, compare the three names or numbers and mark your answer:
> **(A)** if ALL THREE names or numbers are exactly ALIKE
> **(B)** if only the FIRST and SECOND names or numbers are exactly ALIKE
> **(C)** if only the FIRST and THIRD names or numbers are exactly ALIKE
> **(D)** if only the SECOND and THIRD names or numbers are exactly ALIKE
> **(E)** if ALL THREE names or numbers are DIFFERENT

1.	Thomas L. Kershaw	Thomas L. Kershaw	Thomas J. Kershaw
2.	Takahide E. Moro	Takahide E. Moru	Takahide E. Moru
3.	Carlota Cosentino	Carlotta Cosentino	Carlotta Constentino
4.	Albertina Andriuolo	Albertina Andriuolo	Albertina Andriuolo
5.	Francis J. Czukor	Francis Z. Czukor	Frances J. Czukor
6.	7692138	7692138	7692138
7.	2633342	2633342	2633342
8.	2454803	2548403	2454803
9.	9670243	9670423	9670423
10.	2789350	2789350	2798350
11.	Darlene P. Tenenbaum	Darlene P. Tenenbaum	Darlene P. Tanenbaum
12.	Maxwell Macmillan	Maxwell MacMillan	Maxwell Macmillian
13.	Frank D. Stanick	Frank D. Satanic	Frank D. Satanich
14.	J. Robert Schunk	J. Robert Schunh Robert	J. Schunk
15.	Fernando Silva Jr.	Fernando Silva Jr.	Fernand Silva Jr.
16.	2797630	2797360	2797360
17.	6312192	6312192	6312192
18.	7412032	7412032	7412032
19.	2789327	2879327	2789327
20.	5927681	5927861	5927681
21.	Wendy A. Courtney	Wendy A. Courtney	Wendy A. Courtnay
22.	Lambert Forman, MD	Lambert Forman, MD	Lambert Forman, MD

23. Joseph A. Gurreri	Joseph A. Gurreri	Joseph A. Gurreri
24. Sylnette Lynch	Sylnette Lynch	Sylnette Lynch
25. Zion McKenzie Jr.	Zion McKenzie Sr.	Zion MacKenzie Jr.
26. 6932976	6939276	6932796
27. 9631695	9636195	9631695
28. 7370527	7375027	7370537
29. 2799379	2739779	2799379
30. 5261383	5261383	5261338
31. J. Randolph Rea	J. Randolph Rea	J. Randolphe Rea
32. W.E. Johnston	W.E. Johnson	W.E. Johnson
33. Vergil L. Muller	Vergil L. Muller	Vergil L. Muller
34. Atherton R. Warde	Asheton R. Warde	Atherton P. Warde
35. E. Owens McVey	E. Owen McVey	E. Owen McVay
36. 8125690	8126690	8125609
37. 2395890	2395890	2395890
38. 1926341	1926347	1926314
39. 6219354	6219354	6219354
40. 2312793	2312793	2312793
41. Alexander Majthenyi	Alexander Majthenyi	Alexander Majthenyi
42. James T. Harbison	James T. Harbinson	James T. Harbison
43. Margareta Goldenkoff	Margaretta Goldenkoff	Margaretha Goldenkoff
44. Cornelius Detwiler	Cornelius Detwiler	Cornelius Detwiler
45. Benjamin A. D'Ortona	Benjamin A. D'Ortoni	Benjamin D'Ortonia
46. 1065407	1065407	1065047
47. 6452054	6452654	6452054
48. 8501268	8501268	8501286
49. 3457988	3457986	3457986
50. 4695682	4695862	4695682

Part B: Reading Comprehension

30 QUESTIONS • 60 MINUTES

> **Directons:** For each reading question you will be given a paragraph that contains all the information necessary to answer the question that follows. Use only the information provided in the paragraph. Do not speculate or make assumptions that go beyond this information. Also, assume that all information given in the paragraph is true, even if it conflicts with facts you may already know. Only one correct answer can be validly inferred from the information contained in the paragraph. Mark its letter on your answer sheet.

1. A member of the department shall not indulge in liquor while in uniform. A member of the department not required to wear a uniform and a uniformed member while out of uniform shall not indulge in intoxicants to an extent unfitting the member for duty.

   The paragraph best supports the statement that a(n)

   (A) off-duty member, not in uniform, may drink liquor to the extent that it does not unfit the member for duty

   (B) member not on duty, but in uniform and not unfit for duty, may drink liquor

   (C) on-duty member, unfit for duty in uniform, may drink intoxicants

   (D) uniformed member in civilian clothes may not drink intoxicants unless unfit for duty

   (E) civilian member of the department, in uniform, may drink liquor if fit for duty

2. Tax law specialists may authorize their assistants to sign their names to reports, letters, and papers that are not specially required to be signed personally by the tax law specialist. The signature should be: "Jane Doe, tax law specialist, by Richard Roe, tax technician." The name of the tax law specialist may be written or stamped, but the signature of the tax technician shall be in ink.

   The paragraph best supports the statement that

   (A) if a tax law specialist's assistant signs official papers both by rubber stamp and in ink, the assistant has authority to sign

   (B) if a tax technician does not neglect to include his or her title in ink along with his or her signature following the word "by," the technician may sign papers that are not specially required to be signed personally by the tax law specialist

   (C) no signatory authority delegated to the tax technician by the tax law specialist maybe redelegated by the tax technician to an assistant unless so authorized in ink by the tax law specialist

   (D) if a tax law specialist personally signs written requisitions in ink, the technician is not required to identify the source of the order with a rubber stamp

   (E) when a tax technician signs authorized papers for a tax law specialist, the tax technician must write out the tax law specialist's signature in full with pen and ink

230   **PART III: Five Practice Tests**

3. Upon retirement from service, a member shall receive a retirement allowance consisting of an annuity that shall be the actuarial equivalent of his accumulated deductions at the time of retirement; a pension in addition to his annuity that shall be one service-fraction of his final compensation multiplied by the number of years of government service since he last became a member; and a pension that is the actuarial equivalent of their serve-for-increased-take-home-pay to which he may then be entitled, if any.

The paragraph best supports the statement that

(A) a retirement allowance shall consist of an annuity plus a pension plus an actuarial equivalent of a service-fraction

(B) upon retirement from service, a member shall receive an annuity plus a pension plus an actuarial equivalent of reserve-for-increased-take-home-pay if he is entitled

(C) a retiring member shall receive an annuity plus reserve-for-increased-take-home-pay, if any, plus final compensation

(D) a retirement allowance shall consist of a pension plus reserve-for-increased-take-home-pay, if any, plus accumulated deductions

(E) a retirement allowance shall consist of an annuity that is equal to one service-fraction of final compensation, a pension multiplied by the number of years of government service, and the actuarial equivalent of accumulated deductions from increased take-home-pay

4. If you are in doubt as to whether any matter is legally mailable, you should ask the postmaster. Even though the Postal Service has not expressly declared any matter to be nonmailable, the sender of such matter may be held fully liable for violation of law if he or she does actually send nonmailable matter through the mail.

The paragraph best supports the statement that if

(A) the postmaster is in doubt as to whether any matter is legally mailable, the postmaster may be held liable for any sender's sending nonmailable matter through the mail

(B) the sender is ignorant of what it is that constitutes nonmailable matter, the sender is relieved of all responsibility for mailing nonmailable matter

(C) a sender sends nonmailable matter, the sender is fully liable for law violation even though doubt may have existed about the mailability of the matter

(D) the Postal Service has not expressly declared material mailable, it is nonmailable

(E) the Postal Service has not expressly declared material nonmailable, it is mailable

5. In evaluating education for a particular position, education in and of itself is of no value except to the degree in which it contributes to knowledge, skills, and abilities needed in the particular job. On its face, such a statement would seem to contend that general educational development need not be considered in evaluating education and training. Much to the contrary, such a proposition favors the consideration of any and all training, but only as it pertains to the position for which the applicant applies.

The paragraph best supports the statement that

(A) if general education is supplemented by specialized education, it is of no value

(B) if a high school education is desirable in any occupation, special training need not be evaluated

(C) in evaluating education, a contradiction arises in assigning equal weight to general and specialized education

www.petersons.com/arco

(D) unless it is supplemented by general education, specialized education is of no value

(E) education is of value to the degree to which it is needed in the particular position

6. Statistics tell us that heart disease kills more people than any other illness, and the death rate continues to rise. People over 30 have a fifty-fifty chance of escaping, for heart disease is chiefly an illness of people in late middle age and advanced years. Because there are more people in this age group living today than there were some years ago, heart disease is able to find more victims.

The paragraph best supports the statement that

(A) if a person has heart disease, there is a 50 percent chance that he or she is over 30 years of age

(B) according to statistics, more middle-aged and elderly people die of heart disease than of all other causes

(C) because heart disease is chiefly an illness of people in late middle age, young people are less likely to be the victims of heart disease

(D) the rising birth rate has increased the possibility that the average person will die of heart disease

(E) if the stress of modern living were not increasing, there would be a slower increase in the risk of heart disease

7. Racketeers are primarily concerned with business affairs, legitimate or otherwise, and prefer those that are close to the margin of legitimacy. They get their best opportunities from business organizations that meet the need of large sections of the public for goods or services that are defined as illegitimate by the same public, such as prostitution, gambling, illicit drugs, or liquor. In contrast to the thief, the racketeer and the establishments he or she controls deliver goods and services for money received.

The paragraph best supports the statement that

(A) since racketeers deliver goods and services for money received, their business affairs are not illegitimate

(B) since racketeering involves objects of value, it is unlike theft

(C) victims of racketeers are not guilty of violating the law, therefore racketeering is a victimless crime

(D) since many people want services that are not obtainable through legitimate sources, they contribute to the difficulty of suppressing racketeers

(E) if large sections of the public are engaged in legitimate business with racketeers, the businesses are not illegitimate

8. The housing authority not only faces every problem of the private developer, but it must also assume responsibilities of which private building is free. The authority must account to the community; it must conform to federal regulations; it must provide durable buildings of good standard at low cost; and it must overcome the prejudices of contractors, bankers, and prospective tenants against public operations. These authorities are being watched by anti-housing enthusiasts for the first error of judgment or the first evidence of high costs that can be torn to bits before a Congressional committee.

The paragraph best supports the statement that

(A) since private developers are not accountable to the community, they do not have the opposition of contractors, bankers, and prospective tenants

(B) if Congressional committees are watched by antihousing enthusiasts, they may discover errors of judgment and high costs on the part of a housing authority

(C) while a housing authority must deal with all the difficulties encountered by a private builder, it must also deal with antihousing enthusiasts

(D) if housing authorities are not immune to errors in judgment, they must provide durable buildings of good standard and low cost just like private developers

(E) if a housing authority is to conform to federal regulations, it must overcome the prejudices of contractors, builders, and prospective tenants

9. Security of tenure in the public service must be viewed in the context of the universal quest for security. If we narrow our application of the term to employment, the problem of security in the public service is seen to differ from that in private industry only in the need to meet the peculiar threats to security in governmental organizations—principally the danger of making employment contingent upon factors other than the performance of the workers.

The paragraph best supports the statement that

(A) if workers seek security, they should enter public service

(B) if employment is contingent upon factors other than work performance, workers will feel more secure

(C) if employees believe that their security is threatened, they are employed in private industry

(D) the term of employment in public service differs from that in private industry

(E) the employment status of the public servant with respect to security of tenure differs from that of the private employee by encompassing factors beyond those affecting the private employee

10. The wide use of antibiotics has presented a number of problems. Some patients become allergic to the drugs, so that they cannot be used when they are needed. In other cases, after prolonged treatment with antibiotics, certain organisms no longer respond to them. This is one of the reasons for the constant search for more potent drugs.

The paragraph best supports the statement that

(A) since a number of problems have been presented by long-term treatment with antibiotics, antibiotics should never be used on a long-term basis

(B) because some people have developed an allergy to specific drugs, potent antibiotics cannot always be used

(C) since antibiotics have been used successfully for certain allergies, there must be a constant search for more potent drugs

(D) if antibiotics are used for a prolonged period of time, certain organisms become allergic to them

(E) since so many diseases have been successfully treated with antibiotics, there must be a constant search for new drugs

11. The noncompetitive class consists of positions for which there are minimum qualifications but for which no reliable exam has been developed. In the noncompetitive class, every applicant must meet minimum qualifications in terms of education, experience, and medical or physical qualifications. There may even be an examination on a pass/fail basis.

The paragraph best supports the statement that if

(A) an exam is unreliable, the position is in the noncompetitive class

(B) an applicant has met minimum qualifications in terms of education, experience, medical, or physical requirements, the applicant must pass a test

(C) an applicant has met minimum qualifications in terms of education, experience, medical, or physical requirements, the applicant may fail a test

(D) an applicant passes an exam for a noncompetitive position, the applicant must also meet minimum qualifications

(E) there are minimum qualifications for a position, the position is in the noncompetitive class

12. Two independent clauses cannot share one sentence without some form of connective. If they do, they form a run-on sentence. Two principal clauses may be joined by a coordinating conjunction, by a comma followed by a coordinating conjunction, or by a semicolon. They may also form two distinct sentences. Two main clauses may never be joined by a comma without a coordinating conjunction. This error is called a comma splice.

The paragraph best supports the statement that

(A) if the violation is called a comma splice, two main clauses are joined by a comma without a coordinating conjunction

(B) if two distinct sentences share one sentence and are joined by a coordinating conjunction, the result is a run-on sentence

(C) when a coordinating conjunction is not followed by a semicolon, the writer has committed an error of punctuation

(D) while a comma and a semicolon may not be used in the same principal clause, they maybe used in the same sentence

(E) a bad remedy for a run-on sentence is not a comma splice

13. The pay in some job titles is hourly; in others it is annual. Official work weeks vary from 35 hours to $37\frac{1}{2}$ hours to 40 hours. In some positions, overtime is earned for all time worked beyond the set number of hours, and differentials are paid for night, weekend, and holiday work. Other positions offer compensatory time off for overtime or for work during unpopular times. Still other positions require the jobholder to devote as much extra time as needed to do the work without any extra compensation. And in some positions, employees who work overtime are given a meal allowance.

The paragraph best supports the statement that if

(A) a meal allowance is given, there is compensation for overtime

(B) the work week is 35 hours long, the job is unpopular

(C) overtime is earned, pay in the job title is hourly

(D) a jobholder has earned a weekend differential, the employee has worked beyond the set number of hours

(E) compensatory time is offered, it is offered as a substitute for overtime pay

14. All applicants must be of satisfactory character and reputation and must meet all requirements set forth in the Notice of Examination for the position for which they are applying. Applicants may be summoned for the written test prior to investigation of their qualifications and background. Admission to the test does not mean that the applicant has met the qualifications for the position.

The paragraph best supports the statement that if an applicant has

(A) been admitted to the test, the applicant has not met requirements for the position

(B) not been investigated, the applicant will not be admitted to the written test

(C) met all requirements for the position, the applicant will be admitted to the test

(D) satisfactory character and reputation, the applicant will not have his or her background investigated

(E) met all the requirements set forth in the Notice of Examination, the applicant will pass the test

15. Although it has in the past been illegal for undocumented aliens to work in the United States, it has not, until now, been unlawful for employers to hire these aliens. With the passage of the new immigration law, employers will now be subject to civil penalties and ultimately imprisonment if they "knowingly" hire, recruit, or refer for a fee any unauthorized alien. Similarly, it is also unlawful for employers to continue to employ an undocumented alien who was hired after November 6, 1986, knowing that he or she was or is unauthorized to work.

The paragraph best supports the statement that

(A) under the new immigration law, it is no longer illegal for undocumented aliens to be denied employment in the United States

(B) if an undocumented alien is not remaining on the job illegally, the worker was not hired after November 6, 1986

(C) if a person wishes to avoid the penalties of the new immigration law, the person must not knowingly employ aliens

(D) if an employer inadvertently hires undocumented aliens, the employer may be subject to fine or imprisonment but not both

(E) if an unauthorized alien is able to find an employer who will hire him or her after November 6, 1986, the alien is welcome to go to work

16. The law requires that the government offer employees, retirees, and their families the opportunity to continue group health and/or welfare fund coverage at 102 percent of the group rate in certain instances where the coverage would otherwise terminate. All group benefits, including optional benefits riders, are available. Welfare fund benefits that can be continued under COBRA are dental, vision, prescription drugs, and other related medical benefits. The period of coverage varies from 18 to 36 months, depending on the reason for continuation.

The paragraph best supports the statement that

(A) the period of coverage continuation varies depending on the reason for termination

(B) upon retirement, welfare fund benefits continue at a 102 percent rate

(C) the law requires employees, retirees, and their families to continue health coverage

(D) COBRA is a program for acquiring welfare fund benefits

(E) if retirees or their families do not desire to terminate them, they can continue group benefits at 102 percent of the group rate

17. Historical records as such rarely constitute an adequate or, more importantly, a reliable basis for estimating earthquake potential. In most regions of the world, recorded history is short relative to the time between the largest earthquakes. Thus, the fact that there have been no historic earthquakes larger than a given size does not make us confident that they will also be absent in the future. It may, alternatively, be due to the short length of available historical records relative to the long repeat time for large earthquakes.

    The paragraph best supports the statement that
    (A) if historic earthquakes are no larger than a given size, they are unlikely to recur
    (B) potential earthquakes do not inspire confidence in historical records as predictors of time between earthquakes
    (C) if the time span between major earthquakes were not longer than the length of available records, history would have greater predictive value
    (D) since there have been no historic earthquakes larger than a given size, we are confident that there will be a long time span between major earthquakes
    (E) in those regions of the world where recorded history is long, the time between the largest earthquakes is short

18. A language can be thought of as a number of strings or sequences of symbols. The definition of a language defines which strings belong to the language, but since most languages of interest consist of an infinite number of strings, this definition is impossible to accomplish by listing the strings (or sentences). While the number of *sentences* in a language can be infinite, the rules by which they are constructed are not. This may explain why we are able to speak sentences in a language that we have never spoken before, and to understand sentences that we have never heard before.

    The paragraph best supports the statement that
    (A) if there is an infinite number of sequences of symbols in a language, there is an infinite number of rules for their construction
    (B) if we have never spoken a language, we can understand its sentences provided that we know the rules by which they were constructed
    (C) a language is defined by its strings
    (D) if the number of sentences in an unnatural language were not infinite, we would be able to define it
    (E) if sequences of symbols are governed by rules of construction, then the number of sentences can be determined

19. An assumption commonly made in regard to the reliability of testimony is that when a number of persons report the same matter, those details upon which there is an agreement may generally be considered substantiated. Experiments have shown, however, that there is a tendency for the same errors to appear in the testimony of different individuals, and that, apart from any collusion, agreement of testimony is no proof of dependability.

    The paragraph best supports the statement that
    (A) if details of the testimony are true, all witnesses will agree to it
    (B) unless there is collusion, it is impossible for a number of persons to give the same report
    (C) if most witnesses do not independently attest to the same facts, the facts cannot be true
    (D) if the testimony of a group of people is in substantial agreement, it cannot be ruled out that those witnesses have not all made the same mistake
    (E) under experimental conditions, witnesses tend to give reliable testimony

20. In some instances, changes are made in a contract after it has been signed and accepted by both parties. This is done either by inserting a new clause in a contract or by annexing a *rider* to the contract. If a contract is changed by a rider, both parties must sign the rider in order for it to be legal. The basic contract should also note that a rider is attached by inserting new words to the contract, and both parties should also initial and date the new insertion. The same requirement applies if they later change any wording in the contract. What two people agree to do, they can mutually agree not to do—as long as they both agree.

The paragraph best supports the statement that if

(A) two people mutually agree not to do something, they must sign a rider

(B) both parties to a contract do not agree to attach a rider, they must initial the contract to render it legal

(C) a rider to a contract is to be legal, that rider must be agreed to and signed by both parties, who must not neglect to initial and date that portion of the contract to which the rider refers

(D) a party to a contract does not agree to a change, that party should initial the change and annex a rider detailing the disagreement

(E) the wording of a contract is not to be changed, both parties must initial and date a rider

21. Personnel administration begins with the process of defining the quantities of people needed to do the job. Thereafter, people must be recruited, selected, trained, directed, rewarded, transferred, promoted, and perhaps released or retired. However, it is not true that all organizations are structured so that workers can be dealt with as individuals. In some organizations, employees are represented by unions, and managers bargain directly only with these associations.

The paragraph best supports the statement that

(A) no organizations are structured so that workers cannot be dealt with as individuals

(B) some working environments other than organizations are structured so that workers can be dealt with as individuals

(C) all organizations are structured so that employees are represented by unions

(D) no organizations are structured so that managers bargain with unions

(E) some organizations are not structured so that workers can be dealt with as individuals

22. Explosives are substances or devices capable of producing a volume of rapidly expanding gases that exert a sudden pressure on their surroundings. Chemical explosives are the most commonly used, although there are mechanical and nuclear explosives. All mechanical explosives are devices in which a physical reaction is produced, such as that caused by overloading a container with compressed air. While nuclear explosives are by far the most powerful, all nuclear explosives have been restricted to military weapons.

The paragraph best supports the statement that

(A) all explosives that have been restricted to military weapons are nuclear explosives

(B) no mechanical explosives are devices in which a physical reaction is produced, such as that caused by overloading a container with compressed air

(C) some nuclear explosives have not been restricted to military weapons

(D) all mechanical explosives have been restricted to military weapons

(E) some devices in which a physical reaction is produced, such as that caused by overloading a container with compressed air, are mechanical explosives

23. The modern conception of the economic role of the public sector (government), as distinct from the private sector, is that every level of government is a link in the economic process. Government's contribution to political and economic welfare must, however, be evaluated not merely in terms of its technical efficiency, but also in the light of its acceptability to a particular society at a particular state of political and economic development. Even in a dictatorship, this principle is formally observed, although the authorities usually destroy the substance by presuming to interpret to the public its collective desires.

The paragraph best supports the statement that

(A) it is not true that some levels of government are not links in the economic process

(B) all dictatorships observe the same economic principles as other governments

(C) all links in the economic process are levels of government

(D) the contributions of some levels of government do not need to be evaluated for technical efficiency and acceptability to society

(E) no links in the economic process are institutions other than levels of government

24. All property is classified as either personal property or real property, but not both. In general, if something is classified as personal property, it is transient and transportable in nature, while real property is not. Things such as leaseholds, animals, money, and intangible and other moveable goods are examples of personal property. Permanent buildings and land, on the other hand, are fixed in nature and are not transportable.

The paragraph best supports the statement that

(A) if something is classified as personal property, it is not transient and transportable in nature

(B) some forms of property are considered to be both personal property and real property

(C) permanent buildings and land are real property

(D) permanent buildings and land are personal property

(E) tangible goods are considered to be real property

25. The Supreme Court's power to invalidate legislation that violates the Constitution is a strong restriction on the powers of Congress. If an Act of Congress is deemed unconstitutional by the Supreme Court, then the Act is voided. Unlike a presidential veto, which can be overridden by a two-thirds vote of the House and the Senate, a constitutional ruling by the Supreme Court must be accepted by the Congress.

The paragraph best supports the statement that if an Act of Congress

(A) is voided, then it has been deemed unconstitutional by the Supreme Court

(B) has not been voided, then it has not been deemed unconstitutional by the Supreme Court

(C) has not been deemed unconstitutional by the Supreme Court, then it is voided

(D) is deemed unconstitutional by the Supreme Court, then it is not voided

(E) has not been voided, then it has been deemed unconstitutional by the Supreme Court

26. All child-welfare agencies are organizations that seek to promote the healthy growth and development of children. Supplying or supplementing family income so that parents can maintain a home for their children is usually the first such service to be provided. In addition to programs of general family relief, some special programs for broken families are offered when parental care is temporarily or permanently unavailable.

The paragraph best supports the statement that

(A) it is not true that some organizations that seek to promote the healthy growth and development of children are child-welfare agencies

(B) some programs offered when parental care is temporarily or permanently unavailable are not special programs for broken families

(C) it is not true that no special programs for broken families are offered when temporary or permanent parental care is unavailable

(D) all programs offered when parental care is temporarily or permanently unavailable are special programs for broken families

(E) some organizations that seek to promote the healthy growth and development of children are not child-welfare agencies

27. Information centers can be categorized according to the primary activity or service they provide. For example, some information centers are document depots. These depots, generally government-sponsored, serve as archives for the acquisition, storage, retrieval, and dissemination of a variety of documents. All document depots have the capacity to provide a great range of user services, which may include preparing specialized bibliographies; publishing announcements, indexes, and abstracts; as well as providing copies.

The paragraph best supports the statement that

(A) some information centers are categorized by features other than the primary activity or service they provide

(B) some document depots lack the capacity to provide a great range of user services

(C) no document depot lacks the capacity to provide a great range of user services

(D) all information centers are document depots

(E) some places that provide a great range of user services are not document depots

28. Authorities generally agree that the use of hyphens tends to defy most rules. The best advice that can be given is to consult the dictionary to determine whether a given prefix is joined solidly to a root word or is hyphenated. One reliable rule, however, is that if an expression is a familiar one, such as overtime and hatchback, then it is a nonhyphenated compound.

The paragraph best supports the statement that if an expression is

(A) a familiar one, then it is a hyphenated compound

(B) a nonhyphenated compound, then it is a familiar expression

(C) not a familiar one, then it is a hyphenated compound

(D) a hyphenated compound, containing a suffix rather than a prefix, then it is not a familiar one

(E) a hyphenated compound, then it is not a familiar one

29. One use for wild land is the protection of certain species of wild animals or plants in wildlife refuges or in botanical reservations. Some general types of land use are activities that conflict with this stated purpose. All activities that exhibit such conflict are, of course, excluded from refuges and reservations.

The paragraph best supports the statement that

(A) all activities that conflict with the purpose of wildlife refuges or botanical reservations are general types of land use

(B) all activities excluded from wildlife refuges and botanical reservations are those that conflict with the purpose of the refuge or reservation

(C) some activities excluded from wildlife refuges and botanical reservations are general types of land use

(D) no activities that conflict with the purpose of wildlife refuges and botanical reservations are general types of land use

(E) some general types of land use are not excluded from wildlife refuges and botanical reservations

30. Many kinds of computer programming languages have been developed over the years. Initially, programmers had to write instructions in machine language. If a computer programming language is a machine language, then it is a code that can be read directly by a computer. Most high-level computer programming languages, such as Fortran and Cobol, use strings of common English phrases that communicate with the computer only after being converted or translated into a machine code.

The paragraph best supports the statement that

(A) all high-level computer programming languages use strings of common English phrases that are converted to a machine code

(B) if a computer programming language is a machine language, then it is not a code that can be read directly by a computer

(C) if a computer programming language is a code that can be read directly by a computer, then it is not a machine language

(D) if a computer programming language is not a code that can be read directly by a computer, then it is not a machine language

(E) if a computer programming language is not a machine language, then it is a code that can be read directly by a computer

Part C: Arithmetic Reasoning

20 QUESTIONS • 50 MINUTES

> **Directons:** Read each problem carefully and mark your answer sheet with the letter of the correct answer. If the correct answer is not given as one of the response choices, you should select choice (E), "none of these."

1. Twelve clerks are assigned to enter certain data on index cards. This number of clerks could perform the task in 18 days. After these clerks have worked on this assignment for 6 days, 4 more clerks are added to the staff to do this work. Assuming that all the clerks work at the same rate of speed, the entire task, instead of taking 18 days, will take
   (A) 9 days
   (B) 12 days
   (C) 15 days
   (D) 16 days
   (E) none of these

2. In a low-cost public-health dental clinic, an adult cleaning costs twice as much as the same treatment for a child. If a family of three children and two adults can visit the clinic for cleanings for a cost of $49, what is the cost for each adult?
   (A) $7
   (B) $10
   (C) $12
   (D) $14
   (E) none of these

3. A government employee is relocated to a new region of the country and purchases a new home. The purchase price of the house is $87,250. Taxes to be paid on this house include: county tax of $424 per year; town tax of $783 per year; and school tax of $466 every six months. The aggregate tax rate is $.132 per $1000 of assessed value. The assessed value of this house is what percent of the purchase price?
   (A) 14.52%
   (B) 18.57%
   (C) 22.81%

   (D) 29.05%
   (E) none of these

4. The Social Security Administration has ordered an intensive check of 756 SSI payment recipients who are suspected of having above-standard incomes. Four clerical assistants have been assigned to this task. At the end of six days at 7 hours each, they have checked on 336 recipients. In order to speed up the investigation, two more assistants are assigned at this point. If they work at the same rate, the number of additional 7-hour days it will take to complete the job is, most nearly
   (A) 1
   (B) 2
   (C) 3
   (D) 4
   (E) none of these

5. A family spends 30 percent of its take-home income for food, 8 percent for clothing, 25 percent for shelter, 4 percent for recreation, 13 percent for education, and 5 percent for miscellaneous items. The remainder goes into the family savings account. If the weekly net earnings of this household are $500, how many weeks will it take this family to accumulate $15,000 in savings, before interest?
   (A) 200
   (B) 175
   (C) 150
   (D) 100
   (E) none of these

6. An Internal Revenue Service (IRS) officer is making spot-checks of income reported on income tax returns. A cab driver being audited works on a commission basis, receiving $42\frac{1}{2}$ percent of fares collected. The IRS allocates that earnings from tips should be valued at 29 percent of commissions. If the cab driver's weekly fare collections average $520, then the IRS projects his reportable monthly earnings to be

(A) between $900 and $1,000
(B) between $1,000 and $1,100
(C) between $1,100 and $1,200
(D) between $1,200 and $1,250
(E) none of these

7. A department head hired a total of 60 temporary employees to handle a seasonal increase in the department's workload. The following lists the number of temporary employees hired, their rates of pay, and the duration of their employment:

> One-third of the total were hired as clerks, each at the rate of $12,700 a year, for two months

> 30 percent of the total were hired as office machine operators, each at the rate of $13,150 a year, for four months

> 22 stenographers were hired, each at the rate of $13,000 a year, for three months.

The total amount paid to these temporary employees to the nearest dollar was

(A) $194,499
(B) $192,900
(C) $130,000
(D) $127,500
(E) none of these

8. A government worker whose personal car gets 24 miles to the gallon was required to use this car for government business. He filled the tank before he began, requiring 18 gallons, for which he paid $1.349 per gallon. He drove 336 miles, then filled the tank again at a cost of $1.419 per gallon. The government reimburses him at the rate of $.20 per mile. What was the actual cost of gasoline for this trip?

(A) $19.87
(B) $23.05
(C) $24.28
(D) $44.15
(E) none of these

9. The visitors' section of a courtroom seats 105 people. The court is in session 6 hours a day. On one particular day, 486 people visited the court and were given seats. What is the average length of time spent by each visitor in the court? Assume that as soon as a person leaves a seat it is immediately filled and that at no time during the day is one of the 105 seats vacant. Express your answer in hours and minutes.

(A) 1 hour 18 minutes
(B) 1 hour 20 minutes
(C) 1 hour 30 minutes
(D) 2 hours
(E) none of these

10. A worker is paid at the rate of $8.60 per hour for the first 40 hours worked in a week and time-and-a-half for overtime. The FICA (social security) deduction is 7.13 percent; federal tax withholding is 15 percent; state tax withholding, 5 percent; and local tax withholding, $2\frac{1}{2}$ percent. If a worker works 48 hours a week for two consecutive weeks, she will take home

(A) $314.69
(B) $580.97
(C) $629.39
(D) $693.16
(E) none of these

11. A court clerk estimates that the untried cases on the docket will occupy the court for 150 trial days. If new cases are accumulating at the rate of 1.6 trial days per day and the court sits five days a week, how many days' business will remain to be heard at the end of 60 trial days?

   (A) 168
   (B) 184
   (C) 185
   (D) 186
   (E) none of these

12. A criminal investigator has an appointment to meet with an important informant at 4p.m. in a city that is 480 kilometers from his base location. If the investigator estimates that his average speed will be 40 mph, what time must he leave home to make his appointment?

   (A) 8:15 a.m.
   (B) 8:30 a.m.
   (C) 8:45 a.m.
   (D) 9:30 a.m.
   (E) none of these

13. A program analysis office is taking bids for a new office machine. One machine is offered at a list price of $1,360 with successive discounts of 20 percent and 10 percent, a delivery charge of $35, and an installation charge of $52. The other machine is offered at a list price of $1,385 with a single discount of 30 percent, a delivery charge of $40, and an installation charge of $50. If the office chooses the less expensive machine, the savings will amount to just about

   (A) 0.6 percent
   (B) 1.9 percent
   (C) 2.0 percent
   (D) 2.6 percent
   (E) none of these

14. An assignment is completed by 32 clerks in 22 days. Assuming that all the clerks work at the same rate of speed, the number of clerks that would be needed to complete this assignment in 16 days is

   (A) 27
   (B) 38
   (C) 44
   (D) 52
   (E) none of these

15. The paralegals in a large legal department have decided to establish a "sunshine fund" for charitable purposes. Paralegal A has proposed that each worker chip in one-half of 1 percent of weekly salary; paralegal B thinks 1 percent would be just right; paralegal C suggests that one-third of 1 percent would be adequate; and paralegal D, who is strapped for funds, argues for one-fifth of 1 percent. The payroll department will cooperate and make an automatic deduction, but the paralegals must agree on a uniform percentage. The average of their suggested contributions is approximately

   (A) $\frac{1}{4}$ percent
   (B) $\frac{1}{3}$ percent
   (C) $\frac{1}{2}$ percent
   (D) $\frac{5}{8}$ percent
   (E) none of these

16. A federal agency had a personal computer repaired at a cost of $49.20. This amount included a charge of $22 per hour for labor and a charge for a new switch that cost $18 before a 10 percent government discount was applied. How long did the repair job take?

   (A) 1 hour 6 minutes
   (B) 1 hour 11 minutes
   (C) 1 hour 22 minutes
   (D) 1 hour 30 minutes
   (E) none of these

17. In a large agency where mail is delivered in motorized carts, two tires were replaced on a cart at a cost of $34 per tire. If the agency had expected to pay $80 for a pair of tires, what percent of its expected cost did it save?

(A) 7.5 percent
(B) 17.6 percent
(C) 57.5 percent
(D) 75.0 percent
(E) none of these

18. An experimental antipollution vehicle powered by electricity traveled 33 kilometers (km) at a constant speed of 110 kilometers per hour (km/h). How many minutes did it take this vehicle to complete its experimental run?

(A) 3
(B) 10
(C) 18
(D) 20
(E) none of these

19. In one Federal office, $\frac{1}{6}$ of the employees favored abandoning a flexible work schedule system. In a second office that had the same number of employees, $\frac{1}{4}$ of the workers favored abandoning it. What is the average of the fractions of the workers in the two offices who favored abandoning the system?

(A) $\frac{1}{10}$

(B) $\frac{1}{5}$

(C) $\frac{5}{24}$

(D) $\frac{5}{12}$

(E) none of the these

20. A clerk is able to process 40 unemployment compensation claims in one hour. After deductions of 18 percent for benefits and taxes, the clerk's net pay is $6.97 per hour. If the clerk processed 1,200 claims, how much would the government have to pay for the work, based on the clerk's hourly wage *before* deductions?

(A) $278.80
(B) $255.00
(C) $246.74
(D) $209.10
(E) none of these

ANSWER KEY AND EXPLANATIONS

Part A: Name and Number Comparisons

1. B	11. B	21. B	31. B	41. A
2. D	12. E	22. A	32. D	42. C
3. E	13. E	23. A	33. A	43. E
4. A	14. E	24. A	34. E	44. A
5. E	15. B	25. E	35. E	45. E
6. A	16. D	26. E	36. E	46. B
7. A	17. A	27. C	37. A	47. C
8. C	18. A	28. E	38. E	48. B
9. D	19. C	29. C	39. A	49. D
10. B	20. C	30. B	40. A	50. C

1. **The correct answer is (B).** The first two names are exactly alike, but the third name has a different initial.

2. **The correct answer is (D).** In the second and third names, the surname is Moru. In the first name, it is Moro.

3. **The correct answer is (E).** The given name is alike in the second and third names only; the surname is alike in only the first and second names.

4. **The correct answer is (A).** All three names are exactly alike.

5. **The correct answer is (E).** The middle initial in the second name is different from that of the other two. In the third name, Francis becomes Frances.

6. **The correct answer is (A).** All three numbers are exactly alike.

7. **The correct answer is (A).** All three numbers are exactly alike.

8. **The correct answer is (C).** The "254" of the beginning of the second number is different from the "245" opening of the first and third numbers.

9. **The correct answer is (D).** The "243" ending of the first number is different from the "423" ending of the second and third numbers.

10. **The correct answer is (B).** The "2798" opening of the third number is different from the "2789" opening of the first and second numbers.

11. **The correct answer is (B).** In the third name, the surname changes from Tenenbaum to Tanenbaum.

12. **The correct answer is (E).** The surname is different in each of the three names.

13. **The correct answer is (E).** Again, all three surnames are different.

14. **The correct answer is (E).** "Robert J." of the third name is the reverse of "J. Robert" of the first two names; the spelling of the surname in the second name differs from that of the first and third.

15. **The correct answer is (B).** "Fernand" of the third name is different from "Fernando" of the first two.

16. **The correct answer is (D).** The "630" ending of the first number is different from the "360" ending of the second and third.

17. **The correct answer is (A).** All three numbers are exactly alike.

18. **The correct answer is (A).** All three numbers are exactly alike.

19. **The correct answer is (C).** The "287" beginning of the second number is different from the "278" beginning of the first and third numbers.

20. **The correct answer is (C).** The "861" ending of the second number is different from the "681" ending of the first and third.

21. **The correct answer is (B).** "Courtnay" of the third name is different from "Courtney" of the first and second.

22. **The correct answer is (A).** All three names are exactly alike.

23. **The correct answer is (A).** All three names are exactly alike.

24. **The correct answer is (A).** All three names are exactly alike.

25. **The correct answer is (E).** The second name is "Sr.," while the first and third names are "Jr."; the third surname begins with "Mac," while the first and second surnames begin with "Mc."

26. **The correct answer is (E).** The three numbers end 2976, 9276, 2796.

27. **The correct answer is (C).** The first and third numbers end 1695; the second ends 6195.

28. **The correct answer is (E).** The three numbers end 0527, 5027, 0537.

29. **The correct answer is (C).** The first and third numbers are identical; the second number differs in a number of digits.

30. **The correct answer is (B).** The last two digits of the third number are reversed.

31. **The correct answer is (B).** "Randolphe" of the third name is different from "Randolph" of the first two.

32. **The correct answer is (D).** The surname of the second and third names, "Johnson," is different from the surname of the first name, "Johnston."

33. **The correct answer is (A).** All three names are exactly alike.

34. **The correct answer is (E).** The middle initial of the third name differs from the other two. "Asheton" of the second name differs from "Atherton" of the other two.

35. **The correct answer is (E).** The given name in the second and third names is "Owen" while in the first it is "Owens." The surname of the first two names is "McVey" while in the third it is "McVay."

36. **The correct answer is (E).** The three numbers end 5690, 6690, 5609.

37. **The correct answer is (A).** All three numbers are exactly alike.

38. **The correct answer is (E).** The last two digits are, respectively 41, 47, 14.

39. **The correct answer is (A).** All three numbers are exactly alike.

40. **The correct answer is (A).** All three numbers are exactly alike.

41. **The correct answer is (A).** All three names are exactly alike.

42. **The correct answer is (C).** The first and third names are exactly alike, but the second name inserts an "n" in the surname.

43. **The correct answer is (E).** The given name is different in all three names.

44. **The correct answer is (A).** All three names are exactly alike.

45. **The correct answer is (E).** The surname is different in each of the three names.

46. **The correct answer is (B).** In the third number, the fifth and sixth digits are reversed.

47. **The correct answer is (C).** In the second number, the fifth digit is "6" while in the other numbers the fifth digit is "0."

48. **The correct answer is (B).** In the third number, the last two digits are reversed.

49. **The correct answer is (D).** The last digit of the second and third numbers is "6"; the first number ends with "8."

50. **The correct answer is (C).** In the second number, the order of the fifth and sixth digits is reversed.

Part B: Reading Comprehension

1. A	7. D	13. E	19. D	25. B
2. B	8. C	14. C	20. C	26. C
3. B	9. E	15. B	21. E	27. C
4. C	10. B	16. E	22. E	28. E
5. E	11. D	17. C	23. A	29. C
6. C	12. A	18. B	24. C	30. D

1. **The correct answer is (A).** The essential information from which the answer can be inferred is found in the second sentence. Since *a uniformed member while out of uniform* (in other words, an off-duty member) *may **not** indulge in intoxicants to an extent unfitting the member for duty,* it follows that the same member may drink liquor in moderation. Choice (B) is incorrect because it directly contradicts the first sentence. Choice (C) is incorrect because it introduces a concept not addressed in the paragraph—that of the uniformed member who reports unfit for duty. Choice (D) is wrong because it reverses the meaning of the second sentence—the uniformed member in civilian clothes may drink only to the extent that the member remains fit for duty. Choice (E) is incorrect because it raises a topic never mentioned in the paragraph—that of the civilian member of the department in a uniform.

2. **The correct answer is (B).** The paragraph makes the statement that the technician may sign that which it is not required that the specialist personally sign and states the rules that apply to the technician: name and title of tax law specialist followed by "by" and the name and title of the tax technician in ink. Choice (B) is incorrect in that the assistant does not have authority to sign all papers. Choices (C) and (D) are incorrect because they address topics not mentioned in the paragraph—redelegation and requisitions. Choice (E) is

incorrect; the tax law specialist's name may be affixed by rubber stamp.

3. **The correct answer is (B).** The first clause states that the retiree is entitled to an annuity; the second clause tells of the pension that is the equal of one service-fraction of final compensation multiplied by number of years of government service; and the last clause describes an additional pension that is the actuarial equivalent of any reserve-for-increased-take-home-pay to which the retiree might at that time be entitled. Choice (A) is incorrect because it does not complete the explanation of the basis for the second pension. Choices (C), (D), and (E) are all hopelessly garbled misstatements.

4. **The correct answer is (C).** In effect, the paragraph is saying, "When in doubt, check it out." Ignorance of the nature of the material to be mailed or of how the law pertains to it does not excuse the mailer if the material was indeed subject to a prohibition. Choice (A) misinterprets the role of the postmaster. The postmaster is the final authority as to mailability. Choice (B) is incorrect in its direct contradiction of the paragraph, which states, "Ignorance is no excuse." Choices (D) and (E) both interpret beyond the paragraph. The paragraph places all burden on the mailer.

5. **The correct answer is (E).** The last sentence makes the point that *any and all training* is valuable, *but only as it pertains to the position for which the applicant applies.* Choices (A) and (D) miss the point. Any training or

education is valuable *if it contributes to knowledge, skills, and abilities needed in the particular job.* Choices (B) and (C) make statements unsupported by the paragraph.

6. **The correct answer is (C).** The second sentence tells us that heart disease is an illness of late middle age and old age. Choice (A) is totally wrong. Since heart disease is an illness of older people, the odds of a person with heart disease being over 30 are much more than 50%. The fifty-fifty statement refers to the likelihood of persons over 30 sometime developing heart disease. Choice (B) confuses death from *all causes* with death from *all other illnesses.* Choice (D) makes an unsupported assumption that only the rising birth rate contributes to the number of people above a certain age. Actually, the longevity rate is much more crucial to this figure. Choice (E) makes a statement that, whether true or false, is in no way supported by the paragraph.

7. **The correct answer is (D).** If people want what they can't get through legitimate, entirely legal channels, they will turn to those who supply those products or services. The consumers of less than legitimate products or services are unlikely to betray their suppliers. Choice (A) is incorrect. Since racketeers deliver goods and services for money received, they are not engaged in theft, but not all "non-thieves" are engaged in legitimate business. Choice (B) is incorrect because both racketeering and theft involve objects of value; the differences are along other dimensions. Choice (C) makes no sense at all. Choice (E) is unsupported by the paragraph.

8. **The correct answer is (C).** The first sentence tells us that the problems of the housing authority are legion, that it faces all the problems of private developers and problems peculiar to a public authority. Being *watched by antihousing enthusiasts* is one of these

problems. Choice (A) makes an unsupported statement. The paragraph does not enumerate the problems of private developers. Choice (B) is incorrect. It is the anti-housing authorities who watch for errors and cost overruns and then bring them to the attention of Congressional committees. Choices (D) and (E) make unsupported statements that do not make much sense as statements.

9. **The correct answer is (E).** *The peculiar threats to security in governmental organizations* to which the paragraph alludes are factors related to partisan, electoral politics. Other factors—job needs of the marketplace, interpersonal relationships, and internal powerplays—affect private and public employees in about equal proportions. Choice (A) is unsupported by the paragraph. Choice (B) directly contradicts the paragraph. Choices (C) and (D) are entirely unsupported by the paragraph.

10. **The correct answer is (B).** Some people develop allergies to antibiotics so that although those specific antibiotics might be the drug of choice to counter illness, the antibiotics cannot be used for those people. Choice (A) makes a categorical statement that is unsupported by the paragraph. Choice (C) is incorrect because antibiotics do not cure allergies; they may cause allergies. Choice (D) is incorrect because the organisms do not become allergic to antibiotics (people become allergic). Choice (E) is incorrect because there would be no need to search for new drugs if the existing ones were unfailingly effective. We need new drugs precisely because some organisms have become resistant to current ones.

11. **The correct answer is (D).** The paragraph clearly states that *in the competitive class every applicant must meet minimum qualifications....* There may or may not be a pass/fail examination, but there most definitely are minimum qualifications that must be

fulfilled. Choice (A) is a distortion of the first sentence. The sentence means that there are no reliable exams for noncompetitive positions, not that noncompetitive positions are filled by unreliable exams. Choice (B) is incorrect because the paragraph states that there *may* be an exam, not that there will be an exam. Choice (C) is incorrect because if there is a test, the applicant must pass it. Choice (E) goes beyond the scope of the paragraph. The paragraph does not state that *all* positions for which there are minimum qualifications are in the noncompetitive class.

12. **The correct answer is (A).** The paragraph defines a comma splice as the joining of two main clauses by a comma without a coordinating conjunction. Choice (B) is incorrect because a run-on sentence is defined as two independent clauses sharing one sentence with no connective. Choice (C) is incorrect because the paragraph suggests that a semicolon used as a connective can stand alone. Choice (D) touches on a subject not addressed in the paragraph. Choice (E) reverses the intent of the paragraph. A comma splice *is* a bad remedy for a run-on sentence.

13. **The correct answer is (E).** In *some* positions overtime is earned for time worked beyond the set number of hours; *other* positions offer compensatory time for overtime. Compensatory time is an alternative to overtime pay. Choices (A), (B), and (C) make unsupported statements. Choice (D) combines the additional payments for two different classes of services. Overtime pay is for hours in excess of the standard number; weekend differentials are for work on weekends, even if within the standard number of workweek hours.

14. **The correct answer is (C).** The paragraph makes clear that applicants may take the test before their backgrounds and qualifications have been investigated. If qualification is not even prerequisite to testing, certainly a qualified applicant will not be barred from the exam. Choice (A) is incorrect in assuming that all persons admitted to the test are unqualified. The paragraph indicates only that their qualifications need not have yet been verified. Choice (B) contradicts the paragraph. Choice (D) is incorrect. The investigation is made to verify satisfactory character and reputation. Choice (E) is unsupported by the paragraph.

15. **The correct answer is (B).** Since it is illegal to continue employing an undocumented alien hired after November 6, 1986, it must not be illegal to retain an employee who was hired before that date. Choice (A) is incorrect. It never was illegal to *deny* employment to undocumented aliens; it is now illegal to employ them. Choice (C) misinterprets the paragraph. The paragraph applies only to undocumented or unauthorized aliens. Aliens who have authorizing documents or "green cards" may be employed legally. Choice (D) is incorrect. Penalties are for "knowingly" hiring illegal aliens, not for inadvertent hiring. (You must limit your answers to the material presented in the paragraph, even though you may know of the burden on employers to verify documentation or face penalties.) Choice (E) is in contradiction to the paragraph.

16. **The correct answer is (E).** COBRA provides for the continuation of health and welfare benefits upon payment of 102% of the group premium. Choice (A) misinterprets the variation in the length of continuing coverage to depend upon the reason for termination of coverage rather than upon the reason for continuation of coverage. Choice (B) is incorrect because it is the cost to the subscriber that jumps to 102% of the group rate, not the extent of the coverage. Choice (C) is incorrect because the law requires the employer to offer the opportunity to

continue health coverage; it does not require employees, retirees, or their families to continue that coverage. Choice (D) is wrong because under COBRA terminated employees and retirees can continue coverage, but they cannot acquire new benefits.

17. **The correct answer is (C).** Recorded history is short relative to the time span between major earthquakes; therefore, history is inadequate as a predictive tool. Either a much longer period of recorded history or a much shorter span between major earthquakes would enhance the predictive value of historical data. Choice (A) is not supported by the paragraph. Choices (B) and (D) are not only unsupported, but also make no sense. Choice (E) makes an assumption that goes beyond the paragraph.

18. **The correct answer is (B).** Basically, the last sentence of the paragraph is saying that if we know the rules of construction of a language, we can understand it. Choice (A) contradicts the paragraph. The paragraph states that the number of rules is finite. Choice (C) twists the second sentence, which states that definition of a language by listing its strings is impossible because the number of strings is infinite. Choice (D) introduces unnatural languages, which is not a subject of the paragraph. Choice (E) makes an unsupported statement.

19. **The correct answer is (D).** Just as *agreement of testimony is no proof of dependability,* so agreement of testimony is no proof of undependability. Choice (A) is incorrect because the thrust of the paragraph is that people's perceptions are sometimes in error. Choice (B) contradicts the paragraph. It is reported that a number of witnesses may report the same erroneous observation even apart from collusion. Choice (C) misses the point. Since witnesses can make mistakes, they are just as likely to have not

noticed the truth as to have "observed" that which did not happen. Choice (E) is a misstatement.

20. **The correct answer is (C).** If a contract is changed by a rider, both parties must sign the rider. The basic contract should note that a rider is being attached, and both parties should initial and date the notice in the basic contract. Choice (A) is incorrect in that it creates a rider without necessarily having created a contract. A mutual agreement to refrain from an act may be a first point of agreement and not a change. Responses B and D are both incorrect because there can be no change unless both parties agree. Choice (E) is incorrect because if there is to be no change there is no call for a rider.

21. **The correct answer is (E).** The third sentence of the paragraph states that *it is not true that all organizations are structured so that workers can be dealt with as individuals.* From this statement we can infer that *some organizations are not structured so that workers can be dealt with as individuals.* Choice (A) contradicts both the third and fourth sentences by ignoring the information that *in some organizations, employees are represented by unions, and managers bargain with these associations.* Choice (B) is unsupported because the paragraph gives no information about working environments other than organizations. Choices (C) and (D) are incorrect because they generalize some to mean all.

22. **The correct answer is (E).** The third sentence states that *all mechanical explosives are devices in which a physical reaction is produced, such as that caused by overloading a container with compressed air.* From this we can safely conclude that *some devices in which a physical reaction is produced, such as that caused by overloading a container with compressed air, are mechanical explosives.* We cannot infer choice (A) because the

paragraph does not provide sufficient information to enable the conclusion that all explosives that have been restricted to military weapons are nuclear weapons. It may be that other explosives that are not nuclear weapons also have been restricted to military weapons. Choices (B) and (C) contradict the paragraph. Choice (D) is wrong because the paragraph provides no information at all about whether or not mechanical explosives are restricted to military weapons.

23. **The correct answer is (A).** *Every level of government is a link in the economic process.* It can be deduced that its contradictory statement, *some levels of government are not links in the economic process,* cannot be true. Choice (B) is not supported by the paragraph because it goes beyond the information given. It cannot be concluded that dictatorships observe more than one principle in common with other governments. Choices (C) and (E) represent incorrect interpretations of the information that *every level of government is a link in the economic process.* It cannot be inferred from this statement that *all links in the economic process are levels of government,* only that some are. We know that the category "all levels of government" is contained in the category "links in the economic process," but we do not know if other links in the economic process exist that are not levels of government. Choice (D) is not supported by the passage; there is nothing to suggest that the contributions of some levels of society do *not* need to be evaluated.

24. **The correct answer is (C).** The first sentence presents two mutually exclusive alternatives— *all property is classified as either personal property or real property, but not both.* The second sentence states that *if something is classified as personal property, it is transient and transportable in nature.* The fourth sentence states that *permanent buildings and*

land...are fixed in nature and are not transportable. From that we can conclude that since permanent buildings and land are not transient and transportable in nature, they are not personal property; they must, therefore, be real property. All other responses contradict the paragraph in some way.

25. **The correct answer is (B).** The essential information from which the answer is to be inferred is contained in the second sentence, which states that if an Act of Congress has been deemed unconstitutional, then it is voided. In choice (B) we are told that an Act of Congress is not voided; therefore, we can conclude that *it has not been deemed unconstitutional by the Supreme Court.* Choices (A) and (C) are not supported because the paragraph does not indicate whether an Act of Congress is voided *only* when it has been deemed unconstitutional or if it could be voided for other reasons. Choices (D) and (E) contradict the paragraph.

26. **The correct answer is (C).** The last sentence states that *some special programs for broken families are offered when parental care is temporarily or permanently unavailable.* If this statement is true, then its negation cannot be true. Choice (A) contradicts the paragraph. Choices (B) and (D) cannot be validly inferred because the paragraph does not provide sufficient information to support the inferences made. Choice (E) is wrong because the paragraph states that *all child-welfare agencies are organizations that seek to promote the healthy growth and development of children.* There is no way of knowing from this statement whether or not there are organizations other than child-welfare agencies that seek to promote the healthy growth and welfare of children.

27. **The correct answer is (C).** This answer can be inferred from the information presented in the last sentence

of the paragraph, which says in part that *all document depots have the capacity to provide a great range of user services*. In view of this statement, it is clearly the case that *no document depot lacks such a capacity*. Choice (A) goes beyond the information given in the paragraph. Choice (B) contradicts the information presented. Choice (D) draws an overly general conclusion from the information presented. One can infer that *some* document depots are information centers, but one cannot infer that *all* information centers are document depots. Choice (E) goes beyond the information that is implicit in the last sentence.

28. **The correct answer is (E).** The last sentence says that *if an expression is a familiar one...then it is a nonhyphenated compound*. Therefore, if an expression is a hyphenated compound, it cannot be a familiar one. Choice (A) contradicts the information. Choice (B) is incorrect because the paragraph does not give us information about *all* nonhyphenated compounds, only those that are familiar expressions. Choice (C) is incorrect because the paragraph does not give us enough information about all unfamiliar expressions. Choice (D) cannot be correct because the paragraph provides no information about compounds that have suffixes.

29. **The correct answer is (C).** The second sentence tells us that *some general types of land use are activities that conflict with* the purpose of wildlife refuges and botanical reservations. The third sentence explains that *all activities that exhibit such conflict are...excluded from refuges and reservations*. Therefore, we can conclude that *some activities excluded from refuges and reservations* (the ones that conflict with the purpose of refuges and reservations) *are general types of land use*. Choice (A) is wrong because the paragraph does not give any information as to whether all activities that conflict with the purpose of refuges and reservations are general types of land use. Choice (B) cannot be inferred because the paragraph does not give enough information about *all* activities that are excluded. Choice (D) is incorrect because it is too inclusive. Choice (E) is based upon insufficient information.

30. **The correct answer is (D).** The third sentence states that *if a computer programming language is a machine language, then it is a code that can be read directly by a computer*. From this statement it can be seen that all machine languages are codes that can be read directly by a computer and that if a computer programming language is not such a code, then it is not a machine language. Choice (A) goes beyond the information presented in the paragraph. Choices (B) and (C) contradict the paragraph. Choice (E) is incorrect because the paragraph does not say whether or not computer languages that are *not* machine languages are codes that can be read directly by a computer.

Part C: Arithmetic Reasoning

1. C	5. A	9. A	13. A	17. E
2. D	6. C	10. C	14. C	18. C
3. B	7. B	11. D	15. C	19. C
4. E	8. A	12. B	16. D	20. B

1. **The correct answer is (C).** The first 12 clerks complete $\frac{6}{18}$, or $\frac{1}{3}$, of the job in 6 days, leaving $\frac{2}{3}$ of the job to be completed.

One clerk would require $12 \times 18 = 216$ days to complete the job, working alone. Sixteen clerks require $216 \div 16$, or $13\frac{1}{2}$ days for the entire job. But only $\frac{2}{3}$ of the job remains. To do $\frac{2}{3}$ of the job, 16 clerks require

$$\frac{2}{3} \times 13\frac{1}{2} = \frac{2}{3} \times \frac{27}{2} = 9 \text{ days}$$

The entire job takes 6 days + 9 days = 15 days.

2. **The correct answer is (D).** Let x = cost of a child's cleaning
Then $2x$ = cost of an adult's cleaning
$$2(2x) + 3(x) = \$49$$
$$4x + 3x = \$49$$
$$7x = \$49$$
$$x = \$7$$

$7 is the cost of a child's cleaning; $2 \times$ $7 or $14 is the cost of an adult's cleaning.

3. **The correct answer is (B).** First determine the total annual tax:
$424 + $783 + (2)$466 = $424 + $783 + $932 = $2139
Divide the total taxes by the tax rate to find the assessed valuation.
$2139 \div .132 = $16,204
To find what percent one number is of another, create a fraction by putting the part over the whole and convert to a decimal by dividing.
$$\frac{\$16,205}{\$87,250} = \$16,205 \div \$87,250 = 18.57\%$$

4. **The correct answer is (E).** The correct answer, not given, is five additional days.
Four assistants completed 336 cases in 42 hours (6 days at 7 hours per day). Therefore, each assistant completed $336 \div 4$, or 84 cases in 42 hours, for a rate of 2 cases per hour per assistant.
After the first 6 days, the number of cases remaining is $756 - 336 = 420$
It will take 6 assistants, working at the rate of 2 cases per hour per assistant, $420 \div 12$ or 35 hours to complete the work. If each workday has 7 hours, then $35 \div 7$ or 5 days are needed.

5. **The correct answer is (A).** Add what the family spends $30\% + 8\% + 25\% + 4\% + 13\% + 5\% = 85\%$
Since it spends 85 percent, it has 100 percent − 85 percent = 15 percent remaining for savings.
$$15\% \text{ of } \$500 = .15 \times \$500$$
$$= \$75 \text{ per week}$$
$$\$15,000 \div \$75 = 200 \text{ weeks}$$

6. **The correct answer is (C).** Commission $= 42\frac{1}{2}\%$ of fares

$$42\frac{1}{2}\% \text{ of } \$520 = .425 \times \$520$$
$$= \$221 \text{ commission}$$
$$\text{Tips} = 29\% \text{ of commission}$$
$$29\% \text{ of } \$221 = .29 \times \$221$$
$$= \$64.09 \text{ tips}$$

Weekly earnings:
$$\begin{array}{r} \$221.09 \\ +\ \ \ 64.09 \\ \hline \$285.09 \end{array}$$

Monthly earnings, based on four-week month:

$285.09
$\times$ 4
$1,140.36

Earnings in a month a few days longer than four weeks clearly fall between $1,100 and $1,200.

7. **The correct answer is (B).** Take this problem one step at a time. Of the 60 employees, one-third, or 20, were clerks; 30 percent, or 18, were machine operators; 22 were stenographers.
The clerks earned $12,750 ÷ 12 = $1,062.50 per month
Machine operators earned $13,150 ÷ 12 = $1,095.83 per month
Stenographers earned $13,000 ÷ 12 = $1,083.33 per month
20 clerks × $1,062.50 × 2 months = $42,500.00
18 machine operators × $1,095.83× 4 months = $78,899.76
22 stenographers × $1,083.33 × 3 months = $71,499.78
$42,500.00 + $78,889.76 + $71,499.78 = $192,899.54 total cost

8. **The correct answer is (A).** The government worker drove 336 miles, and his car got 24 miles per gallon; therefore, he used 336 ÷ 24 = 14 gallons for which he paid $1.419 per gallon or $1.419 × 14 = $19.87. All other information is irrelevant; disregard it.

9. **The correct answer is (A).** There are 360 minutes in a six-hour day. If each seat is occupied all day there are 105 × 360 = 37,800 minutes of seating time to be divided among 486 people. 37,800 ÷ 486 = 77.77 minutes of seating time per person = 1 hour 17.7 minutes per person.

10. **The correct answer is (C).** The worker earns $8.60 per hour for two 40-hour weeks or $8.60 × 80 hours = $688 and $12.90 per hour for an additional 16 hours ($12.90× 16 hours = $206.40), so her gross pay is $688 + $206.40 = $894.40. From this are deducted: FICA at 7.13% = $63.77 and the three withholding taxes at the combined rate of 22.5% = $201.24. Add the deductions: $63.77 + $201.24 = $265.01, and subtract the sum from the gross pay: $894.40 − $265.01= $629.39.

11. **The correct answer is (D).** Since the court does one day's work per day, at the end of 60 days there will be 150 − 60 = 90 trial days of old cases remaining. New cases are accumulating at the rate of 1.6 trial days per day; therefore, there will be 60 × 1.6 = 96 trial days of new cases at the end of 60 days. 96 new trial days added to the backlog of 90 trial days would make the total backlog 186 trial days.

12. **The correct answer is (B).** A kilometer is of a mile.
$480 \text{ km} \times \dfrac{5}{8} = 300$ miles; 300 miles ÷ 40 mph = 7.5 hours
Subtract 7.5 hours from the required arrival time of 4p.m. to find that he must leave at 8:30 a.m. (noon to 4p.m. is 4 hours + 8:30 to noon is $3\dfrac{1}{2}$ hours).

13. **The correct answer is (A).** Calculate the cost of the first machine:
$1360 − 20% = $1360 × 80% = $1088
then
$1088 − 10% = $1088 × 90% = $979.20 + $35 + $52 = $1066.20
Calculate the cost of the second machine:
$1385 − 30% = $1385 × 70% = $969.50 + $40 + $50 = $1059.50
The second machine is $1066.20 − $1059.50 = $6.70 less expensive; $6.70 ÷ $1066.20 = 0.6% savings by buying the second machine.

14. **The correct answer is (C).** The proportion is $32 \times 22 = x \times 16$
$16 x = 704$
$x = 704 ÷ 16 = 44$

15. The correct answer is (C). Add the suggested contributions and divide by the number of paralegals to get the average.

$$\frac{1}{2}\% = \frac{15}{30}$$

$$\frac{1}{1}\% = \frac{30}{30}$$

$$\frac{1}{3}\% = \frac{10}{30}$$

$$+\frac{1}{5}\% = \frac{16}{30}$$

$$\frac{61}{30}\% = 2\% \div 4 \text{ paralegals} = \frac{1}{2}\%$$

16. The correct answer is (D).
Compute the following:
$$\frac{49.20 - (18 - (18 \times .10))}{22} = x$$

$$x = \frac{33}{22} = 1.5 \text{ hours or 1 hour, 30 minutes}$$

The cost of the switch after the government discount of 10% is applied is $18 - (18 \times .10)$ or $16.20. This amount, when subtracted from the total charge of $49.20, leaves $33, which represents the charge for labor. A charge of $33 at the rate of $22 per hour represents 1.5 hours, or 1 hour 30 minutes, of work.

17. The correct answer is (E). The correct answer is not given as one of the response choices. The answer can be obtained by computing the following:

$$\frac{\left(\frac{80}{2} - 34\right)}{40} = x$$

$$x = \frac{6}{40} = .15$$

$.15 \times 100 = 15\%$

The expected $80 cost for a pair of tires would make the cost of a single tire $40. The difference between the actual cost of $34 per tire and the expected cost of $40 per tire is $6, which is 15% of the $40 expected cost.

18. The correct answer is (C). Obtain the answer by setting up a simple proportion:
$$\frac{110 \text{ km}}{60 \text{ min}} = \frac{33 \text{ km}}{x \text{ min}}$$
Solving this proportion, we obtain 110 $x = 1980$; $x = [1980/110] = 18$.

19. The correct answer is (C). Compute the following:
$$\frac{\left(\frac{1}{6} + \frac{1}{4}\right)}{2} = x$$

This simple arithmetic averaging of two fractions can be accomplished by first finding their lowest common denominator:
$$\frac{1}{6} = \frac{2}{12} \text{ and } \frac{1}{4} = \frac{3}{12}$$

The sum of $\frac{2}{12}$ and $\frac{3}{12}$ is $\frac{5}{12}$. This fraction, when multiplied by $\frac{1}{2}$ (which is the same as dividing by 2) gives the correct answer:
$$\frac{5}{12} \times \frac{1}{2} = \frac{5}{24}$$

20. The correct answer is (B). Compute the following:
(1) $0.82 S = 6.97$
and
(2) $\frac{1200}{40} \times S = Y$

The clerk's net pay of $6.97 per hour represents .82 of his or her gross pay (100% − 18% =82% or .82). Solving equation (1) we find that the clerk's hourly salary (S) before deductions is $8.50. Substituting this figure in equation (2), we compute the total number of hours of work involved (1200 forms divided by 40 forms per hour equals 30 hours of work), and then multiply 30 hours by an hourly wage of $8.50 to get $255.00, the amount the government would have to pay for the work.

Glossary

base salary: A *basic salary* with *COLA* added.

basic salary: Annual, daily, or hourly rate of pay, as indicated by the salary schedule for the employee's assigned position; excludes *COLA*.

career appointment: An appointment to the postal career service without time limitation.

casual appointment: A noncareer, limited-term appointment to positions used as a supplemental work force.

COLA: see *cost of living adjustment.*

cost of living adjustment (COLA): Increase in pay based on increases in the Consumer Price Index (CPI) over a base month; this increase is specified in bargaining unit agreements.

entrance examinations: Tests given to establish eligibility for employment.

grade: Each pay category.

in-service examinations: Tests administered to substitute rural carriers and career postal employees to determine eligibility for advancement and *reassignment;* also used to establish qualification for enrollment in certain postal training courses.

Merit Promotion Program: Provides the means for making selections for promotions according to the relative qualifications of the employees under consideration.

performance test: A procedure in which the applicant is directed to carry out a certain work activity related to the position under consideration.

promotion: The permanent assignment, with or without relocation, of an employee to an established position with a higher grade than the position to which the employee was previously assigned in the same schedule or in another schedule.

quality step increase: An increase in addition to a periodic *step increase*, granted on or before expiration of required waiting periods in recognition of extra competence.

rated application: Applications and other required documents that provide a basis for evaluation against an established rating standard; based on this application, a final rating is established for each competitor.

reassignment: The permanent assignment, with or without relocation, to another established position with the same *grade* in the same schedule, or in a different schedule.

register: A file of eligible employees' names arranged in order of relative standing for appointment consideration.

step increase: An advancement from one step to the next within a specific *grade* of a position; this is dependent on satisfying certain performance and waiting period criteria. See also *quality step increase.*

temporary appointment: A noncareer, limited-term appointment up to, but not exceeding, one year in a position that includes the performance of duties assigned to non-bargaining units.

temporary assignment: The placement of an employee in another established position, for a limited period of time, to perform duties other than those in the position description.

veteran preference: Granted to eligible applicants to be added to the ratings on examinations.